Italian Grammar in Use

via Hoepli 5, 20121 Milano (Italy)
tel. +39 02 864871 – fax +39 02 8052886
e-mail hoepli@hoepli.it

www.hoepli.it

ISBN 978-88-203-6295-9

Copertina realizzata da mncg S.r.l., Milano

Realizzazione editoriale: Thèsis Contents S.r.l., Firenze-Milano

Disegni: Mauro Marchesi

Stampato da LegoDigit S.r.l., Lavis (Trento)

Printed in Italy

LOREDANA LA CIFRA

Italian Grammar in Use

A self-study reference and practice book for elementary and intermediate learners

WITH KEY

EDITORE ULRICO HOEPLI MILANO

Contents

Preface

This handbook is designed for students from total and false beginners to learners at an intermediate level (Levels A1-B1 of the Common European Framework of Reference for Languages).

- It is a user-friendly grammar book with clear and easy explanations of grammar rules and a combined set of exercises aimed at meeting the practical needs of students who are learning Italian as a foreign language.
- The text is divided into 62 units: each of them covers two pages and deals with a particular grammar point.

A drawing presents the grammar topic in a communicative context.

Clear and concise grammar explanation in English.

Exercises that help learners practice and consolidate their knowledge.

Theory **Practice**

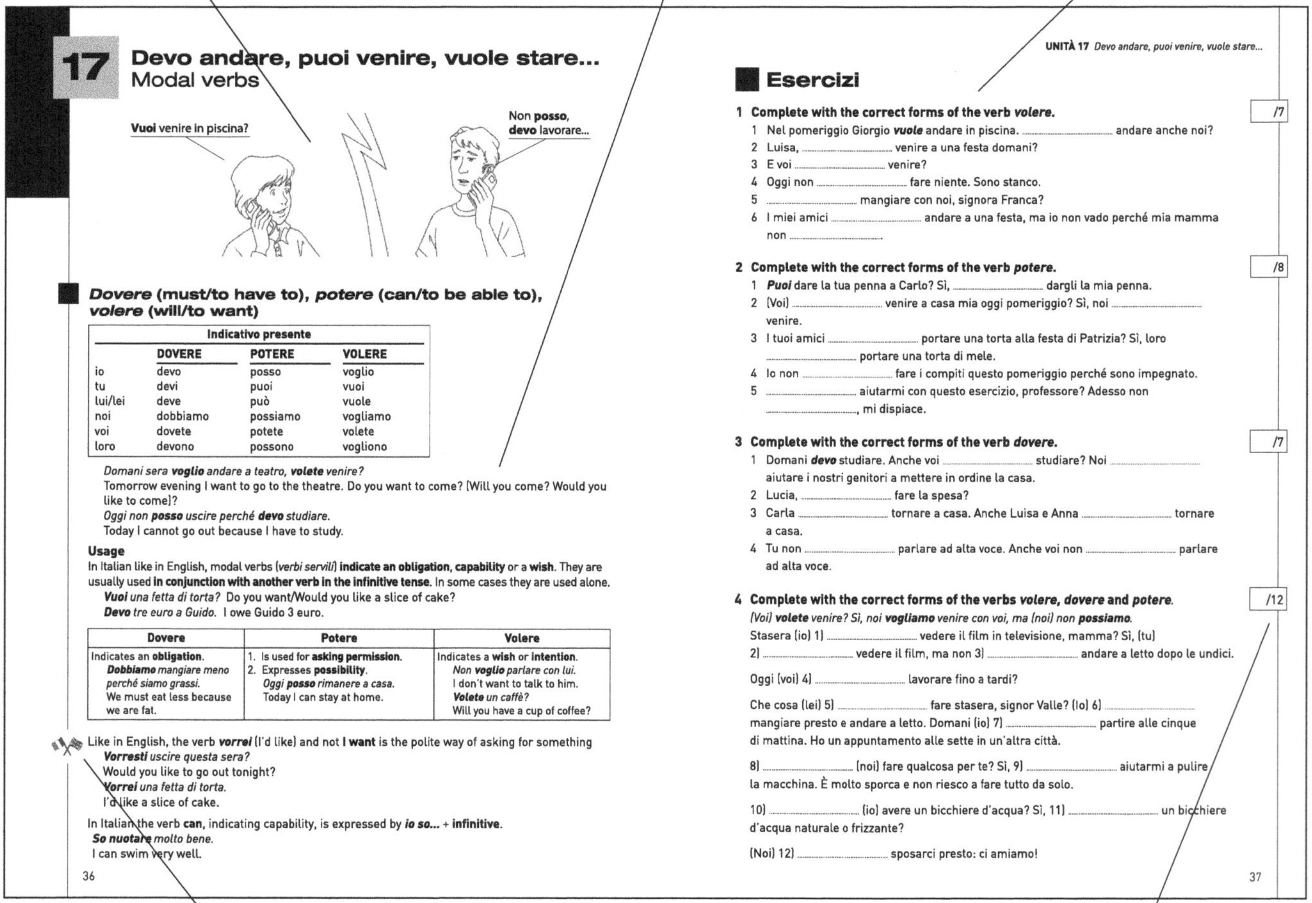

17 Devo andare, puoi venire, vuole stare...
Modal verbs

Vuoi venire in piscina?

Non **posso**, **devo** lavorare...

Dovere (must/to have to), potere (can/to be able to), volere (will/to want)

Indicativo presente			
	DOVERE	POTERE	VOLERE
io	devo	posso	voglio
tu	devi	puoi	vuoi
lui/lei	deve	può	vuole
noi	dobbiamo	possiamo	vogliamo
voi	dovete	potete	volete
loro	devono	possono	vogliono

*Domani sera **voglio** andare a teatro, **volete** venire?*
Tomorrow evening I want to go to the theatre. Do you want to come? (Will you come? Would you like to come)?
*Oggi non **posso** uscire perché **devo** studiare.*
Today I cannot go out because I have to study.

Usage
In Italian like in English, modal verbs (*verbi servili*) **indicate an obligation, capability** or a **wish**. They are usually used **in conjunction with another verb in the infinitive tense.** In some cases they are used alone.
***Vuoi** una fetta di torta?* Do you want/Would you like a slice of cake?
***Devo** tre euro a Guido.* I owe Guido 3 euro.

Dovere	Potere	Volere
Indicates an **obligation**. ***Dobbiamo** mangiare meno perché siamo grassi.* We must eat less because we are fat.	1. Is used for **asking permission**. 2. Expresses **possibility**. *Oggi **posso** rimanere a casa.* Today I can stay at home.	Indicates a **wish** or **intention**. *Non **voglio** parlare con lui.* I don't want to talk to him. ***Volete** un caffè?* Will you have a cup of coffee?

Like in English, the verb ***vorrei*** (I'd like) and not **I want** is the polite way of asking for something
***Vorresti** uscire questa sera?*
Would you like to go out tonight?
***Vorrei** una fetta di torta.*
I'd like a slice of cake.

In Italian the verb **can**, indicating capability, is expressed by ***io so...*** + **infinitive**.
***So nuotare** molto bene.*
I can swim very well.

36

UNITÀ 17 *Devo andare, puoi venire, vuole stare...*

Esercizi

1 Complete with the correct forms of the verb *volere*. /7
1 Nel pomeriggio Giorgio ***vuole*** andare in piscina. .... andare anche noi?
2 Luisa, ... venire a una festa domani?
3 E voi .... venire?
4 Oggi non .... fare niente. Sono stanco.
5 .... mangiare con noi, signora Franca?
6 I miei amici .... andare a una festa, ma io non vado perché mia mamma non ....

2 Complete with the correct forms of the verb *potere*. /8
1 ***Puoi*** dare la tua penna a Carlo? Sì, ... dargli la mia penna.
2 (Voi) .... venire a casa mia oggi pomeriggio? Sì, noi .... venire.
3 I tuoi amici .... portare una torta alla festa di Patrizia? Sì, loro .... portare una torta di mele.
4 Io non .... fare i compiti questo pomeriggio perché sono impegnato.
5 .... aiutarmi con questo esercizio, professore? Adesso non ...., mi dispiace.

3 Complete with the correct forms of the verb *dovere*. /7
1 Domani ***devo*** studiare. Anche voi .... studiare? Noi .... aiutare i nostri genitori a mettere in ordine la casa.
2 Lucia, ... fare la spesa?
3 Carla .... tornare a casa. Anche Luisa e Anna .... tornare a casa.
4 Tu non .... parlare ad alta voce. Anche voi non .... parlare ad alta voce.

4 Complete with the correct forms of the verbs *volere, dovere* and *potere*. /12
*(Voi) **volete** venire? Sì, noi **vogliamo** venire con voi, ma (noi) non **possiamo**.*
Stasera (io) 1) .... vedere il film in televisione, mamma? Sì, (tu) 2) .... vedere il film, ma non 3) .... andare a letto dopo le undici.

Oggi (voi) 4) .... lavorare fino a tardi?

Che cosa (lei) 5) .... fare stasera, signor Valle? (Io) 6) .... mangiare presto e andare a letto. Domani (io) 7) .... partire alle cinque di mattina. Ho un appuntamento alle sette in un'altra città.

8) .... (noi) fare qualcosa per te? Sì, 9) .... aiutarmi a pulire la macchina. È molto sporca e non riesco a fare tutto da solo.

10) .... (io) avere un bicchiere d'acqua? Sì, 11) .... un bicchiere d'acqua naturale o frizzante?

(Noi) 12) .... sposarci presto: ci amiamo!

37

It focuses on cross-cultural aspects of English and Italian grammar.

Self assessment.

- All explanations in the unit are written in English and all examples translated into English.
- The two flags (🏁) indicate a focus on cross-cultural aspects of English and Italian grammar.
- It presents a vast range of exercises inserted in a communicative context.
- There are also *Summary exercises* that will help students revise and reuse the structures and rules learnt.
- The section *Prove CELI* presents mock tests of the Certificate for Italian language.
- In the *Appendix* you can find tables presenting the main grammar rules.
- The *Key to exercises* (at the end of the volume) allow the student to check the progress made.

How to use the book

- The handbook can be used in classroom or for self study purposes.
- Read the theory.
- Do the exercises.
- Check the answers with the keys and write your score.
- If your score is good, it means that you've reached your goal: you've understood the rule.
- If you have made mistakes read the rule, do some exercises again and do the *Summary exercises*.

1 Io sono, tu sei, lui è... C'è, ci sono
Subject pronouns. Verb "to be" (*essere*)

Subject pronouns

Singular		
1st person	**2nd person**	**3rd person**
io	tu	lui (masculine) lei (feminine)

Plural		
1st person	**2nd person**	**3rd person**
noi	voi	loro

Io, ***tu***, ***lui*** are **subject pronouns** (*pronomi personali*). They replace the names of people or things. In Italian subject pronouns are often **omitted**.

Sono Mario. (= ***Io*** *sono Mario).* I am Mario. *Siamo stanchi. (=* ***Noi*** *siamo stanchi).* We are tired.

Present simple (*indicativo presente*) of the verb "to be" (*essere*)

ESSERE	
Indicativo presente	
io	sono
tu	sei
lui/lei	è
noi	siamo
voi	siete
loro	sono

Like in English, the verb ***essere*** is used in numerous grammatical and linguistic situations.

Roma ***è*** *in Italia.* Rome is in Italy.
John ***è*** *americano.* John is American.
Alberto e Marco ***sono*** *qui.* Alberto and Marco are here.
Oggi ***è*** *martedì.* Today is Tuesday.

There is, there are (*c'è, ci sono*)

They state the existence of someone or something in a place.

A Roma ***c'è*** *il Colosseo.* In Rome there is the Colosseum.
Ci sono *ragazze alla festa?* Are there any girls at the party?

Speaking about the weather

Differently from English, ***c'è***, ***ci sono*** are also used for the weather.

C'è *il sole.*
It's sunny.

C'è *il vento.*
It's windy.

Ci sono *le nuvole.*
It's cloudy.

C'è *la nebbia.*
It's foggy.

Exercises

1 Complete with the personal pronouns. /8

.... *sono italiana.* → ***Io** sono italiana.*

1 .... siamo a scuola.
2 .... è italiana, ... siamo francesi.
3 Questo è Giacomo. .... è un amico!
4 .... siete tedeschi, ... sono spagnoli.
5 .... amo Pietro.
6 .... è stanca.

2 Complete with the verb *essere*. /10

Paolo .... al lavoro. → *Paolo **è** al lavoro.*

1 Susanna e Francesca .... amiche.
2 .... le 23, ... notte.
3 I miei colleghi .... simpatici.
4 Io .... malato, per questo oggi non .... in ufficio.
5 (Noi) .... in ritardo?
6 Dove (voi) .... domani? .... a Firenze.
7 Il libro .... sul tavolo.

3 Write the appropriate sentence under the image. /6

a) Lei è a scuola.
b) Tu sei alto.
c) Noi siamo a Parigi.
d) Loro sono giapponesi.
e) Noi siamo bambini.
f) Voi siete amiche.

....

....

....

....

....

....

4 Complete with *c'è/ci sono*. /6

***C'è** un telefono?*

1 .... tre gatti qui!
2 Non .... posto per tutti.
3 .... del latte?
4 In questo mese .... trenta giorni.
5 Purtroppo non .... biscotti per la colazione.
6 Non .... neppure del caffè. Vado a comprarlo!

2 Io ho, tu hai, lui/lei ha... Dove sei?, È italiano?...

Verb "to have" (*avere*). Interrogative form

Present simple (*indicativo presente*) of the verb "to have" (*avere*)

The verb ***avere*** is used in these cases:

- to express **possession**
  *Giorgio **ha** un cane.* Giorgio has a dog.
  *Michela e Gianni **hanno** un gatto.*
  Michela and Gianni have a cat.
- to describe a person's **age**
  *Quanti anni **hai**? Io **ho** 43 anni.*
  How old are you? I'm 43.
  *E tu quanti anni **hai**? **Ho** 12 anni.*
  And you? How old are you? I'm 12.

AVERE	
Indicativo presente	
io	ho
tu	hai
lui/lei	ha
noi	abbiamo
voi	avete
loro	hanno

Expressions with "to have" (*avere*)

In the following expressions you use the verb ***avere*** (differently from English).

***Ho** fame.* I'm hungry.
***Ho** sete.* I'm thirsty.
***Ho** sonno.* I'm sleepy.
***Ho** paura.* I'm afraid.

*Paolo **ha** freddo, noi **abbiamo** caldo.* Paolo is cold, we are warm.
*Mio fratello **ha** paura dei cani.* My brother is afraid of dogs.
*Voi **avete** fame, noi **abbiamo** sete.* You are hungry, we are thirsty.
***Ho** sonno e sono stanco.* I'm sleepy and I'm tired.

Interrogative form

In the interrogative form nothing changes in the word order of the sentence. What changes is the **intonation**.

*Monica **è** italiana? No, **è** inglese.*
Is Monica Italian? No, she is English.
*Dove **siete**? **Siamo** in ufficio.*
Where are you? We are in the office.

Exercises

1 Complete with the verb *avere*. /5

Luca: Marco, ***hai*** fratelli o sorelle?

Marco. Sì, 1) .... una sorella.

Luca: Quanti anni 2) ....?

Marco: Lei 3) .... diciotto anni. 4) .... i capelli biondi ed è molto bella.

Luca: Bene! 5) .... il fidanzato?

Marco: Certo. Ed è grande e grosso!

2 Write these sentences in the plural. /4

Ha la patente. ⟶ ***Hanno*** *la patente.*

1 Hai un lavoro? ....

2 Hai amici in Italia? ....

3 Hai anche un figlio? ....

4 Ho la macchina. ....

3 Answer the following questions. /4

Sei straniero? ⟶ ***Sì, sono straniero.***

1 Quanti anni hai? ....

2 Hai un lavoro? ....

3 Hai figli? ....

4 Hai la macchina? ....

4 *To be* or *to have*? Choose the right alternative. /8

Giorgio *ha*/**è** stanco.

1 Giorgio *è*/*ha* sonno.

2 Io *ho*/*sono* caldo. *È*/*ha* inverno, ma fa ancora caldo!

3 Tu non *hai*/*sei* molto soldi, ma *hai*/*sei* molti amici. Questa *è*/*ha* la cosa più importante!

4 *Hai*/*sei* paura? Non ti preoccupare! *Sono*/*ho* qui io!

5 *Essere* or *avere*? Complete with the right verb. /12

Lui: Di che nazionalità ***sei***?

Lei: 1) Io .... italiana e tu?

Lui: 2) .... ucraino, ma 3) .... in Italia da sette anni.

Lei: Anche la tua famiglia 4) .... qui?

Lui: No, i miei genitori 5) .... in Ucraina. Però 6) .... un fratello che vive a Firenze.

Lei: Ah, Firenze! 7) .... una città molto bella.

Lui: Quanti anni 8) ....?

Lei: 9) .... 23 anni e tu?

Lui: Io 10) .... 25 anni.

Lei: Arrivederci, adesso devo scendere!

Lui: Questo 11) .... il mio numero di cellulare. Se 12) .... voglia di rivedermi, chiamami!

Lei: OK. Ciao...

3 Io non sono... Lei ha...
The negative sentence
Formal and informal speech

The negative sentence

non **+ verb**

The negative sentence can be made simply by placing **not** before the main verb. Unlike English, the auxiliaries do/does/did are not used.

Paolo ***non*** *ha la macchina.*
Paolo doesn't have a car.
Voi ***non*** *avete figli.*
You don't have any children.

If the sentence is interro-negative the negation ***non*** is placed before the verb.

Non *siete stanchi?*
Aren't you tired?
Non *hai fame?*
Aren't you hungry?

If the negative sentence is an answer to a question, you use ***no***.

Siete sposati? ***No, non*** *siamo sposati.*
Are you married? No, we are not married.

Formal and informal form

We use the **you** singular in two ways. ***Tu*** is the familiar form and is used to address relatives, friends and children.

The formal form

Lei è, Lei ha

Lei is the formal form and is used to address people whom you don't know or with whom you are not on familiar terms.

Signore, ***Lei è*** *un medico?*
Are you a doctor, Sir?
Signora, ***Lei*** *può entrare adesso.*
You can enter now, Madam.

Lei is used both for men and for women.

Exercises

1 When do you use the formal form? Tick the right answers. /8

1 Con i tuoi colleghi. ☐
2 Con una persona che incontri in treno. ☐
3 Con tuo fratello. ☐
4 Con il tuo capo. ☐
5 Con il dottore all'ospedale. ☐
6 Con il vigile a cui chiedi informazioni. ☐
7 Con la persona con cui vai a correre. ☐
8 Con il tuo amico d'infanzia. ☐

2 Complete with *è/ha* (formal form of the verb *essere/avere*). /7

***Ha** una bottiglia d'acqua minerale?*
1 .... sposata?
2 .... dei figli, signor Ferrari?
3 .... pronta per partire, signora Villa?
4 So che .... dei libri per me, professore.
5 .... francese, signora? No, sono spagnola.
6 .... la carta di credito o il bancomat, signora?
7 .... in Italia da molto tempo, signor Velez?

3 Write these sentences with the formal form. /5

Sei qui per me? ⟶ ***Lei** è qui per me?*
1 Hai un biglietto dell'autobus?
....
2 Sei italiana o tedesca?
....
3 Hai una caramella?
....
4 Non hai il passaporto?
....
5 Sei libera questa sera?
....

4 *Tu* or *lei*? Complete with the verbs *essere/avere* using *tu* or *lei*. /5

.... *a casa, cara?* ⟶ ***Sei** a casa, cara?*
1 .... una casa grande, signor Manzoni.
2 Non .... pronto per l'esame, Mauro!
3 .... interessata a questa presentazione, dottoressa?
4 .... dei soldi da prestarmi, zio?
5 Non .... una caramella, mamma?

4 Amare, vendere, dormire... Io amo, tu ami...

The three conjugations
Verbs ending with -*are* (first conjugation)

Italian verbs are divided into **three conjugations** according to the ending of the infinitive:

- **first conjugation**: verbs ending with -***are*** (*amare* = to love);
- **second conjugation**: verbs ending with -***ere*** (*vendere* = to sell);
- **third conjugation**: verbs ending with -***ire*** (*dormire* = to sleep).

Usage of the present tense

The present tense in Italian is essentially the same as in English. The only difference is that it can also be used **both as present continuous and as simple present**.

Tutti i giorni ***compriamo*** *del pane.*
We buy some bread every day.
Di sera ***guardi*** *la televisione?*
Do you watch television in the evening?
Giulio ***viaggia*** *molto.* Giulio travels a lot.

The English present continuous, however, can be expressed in a better way by another construction: the present progressive (see pg. 38).

Remember that in Italian the present is also used to talk about plans and intentions for the **future**.

Domani ***lavoriamo*** *tutto il giorno.* We are working all day tomorrow.
Fra due giorni ***torniamo*** *a casa.* In two days we are going back home.

First conjugation: verbs ending with -*are*

AMARE	
Present	
io	am-**o**
tu	am-**i**
lui/lei	am-**a**
noi	am-**iamo**
voi	am-**ate**
loro	am-**ano**

Other common verbs of the first conjugation are: ***cenare*** (to have supper), ***aiutare*** (to help), ***comprare*** (to buy), ***viaggiare*** (to travel), ***guardare*** (to look at), ***tornare*** (to go back), ***lavorare*** (to work).

Marco ***ascolta*** *spesso la musica.* Marco often listens to music.
Noi non ***parliamo*** *italiano.* We don't speak Italian.

Exercises

1 Complete with the verbs in brackets.

/6

Aldo (lavorare) in ufficio. → *Aldo* ***lavora*** *in ufficio.*

1 Giorgio e Stefano (*abitare*) .... a Mantova.
2 Voi (*disegnare*) .... molto bene.
3 La nonna (*cucinare*) .... sempre.
4 Voi (*imparare*) .... l'italiano.
5 Stefano (*tornare*) .... presto.
6 Carlo e Maria (*parlare*) .... francese.

2 Write the questions to these answers.

/4

Domanda: ***Abiti*** *a Pavia?* → *Risposta: Sì, abito a Pavia.*

1 .... Sì, studiamo italiano.
2 .... No, non lavoro.
3 .... Sì, cantiamo spesso.
4 .... Sì, mangia al ristorante.

3 A typical day in Nadia's life. Match the sentences.

/4

1 Di mattina frequenta l'università.
2 Alle tre torna a casa.
3 Alle sei incontra suo fratello.
4 Di sera cucina.
5 Dopo cena guarda la televisione.

☐ a) E poi va a letto.
☐ b) E mangia con i suoi genitori.
☐ c) Con lui passeggia per la città.
[1] d) Dove impara inglese e italiano.
☐ e) E studia tutto il pomeriggio.

4 Write the texts.

/6

Dove essere (tu)? (Io) ti aspettare qui alla stazione. → *Dove* ***sei****? Ti* ***aspetto*** *qui alla stazione.*

1 Oggi (noi) *cucinare* per tutti.
....
....
....
....

2 (Io) *arrivare* tardi. Scusa.
....
....
....
....

3 (Io) ti *amare*.
....
....
....
....
....

4 Domani (voi) *lavorare* di sera?
....
....
....
....

5 Fabio *mangiare* da noi.
....
....
....
....
....

6 (Io) non *ricordare* l'ora dell'appuntamento dal dentista.
....
....
....

5 Io cerco, tu stai, lui dà, lei va, voi fate...
Irregular verbs of the first conjugation

Many important Italian verbs are **irregular**: they do not follow the regular pattern of conjugation shown here. They may have a different stem or different endings.

Irregular verbs ending in *-care* and *-gare*

The verbs ending with -***care*** and -***gare*** change in the 2nd person singular and in the 1st person singular.

CERCARE	
Present	
io	cerco
tu	cer**chi**
lui/lei	cerca
noi	cer**chi**amo
voi	cercate
loro	cercano

Irregular verbs: *stare, dare, andare, fare*

These verbs belong to the first conjugation.

STARE	
Present	
io	sto
tu	stai
lui/lei	sta
noi	stiamo
voi	state
loro	stanno

DARE	
Present	
io	do
tu	dai
lui/lei	dà
noi	diamo
voi	date
loro	danno

ANDARE	
Present	
io	vado
tu	vai
lui/lei	va
noi	andiamo
voi	andate
loro	vanno

FARE	
Present	
io	faccio
tu	fai
lui/lei	fa
noi	facciamo
voi	fate
loro	fanno

Usage of *stare*

The verb *stare* is used in the expression "I'm fine/I'm sick" (*Sto bene/sto male*).

Usage of *fare*

The verb *fare* is used very frequently in different contexts.

- In a **figurative sense**.
  Facciamo *una passeggiata.* Shall we go for a walk?
- To talk about **food or drinks**.
  Facciamo *colazione, Gianni,* ***fai*** *un té, per favore?* Let's have breakfast. Gianni, will you make tea, please?
- To talk about the **weather**.
  Oggi ***fa*** *freddo e piove.* Today it's cold and rainy.
  C'è il sole e ***fa*** *caldo.* Today it's sunny and hot.
- To talk about **school, work, hobby, sport**.
  Che cosa ***fa*** *tua moglie? Fa l'infermiera.* What does your wife do? She's a nurse.

Exercises

1 Choose the right alternative. /6

1 Che cosa *cercate/cerchiate*? *Cercamo/cerchiamo* un lavoro.
2 *Paghi/pagi* in contanti? No, *pago/pagho* con un assegno.
3 Il bambino *giocha/gioca* nel giardino.
4 Non *dimenticamo/dimentichiamo* i soldi, per favore!

2 Complete with the correct forms of the verb *stare*. /6

*Io **sto** bene.*
Tu 1) .... bene? No, non molto. E Vincenzo? Lui 2) .... bene?
Sì, 3) .... molto bene. Anche noi 4) .... bene.
Voi come 5) ....? Così così. Però i nostri fratelli 6) .... benissimo.

3 Complete with the correct forms of the verb *dare*. /4

Martina mi ***dà*** un regalo e io 1) .... un regalo a lei. Anche i miei amici mi 2) .... un bel regalo. Voi che cosa 3) .... ai vostri figli? Niente regali, ai nostri figli noi 4) .... soldi.

4 Complete with the correct forms of the verb *andare*. /5

Tutti viaggiano. Domani noi ***andiamo*** a Roma e Alice 1) .... a Parigi. Dopo Natale, io e Alice 2) .... in Toscana. I miei genitori 3) .... a Venezia. E voi, dove 4) ....? Noi non 5) .... da nessuna parte!

5 Describe the images by completing the sentences with the words below and the verb *fare*. /5

la doccia • i compiti • shopping • il caffè • sport • ~~l'insegnante~~

Marco ....
→ *Marco **fa l'insegnante**.*

1
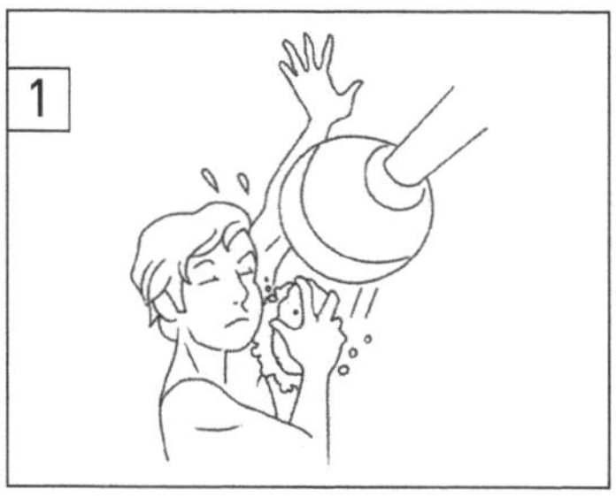

Giorgio ....
....

2

Tu ....
....

3

Lara ....
....

4

Stefania e Lorenzo ....
....

5

Il bambino ....
....

6 Io vendo, tu vendi... lo sento, tu senti... Tu bevi, lei sa, noi diciamo...

Verbs ending with -*ere* and -*ire* (second and third conjugations). Irregular verbs

Second conjugation: verbs ending with -***ere*** (*vendere* = to sell)
Third conjugation: verbs ending with -***ire*** (*dormire* = to sleep)

VENDERE (2nd conjugation)	
Present	
io	vendo
tu	vendi
lui/lei	vende
noi	vendiamo
voi	vendete
loro	vendono

SENTIRE (3rd conjugation)	
Present	
io	sento
tu	senti
lui/lei	sente
noi	sentiamo
voi	sentite
loro	sentono

Chiudete *la porta, per favore.* Close the door, please.
Prende *un caffé, signore?* Will you have a coffee, sir?

Irregular verbs of the second conjugation: ***bere*** (to drink), ***conoscere*** (to know), ***sapere*** (to know), ***rimanere*** (to stay).

BERE	
Present	
io	bevo
tu	bevi
lui/lei	beve
noi	beviamo
voi	bevete
loro	bevono

CONOSCERE	
Present	
io	conosco
tu	conosci
lui/lei	conosce
noi	conosciamo
voi	conoscete
loro	conoscono

SAPERE	
Present	
io	so
tu	sai
lui/lei	sa
noi	sappiamo
voi	sapete
loro	sanno

RIMANERE	
Present	
io	rimango
tu	rimani
lui/lei	rimane
noi	rimaniamo
voi	rimanete
loro	rimangono

Carla ***beve*** *solo acqua minerale.* Carla only drinks mineral water.
Non ***conosco*** *nessuno in questa città.* I don't know anyone in this city.
Sapete *dove abita Lucia?* Do you know where Lucia lives?

Irregular verbs of the third conjugation: ***dire*** (to say), ***salire*** (to climb).

DIRE	
Present	
io	dico
tu	dici
lui/lei	dice
noi	diciamo
voi	dite
loro	dicono

SALIRE	
Present	
io	salgo
tu	sali
lui/lei	sale
noi	saliamo
voi	salite
loro	salgono

Exercises

1 Complete with the verbs in brackets. /5

1 Mio padre *(leggere)* → ***legge*** il giornale, i miei fratellini (*leggere*) .... i fumetti, io (*leggere*) .... un libro.

2 Sergio (*scrivere*) .... una lettera.

3 Stefania e Daniela (*prendere*) .... l'autobus.

4 Il panettiere (*vendere*) .... il pane.

5 Il negozio (*chiudere*) .... alle otto.

2 Mini-quiz. How much do you know about the habits of the Italians? Write the correct form of the verb and choose true or false. /5

*In agosto tanti italiani part**ono** per le vacanze.* V ☒ F ☐

1 Molti be.................. il caffè di mattina. V ☐ F ☐

2 Molti negozi chiud.................. il lunedì mattina. V ☐ F ☐

3 Una volta alla settimana pul.................. le strade di notte. V ☐ F ☐

4 Tutti con.................. molto bene le lingue straniere. V ☐ F ☐

5 Molti parl.................. bene l'inglese. V ☐ F ☐

3 Write the questions to these answers. /5

***Prendi** il tram? → No, non prendo il tram. Prendo l'autobus.*

1 ....? Sì, vivo a Roma.

2 ....? Sì, conosciamo Paolo.

3 ....? No, loro non mangiano carne.

4 ....? Sì, Anna corre ogni giorno.

5 ....? No, non spendo molto.

4 Complete with the irregular verbs *dire, dare, rimanere, salire, stare.* /5

*Le persone sincere **dicono** sempre la verità.*

1 Cosa mi .... di lui?

2 Signora, mi .... un bicchiere d'acqua, per favore?

3 Stasera Paolo e Anna .... a casa perché sono stanchi.

4 (Voi) .... in ascensore o a piedi?

5 Perché (tu) non .... qui con me?

7 Io capisco... Lui viene...
Other irregular verbs of the third conjugation

There are several irregular verbs in the third conjugation in ***-ire.***

Irregular verbs in *-isco*

The verbs ending in ***-isco***, like ***capire*** (to understand), ***preferire*** (to prefer), ***finire*** (to finish), ***pulire*** (to clean) and many others follow this conjugation.

CAPIRE	
Present	
io	capisco
tu	capisci
lui/lei	capisce
noi	capiamo
voi	capite
loro	capiscono

*Non **capisco**. Parla italiano, per favore.*
I don't understand. Speak Italian, please.
*Non **capisci** niente.*
You don't understand anything.

The irregular verb *venire*

Also the verb ***venire*** does not follow the regular pattern of conjugation.

VENIRE	
Present	
io	vengo
tu	vieni
lui/lei	viene
noi	veniamo
voi	venite
loro	vengono

***Venite** in pizzeria con noi?*
Will you come to the pizzeria with us?
*Daniele e Cinzia non **vengono**.*
Daniele and Cinzia are not coming.

You find the conjugation of other irregular verbs, like ***dire***, ***salire*** on pg. 12.

Exercises

1 Choose the right alternative. /5

1 Marta parla il russo ma non lo ....

☐ a) capisca ☐ b) capisce ☐ c) capie

2 Adesso (noi) .... di studiare.

☐ a) finissiamo ☐ b) finiamo ☐ c) finisciamo

3 Giorgio .... la sua stanza ogni giorno.

☐ a) pulisca ☐ b) pulise ☐ c) pulisce

4 (Io) .... un pacco a mio fratello.

☐ a) spedo ☐ b) spediso ☐ c) spedisco

5 Mio fratello non .... alla mamma.

☐ a) obbedisce ☐ b) obbedisci ☐ c) obbedie

2 Complete with the correct forms of the verb *venire*. /6

1 (Tu) ***vieni*** al cinema con noi? No (io) non ....

2 I miei amici .... alle quattro.

3 Voi .... a casa più tardi? No, (noi) non .... a casa questa sera.

4 Qui ci sono tante persone che vanno e ....

5 Maria non .... alla festa.

3 Write questions to these answers. /5

Dove vai? ⟶ *Vado a Londra.*

1 ....? Andiamo in ufficio.

2 ....? Arriviamo alle otto.

3 ....? Vengo da te di mattina.

4 ....? Partiamo domenica.

5 ....? Vado al mare.

4 Revise the verbs in *-are*, *-ere*, *-ire* and answer the following questions. /5

1 Prendi l'autobus o la macchina?

....

2 Bevi il caffè o il tè?

....

3 Quale musica preferisci? Quella italiana o quella del tuo Paese?

....

4 Vivi in una città o in un piccolo paese?

....

5 Scrivi cartoline o e-mail ai tuoi amici?

....

8 Il gatto, lo zaino, gli sci...
Definite articles

Ho **la** macchina,
ho **una** moglie e **dei** bambini.

In Italian there are mainly **3 types of articles**:
- **definite** (*determinativi*): *il, lo, la, i, gli, le*;
- **indefinite** (*indeterminativi*): *un, uno, una*;
- **partitive** (*partitivi*): *del, dello, della, dei, degli, delle*.

Definite articles are used to introduce nouns which refer to specific items.

Masculine			
Singular		**Plural**	
il	bambino	**i**	bambini
l'	albero	**gli**	alberi
lo	studente	**gli**	studenti

Feminine			
Singular		**Plural**	
la	bambina	**le**	bambine
l'	ape	**le**	api

__Il__ tavolo e __le__ sedie sono in cucina.
The table and the chairs are in the kitchen.
Claudia mangia sempre __gli__ spinaci con __lo__ yoghurt.
Claudia always eats spinach with yogurt.
__Le__ finestre di questa casa sono grandi.
The windows of this house are big.

il **i**	Are used before **masculine nous** beginning with a **consonant**. *__Il__ ragazzo fa __i__ compiti di pomeriggio.* The boy does his homework in the afternoon.
la **le**	Are used before **feminine nouns** beginning with a **consonant**. *__La__ sorella di Giacomo ha una bella borsa.* Giacomo's sister has a beautiful bag.
lo **gli/le**	Are used before **masculine and feminine nouns** beginning with a **vowel** (*a, e, i, o, u*) or with ***h-***. The plural is ***gli*** if it is a masculine noun, ***le*** if it is a feminine noun. *Non amo __l'__inverno, preferisco __l'__estate; tutti __gli__ anni vado al mare.* I don't like winter, I prefer summer. I go to the seaside every year.
lo **gli**	Are used before **masculine nouns** beginning with ***s-* + consonant**, ***i-* + vowel**, ***z-***, ***x-***, ***y-***, ***j-***, ***gn-***, ***ps-*** and ***pn-***. *__Lo__ zio di Paolo beve tanto caffè.* Paolo's uncle drinks a lot of coffee.

Exercises

1 List each word under the right article. /35

studente • biglietto • fiume • mamma • genitore • città • ombrello • famiglia • padre • madre • amica • moglie • marito • zio • classe • pesce • mare • bicchiere • forchetta • estate • tovaglia • stagione • gatto • cane • sole • sete • gamba • amore • sale • fiume • monte • piatto • cuore • sbaglio • errore

il			lo	l' (masculine)
nonno,	....	....	....	....
....	....	....	....	....
....	....	....	....	....
....	....	....	....	....
....	....	....	....	....
....	....	....	....	....

la			l' (feminine)
....	....	....	....
....	....	....	....
....	....	....	
....	....	....	

2 What is in the sitting room? Add the article *il, la, i, le*. /11

Il divano
1 .... tavolo
2 .... poltrone
3 .... televisione
4 .... finestra
5 .... fotografie
6 .... lampade
7 .... vasi
8 .... tenda
9 .... pianta
10 .... tappeti
11 .... divano

3 What is in the bathroom? Add the article *il, lo, l', gli*. /8

Il dentifricio
1 .... lavandino
2 .... spazzolini
3 .... sapone
4 .... asciugamano
5 .... shampoo
6 .... rossetto
7 .... specchi
8 .... asciugacapelli

4 Complete with the right definite article. /10

Gli *occhiali di Carlo sono rotti.*

1 Devo pulire .... pavimento e lavare .... piatti.
2 .... esercizi di francese sono difficili.
3 .... zia di Aldo è inglese.
4 Vasco Rossi è .... cantante preferito di Daniele.
5 Mangiamo .... spaghetti quasi tutti .... giorni.
6 .... signore con .... cappello è .... zio di Mauro.

9 Un libro, uno scudo, un'armatura...
Indefinite articles

Masculine singular	
un	bambino
uno	studente
un	amico

Feminine singular	
una	bambina
una	studentessa
un'	amica

Stefano è ***uno*** *studente intelligente e* ***un*** *ragazzo onesto.*
Stefano is a clever boy and an honest boy.
Questo è ***un*** *tablet?*
Is this a tablet?
Giulia è ancora ***una*** *bambina.*
Giulia is still a child.
Ho ***un'****amica che si chiama Sara.*
I've got a friend whose name is Sara.

Uno, ***un***, ***una***, ***un'*** are **indefinite articles** (*articoli indeterminativi*). They are used to introduce nouns which do not refer to specific items.
I use the indefinite when I do not refer to a precise tie but to a tie in general.
The indefinite **doesn't have a plural form**. For the plural of this kind of articles we adopt the partitive articles (see Appendix on pg. 139).

un	Is used before **masculine nouns** beginning with a **consonant** or a **vowel**. *Mio cugino ha* ***un*** *cane e* ***un*** *gatto.* My cousin has a dog and a cat.
una	Is used before **feminine nouns** beginning with a **consonant**. *Franco ha* ***una*** *sorella.* Franco has a sister.
un'	Is used before **feminine nouns** beginning with a **vowel** (a, e, i, o, u) or with ***h***-. *Giulio ha* ***un'****amica molto bella.* Giulio has a very beautiful friend.
uno	Is used before masculine nouns beginning with ***s***- + **consonant**, ***i***- + **vowel**, ***z***-, ***x***-, ***y***-, ***j***-, ***gn***-, ***ps***- and ***pn***-. ***Uno*** *zio di Luca vive a Firenze.* One of Luca's uncles lives in Florence.

Pay attention: ***un'*** and not ***un*** is used before a feminine noun.
Mio zio Carlo è un'abile nuotatore. (marked ×) → *Mio zio Carlo è* ***un*** *abile nuotatore.*
My uncle Carlo is a good swimmer.

Exercises

1 Complete with the article *un, uno, una, un'*. /20

Feminine singular nouns		**Masculine singular nouns**	
Una zia			
1 .... estate	6 .... bambina	11 .... uomo	16 .... zaino
2 .... donna	7 .... anima	12 .... bambino	17 .... bicchiere
3 .... pagella	8 .... moto	13 .... viale	18 .... cinema
4 .... strada	9 .... camicia	14 .... errore	19 .... abito
5 .... chiave	10 .... gonna	15 .... zio	20 .... sport

2 What is in the fridge? Add the article *un, una, un'*. /13

Un'anguria
1 .... banana
2 .... arancia
3 .... ananas
4 .... ciliegia
5 .... fragola
6 .... albicocca
7 .... prugna
8 .... pesca
9 .... bottiglia
10 .... panino
11 .... budino
12 .... limone
13 .... pomodoro
14 .... oliva
15 .... pesce
16 .... torta
17 .... pollo
18 .... maiale
19 .... salame
20 .... patata

3 Complete with the definite or indefinite article. /12

1 ***La*** madre di Paola è .... signora molto simpatica e .... brava pianista.
2 .... mia bicicletta è molto vecchia ma funziona ancora bene.
3 C'è .... moneta da due euro per terra!
4 Mio fratello vuole trovare .... lavoro per .... estate.
5 Babacar è .... studente senegalese.
6 Non posso venire con voi perché ho .... febbre e .... mal di testa.
7 Oggi c'è .... mercato. Voglio comprare gli ingredienti per fare .... dolce. Conosco .... ricetta fantastica!

4 Choose the right alternative. /15

a) ***un'aranciata*** *b) un aranciata*
1 a) un amico b) un'amico
2 a) un studente b) uno studente
3 a) un animale b) un'animale
4 a) un'ospedale b) un ospedale
5 a) una limonata b) un'limonata
6 a) uno sbaglio b) un sbaglio
7 a) un'eccezione b) un eccezione
8 a) un illusione b) un'illusione
9 a) uno scoglio b) un scoglio
10 a) un'operazione b) un operazione
11 a) una decisione b) un decisione
12 a) una problema b) un problema
13 a) un'ipotesi b) uno ipotesi
14 a) un psicologo b) uno psicologo
15 a) un'autobus b) un autobus

10 Libro, penne, quaderni... The noun

Nouns can refer to **people, places**, or **things**. All nouns in Italian have a **gender** (*genere*); that is, they are either **masculine** or **feminine**.

Masculine

Generally, nouns ending in -***o*** are masculine, nouns ending in -***a*** are feminine.

Masculine	
Singular	**Plural**
bambin-**o**	bambin-**i**
can-**e**	can-**i**

Feminine	
Singular	**Plural**
bambin-**a**	bambin-**e**
chiav-**e**	chiav-**i**

Nouns ending in a **consonant** are usually **masculine**: sport, hotel, etc.
Nouns ending in -***e***, -***i***, -***u*** can be **masculine** (*ponte* bridge, *fiume* flower) or **feminine** (*valle* valley, *ipotesi* hypothesis).

*Io ho un can-**e**.* I have got a dog.
*Tu hai due can-**i**.* You have two dogs.
*Lui ha la chia-**ve*** He has a key.
*Tu hai le chiav-**i**?* Have you got the keys?

Masculine: *anello* (ring), *libro* (book), *documento* (document) etc
Feminine: *amica* (friend), *bicicletta* (bicycle), *studentessa* (student) etc

Capitalisation

Proper nouns are usually capitalized in Italian.

*Mi chiamo **Alberto Grossi** e abito in Italia a **Perugia**.*
My name is Alberto Grossi and I live in Italy in Perugia.
***Parigi** è la capitale della **Francia**.*
Paris is the capital of France.

Many words that are capitalized in English are not capitalized in Italian. These include: the **days of the week**, the **months** of the year, adjectives referring to **nationality**, **titles** such as Mr., Mrs., and Miss.

*Oggi è **lunedì**.*
Today is Monday.
*La signora Rossi è **italiana**.*
Mrs Rossi is Italian.

Exercises

1 Change the nouns to the plural.

/10

quaderno → ***quaderni***

1 matita ....
2 segretaria ....
3 zaino ....
4 ponte ....
5 lavoro ....
6 porta ....
7 pesce ....
8 studente ....
9 legge ....
10 appartamento ....

2 Complete.

/13

*Le matit**e** di Giorgio sono nuove.*

1 Il pesc.......... rosso è malato.
2 Gli alber.......... sono verdi.
3 Sul banco ci sono le penn...........
4 Quel quadern.......... ha poche pagin...........
5 Mi piacciono le banan.......... fritte.
6 L'estat.......... è una stagion.......... calda.
7 Mia cugina vive con i nonn...........
8 Pluto è un can...........
9 Due ett.......... di prosciutto e un litr.......... di latt...........

3 Match the words in the two columns.

/13

1 Via Gramsci, viale Libertà, corso Vittorio Emanuele sono
2 India, Germania e Marocco sono
3 Marta, Stefania e Rupali sono
4 Il professor Verdi e la professoressa Bianchi sono
5 Milan, Inter e Juventus sono
6 Aldo, Alì e Enrique sono
7 Milano, Firenze e Roma sono
8 Cane, gatto e maiale sono
9 Atlantico, Pacifico e Indiano sono
10 Europa, Africa e America sono
11 Bianco, rosso e verde sono
12 Calcio, pallavolo e tennis sono
13 Mela, banana e arancia sono
14 Sicilia, Sardegna e Corsica sono

☐ a) continenti
[1] b) strade
☐ c) città
☐ d) frutti
☐ e) sport
☐ f) colori
☐ g) nazioni
☐ h) studentesse
☐ i) squadre
☐ l) studenti
☐ m) animali
☐ n) isole
☐ o) oceani
☐ p) insegnanti

4 Find the odd word.

/6

mele, pere, fragole, ~~carne~~, banane

1 penne, matite, quaderni, libri, letti
2 calze, magliette, gonne, sedie, guanti
3 piatti, bicchieri, coltelli, forchette, pettini
4 gatti, bicchieri, cani, uccelli, pesci
5 biciclette, automobili, semafori, treni, navi
6 sedie, poltrone, divani, farfalle, tavoli.

Units 1-10 Summary exercises

1 Complete with *essere, avere, stare, c'è, ci sono.* /15

*Noi .... un gatto. → Noi **abbiamo** un gatto.*

1 Voi .... europei? Sì, noi .... francesi.
2 Paola, ... stanca? Sì, ... stanca e .... mal di testa.
3 Oggi .... le nuvole e non .... il sole.
4 Quanti anni ....? Io .... 32 anni.
5 Come ...., signora Bianchi? Io .... bene, e tu come ....?
6 I bambini .... sonno perché .... tardi.
7 Dottor Poli, ... i documenti?

2 Complete with the present tense of the verbs. /10

*Giulio (leggere) .... il giornale. → Giulio **legge** il giornale.*

1 Io non (*trovare*) .... una camera in affitto.
2 Dove (*abitare*) ...., signora Sereni?
3 Luisa non (*rispondere*) .... al telefono.
4 Le lezioni (*cominciare*) .... alle otto.
5 Ragazzi, (*accendere*) .... la luce, per favore?
6 A che ora (*partire*) .... il treno per Bari?
7 Paolo e Anna (*ascoltare*) .... la musica.
8 Voi non (*sentire*) .... un rumore in cucina?
9 Loro a colazione (*prendere*) .... un caffè, noi (*prendere*) .... un tè.

3 Complete with the present tense of the regular and irregular verbs. /13

*A che ora (finire, tu) .... di mangiare? → A che ora **finisci** di mangiare?*

1 Dove (*andare*) ...., Giacomo? (*andare*) .... in centro.
2 Noi (*capire*) .... il francese, ma (*preferire*) .... l'inglese.
3 Paola, (*venire*) .... con noi? Dove (*andare*) ....? Andiamo al cinema. Sì, (*venire*) .... volentieri.
4 Che cosa (*bere, voi*) ....? (*bere, noi*) .... un tè.
5 Franco e Zeno (*conoscere*) .... tre lingue.
6 Lucia e Maria (*avere*) .... tre figli.
7 Aldo (*spendere*) .... poco per l'affitto.
8 Noi (*chiedere*) .... un'indicazione al vigile.

4 Complete with the right verb. /10

bere • essere (x2) • venire • andare • spedire • stare • chiudere • avere • fare • guardare

*Paola .... gli auguri di Natale. → Paola **spedisce** gli auguri di Natale.*

1 La sera noi .... la televisione.
2 Loro non .... vino.
3 Sonia, sabato sera .... al cinema con me?
4 In agosto voi .... al mare?
5 Oggi c'............ vento.
6 Dov'............ la farmacia?

7 Laura oggi non .... bene perché .... mal di denti.
8 Loro .... la finestra perché .... freddo.

5 Choose the right word. /5

*Aprite **la porta**, per favore. (la radio/la porta)*

1 La sera prepariamo .... (*la colazione/il pranzo/la cena*)
2 Sono stanco, stasera vado .... presto. (*al cinema/a letto/in ufficio*)
3 La sera Carlo e Maria guardano .... (*la televisione/la radio/il cinema*)
4 Prendiamo il treno .... (*all'aeroporto/alla stazione/in autostrada*)
5 Chiudi ...., per favore? (*la finestra/la sedia/la luce*)

6 Complete. /13

1 L'appartamento di Gennaro ha due bagn.......
2 Josè è uno student...... brasiliano.
3 Vorrei cinque pomodor...... e un chilo di patat.......
4 Voi avete la patent...... di guida?
5 Preferite il pan...... con il salam...... o con il formaggi.......
6 I miei document...... sono pronti.
7 I signori Rossi hanno due bambin......: Chiara e Valentina.
8 Le medicin...... di papà sono sul tavolo in cucin.......
9 Ti piacciono le verdur......?

7 Complete with the right article. /18

***Lo** spazzolino da denti e **il** dentifricio sono in bagno.*

1 Se fai .... errore, devi correggere con .... penna rossa.
2 Vorrei .... bicchiere di latte e .... fetta di torta, per favore.
3 .... sport che .... ragazzi italiani praticano di più è .... calcio.
4 .... Sicilia è .... isola ricca di storia e cultura.
5 Mi servono .... forbici perché ho .... unghia rotta.
6 Ho trovato .... chiavi di casa di mio marito in frigorifero: è proprio .... uomo distratto!
7 Non uso mai .... zucchero, preferisco .... miele per preparare .... dolci.
8 .... ospiti sono in ritardo di .... ora.

8 Translate these sentences into Italian. /8

Are you looking for your bag? ⟶ Cerchi la tua borsa?

1 It's sunny today. ....
2 There are two books here. ....
3 Is there a present for me? ....
4 Do you love Italy? ....
5 I love cheese. ....
6 Paul understands Italian and French.
....
7 We speak Spanish. ....
8 I've got a pen. Have you got an exercise book?
....

11 Programma, ferie, maghi...
Irregular nouns

Nouns with irregular gender

Masculine nouns ending in -***a*** have a plural ending in -***i***.

il problem**a** (the problem)	→ i problem**i**	il pilot**a** (the pilot)	→ i pilot**i**
il programm**a** (the programme)	→ i programm**i**	il poet**a** (the poet)	→ i poet**i**
il clim**a** (the climate)	→ i clim**i**	il sistem**a** (the system)	→ i sistem**i**

Masculine nouns ending in -***o*** have a feminine plural ending in -***a***.

il bracci**o** (the arm) → le bracci**a**	l'uov**o** (the egg) → le uov**a**	il dit**o** (the finger) → le dit**a**

Nouns with irregular number

Some nouns have **only the singular form**: *il latte* (milk), *la sete* (thirst), *la fame* (hunger), *il sangue* (blood). Some nouns are used **only in the plural form**: *occhiali* (glasses), *forbici* (scissors), *mutande* (underwear), *pantaloni* (trousers), *ferie* (holiday).

Some other nouns have the same form for the singular and the plural.

Ending in a **consonant**	*l'autobus/gli autobus, il film/i film, l'hotel/gli hotel*, etc.
Ending in -***ie***	*la specie/le specie, la serie/le serie*, etc.
Ending in -***i***	*il brindisi/i brindisi, l'ipotesi/le ipotesi, la crisi/le crisi*, etc.
Having **only one vowel**	*il re/i re, la gru/le gru*, etc.
Ending with an accented vowel	*la città/le città, il papà/i papà, il caffè/i caffè*, etc.
Shortened	*la foto/le foto (= fotografia), la moto/le moto (= motocicletta), l'auto /le auto (= automobile), il cinema/i cinema (= cinematografo)*, etc.

Nouns with irregular plural

Singular	Plural	Example
Feminine in -***ca***, -***ga***	-***che***, -***ghe***	*colle**ghe***
Masculine in -***ca***, -***go***	-***chi***, -***ghi***, -***ci***, -***gi***	*alber**ghi**, medi**ci***
Masculine in -***io***	-***ii***/-***i***	***addii**, stu**di***
Feminine in -***cia***, -***gia***	-***cie***/-***gie***, -***ce***/-***ge***	*cilie**gie**, aran**ce**, nevral**gie***
Masculine in -***logo***	-***logi*** (things), -***loghi*** (people)	*psico**logi**, cata**loghi***

For the irregular nouns see Appendix on pg. 141.

Exercises

1 Write these words in the plural. /12

mano → ***mani***

1 uomo ....
2 dio ....
3 clima ....
4 braccio ....
5 dito ....
6 poeta ....
7 autobus ....
8 serie ....
9 brindisi ....
10 città ....
11 foto ....
12 re ....

2 Complete the sentences with these words. /8

papà • poeti • ipotesi • telegrammi • mani • serie • hotel • auto

1 Ho una .... di film che ti voglio far vedere.
2 Amo i .... italiani e leggo spesso poesie.
3 Ho ricevuto due ...., ma non so chi li ha mandati.
4 Gli .... di questa città sono molto belli.
5 Fammi vedere le tue .... Ah, come sono sporche!
6 C'erano le mamme e i .... alla recita di classe.
7 Dove sono le vostre ....? In garage.
8 Abbiamo un'.......... riguardo questo fenomeno.

3 Write these words in the plural. /8

studio → ***studi***

1 farmacia ....
2 catalogo ....
3 amico ....
4 mago ....
5 maga ....
6 astrologo ....
7 cuoca ....
8 cuoco ....

4 Choose the right alternative. /8

1 Voglio vedere questi *alberghi/albergi*.
2 Dovete parlare con dei *medichi/medici*.
3 Queste sono le mie *colleghe/college*.
4 È importante non avere *nemici/nemichi*.
5 Gli *addii/addi* sono spesso dolorosi.
6 Quante *ciliegie/ciliege* desidera, signore?
7 Desidero due chili di *arancie/arance*.
8 Vorrebbero diventare *psicologi/psicologhi*.

12 Perché? Come? Quando?...
Interrogative and quantity adverbs

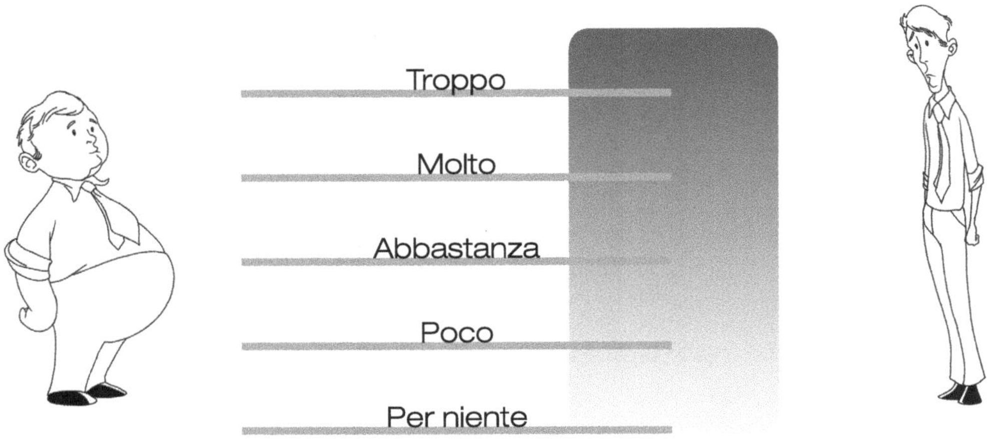

Interrogative adverbs

Interrogative and quantity adverbs are used in the **formation of questions**. They may also be used in answers (in this case they are adverbs or conjunctions).

- ***Perché*** Why: is used both in the question and in the answer.
  Perché *non parli?* ***Perché*** *ho mal di gola.*
  Why don't you talk? Because I have sore throat.
- ***Come mai?*** How come/Why ever?
  Come mai *non sei a casa?* How come you are not home?
- ***Dove?*** Where?
  Dove *andate questo pomeriggio?*
  Where are you going this afternoon?
- ***Quando?*** When?
  Quando *posso chiamarti?* When can I call you?
- ***A che ora?*** What time?
  A che ora *torni a casa di solito?*
  What time do you usually go back home?
- ***Come?*** How?
  Come *stai? Sto bene, grazie.*
  How are you? I'm fine, thank you.

Adverbs of quantity

The adverbs of quantity answer the question: ***Quanto?*** (How much?)
Like the other adverbs, they **do not vary in form**.

per niente	***poco/un po'***	***abbastanza***	***molto/tanto/parecchio***	***troppo***
not at all	a little/a little bit	quite/rather	very much/a lot	too much

Sono ***molto*** *stanco perché ho lavorato* ***troppo****.*
I'm very tired because I've worked too much.
Studio ***un po'****, poi esco con i miei amici.*
I study a little bit then I go out with my friends.
È buono? ***Abbastanza****.* Is it good? Quite.
Non mangio adesso perché non ho ***per niente*** *fame.*
I'm not eating now because I'm not hungry at all.

Exercises

1 Complete the questions with *come* or *perché*. /5

.... *è la tua ragazza? Bella, molto bella.* ⟶ ***Come è** la tua ragazza?*

1 .... sei qui? Aspetto mia sorella.
2 .... dormite in questa stanza in tre? Abbiamo pochi soldi.
3 .... trovi la mia nuova auto? Fantastica!
4 .... parli l'italiano? Ancora non molto bene.
5 .... giocate a pallone? Giochiamo abbastanza bene!

2 Choose the correct alternative. /5

***Come** sono i mobili della tua casa?*

☒ a) Come ☐ b) Come mai

1 Siamo qui .... cerchiamo lavoro.

☐ a) perché ☐ b) come mai

2 .... dormite? Perché siamo stanchi!

☐ a) Come ☐ b) Come mai

3 Tua mamma .... male?

☐ a) sta ☐ b) è

Sì, ... mal di denti.

☐ a) ha ☐ b) sta

4 Io .... qui perché non so dove andare.

☐ a) sta ☐ b) sto

3 Write the questions to these answers. /5

Dove vai? ⟶ *Vado a Londra.*

1 ....? Andiamo in ufficio.
2 ....? Arriviamo alle otto.
3 ....? Vengo da te di mattina.
4 ....? Partiamo domenica.
5 ....? Vado al mare.

4 Complete the sentences with the listed adverbs. /7

per niente • abbastanza (x2) • un po' • molto (x2) • troppo

*Marco ha parecchi chili in più. Mangia **troppo**!*

1 Non dormo ...., meno di cinque ore ogni notte, e sono stanco.
2 Non lavoriamo .... e stiamo tutto il giorno a casa.
3 Hai mangiato ....? No, ho ancora fame.
4 Il film mi è piaciuto .... È davvero bello!
5 Franco beve ....: spesso è ubriaco.
6 Sei preoccupato per l'esame? Un po', perché non sono .... preparato.
7 Adesso dormo ...., poi esco con la mia ragazza.

13 Dolcemente, bene, spesso...
Adverbs of manner, of time, of doubt...

Adverbs deriving from adjectives

In English, adverbs deriving from adjectives are often formed by adding the suffix ***-ly***. In Italian many adverbs are formed by adding the **suffix *-amente*** to the singular feminine form of the adjective (*sincer-**amente*** ⟶ sincerely, *improvvis-**amente*** ⟶ suddenly).

*Leggi **lentamente** per favore.* Read slowly, please.
*Non parla **chiaramente**. Non lo capisco.* He doesn't speak clearly. I don't understand him.

If the adjectives belong to the second group (dolce, facile etc). the adverb is formed by adding the suffix ***-emente***: *dolce* (sweet) ⟶ *dolcemente* (sweetly); *breve* (brief) ⟶ *brevemente* (briefly).

There are other adverbs that do not derive from adjectives. They are adverbs of:

- **time** ⟶ *ora* (now), *adesso* (now), *sempre* (always), *mai* (never), *a volte* (sometimes), *raramente* (seldom), *prima* (first), *poi* (then), *presto* (soon/early), *tardi* (late)
- **manner** ⟶ *bene* (well), *male* (badly), *piano* (slowly), *forte* (loud), *chiaramente* (clearly), etc.
- **place or location** ⟶ *qui/qua* (here), *lì/là* (there), *laggiù/lassù* (over there), *vicino* (nearby), *lontano* (far), *fuori* (outside), *dentro* (inside), *dappertutto* (everywhere), etc.
- **probability** ⟶ *sicuramente* (certainly), *davvero* (indeed), *certo* (surely), *forse* (maybe), *probabilmente* (probably), etc.
- **degree/quantity** ⟶ *molto* (a lot), *troppo* (too much) (see Unit 12)
- **interrogative** ⟶ *come* (how), *dove* (where) (see Unit 12)

The most common ones are the adverbs of time and of degree/quantity.

Adverbs of time

sempre always	***spesso*** often	***talvolta/raramente*** sometimes/seldom	***mai*** never

ieri yesterday	***oggi*** today	***domani*** tomorrow
prima before/first	***ora/adesso*** now	***poi/dopo*** after/then

The adverbs **do not vary** in form for the feminine, masculine, singular, plural.

*Mio padre gioca **sempre** a tennis di sera.* My father always plays tennis in the evening.
***Prima** ha piovuto, **poi** ha nevicato.* First it rained, then it snowed.

Exercises

1 Build adverbs.

/8

Difficile mi trovo male quando sono in vacanza. → ***Difficilmente** mi trovo male quando sono in vacanza.*

1 Svolgo tutti i miei compiti *facile*. ....
2 È uscito *improvviso*. ....
3 Ha lavorato *diligente*. ....
4 Ha guidato *lento*. ....
5 Quella macchina viaggia *veloce*. ....
6 L'ho amato *profondo*. ....
7 Lo saluto *cordiale*. ....
8 Sorride *stupido*. ....

2 Replace the expression with the right adverb.

/4

Stefano non fa i compiti tutti i giorni. → *Stefano **non** fa **sempre** i compiti.*

mai • talvolta • spesso • sempre

1 Mangiamo la carne una volta alla settimana. ....
2 Vado al cinema due volte alla settimana. ....
3 Non andiamo a teatro neanche una volta all'anno. ....
4 Ogni mattina vado al lavoro. ....

3 Choose the right alternative.

/6

1 C'è troppa gente in questo posto. In realtà c'è troppa gente *dappertutto/fuori/lontano*.
2 Veniamo *giù/su/vicino* subito. Dobbiamo solo scendere le scale.
3 Noi abitiamo *su/laggiù/sopra*, loro abitano sotto.
4 Sta sempre chiuso *là fuori/sopra/là dentro* e non esce mai.
5 Abita troppo *lontano/laggiù/lassù*, perciò non riusciamo ad andare in visita da lui e tornare in giornata.
6 Sono a casa, vieni *là/qua/giù*. Ti aspetto.

4 Tick the right answer.

/6

1 Sei pronto? *Davvero/sì, certo/appunto*.
2 Avete studiato? *Certamente/appunto/davvero*.
3 È una bella macchina *davvero/appunto/non sicuramente*!
4 *Probabilmente/sicuramente/davvero* verrà domani. Però non ne sono sicurissimo.
5 *Certo/sicuramente/magari* piovesse!
6 Il tuo bambino gioca molto? *Appunto no/certamente/proprio*!

14 Alto, alti, alta, alte... Bello/brutto...
Descriptive adjectives of the first group

Descriptive adjectives of the first group ending in:

- -***o*** are masculine singular: *piccolo*
- -***i*** masculine plural: *piccoli*
- -***a*** feminine singular: *piccola*
- -***e*** feminine plural: *piccole*

  *La stazione è lontan**a** da qui? No, è vicin**a**.*
  Is the station far from here? No, it's near.
  *Mio fratello ha gli occhi azzurr**i**, io ho gli occhi ner**i**.*
  My brother has blue eyes, I've got black eyes.

This is a list of the **most common opposite adjectives** of the first group.

alto/basso tall/short	***corto/lungo*** short/long	***pieno/vuoto*** full/empty
bello/brutto beautiful/ugly	***giusto/sbagliato*** right/wrong	***ricco/povero*** rich/poor
buono/cattivo good/bad	***grasso/magro*** fat/thin	***simpatico/antipatico*** nice/unpleasant
chiaro/scuro fair/dark	***nuovo/vecchio*** new/old	***vero/falso*** right/false

The **adjective and noun have to agree** in number and gender.
*Marina e Daniele hanno un bambino piccol-**o**.*
Marina and Daniele have a little child.
*Alice e Andrea hanno due bambini piccol-**i**.*
Alice and Andrea have two little children.
*Paolo ha una bambina biond-**a**.*
Paolo has a blonde baby girl.
*Carlo ha due bambine piccol-**e**.*
Carlo has two baby girls.

When an adjective refers **to more nouns of feminine plural**, the feminine plural of the adjective is used.
*Le ragazze e le donne in questa stanza sono tutte alt-**e**?*
Are all girls and women in this room tall?

If an adjective refers to nouns of a different gender, the **masculine plural** of that adjective is used.
*Paolo, Carla, Anna e Marco sono italian**i**.*
Paolo, Carla, Anna e Marco are Italian.

Exercises

1 Complete with the correct ending: *-o/-i/-a/-e.* /9

*La bicicletta di Stefano è nuov***a**.

1 Per il suo compleanno mio padre regala sempre a mia madre delle rose giall..........
2 Molti compagni dicono che Sara è una ragazza carin..........
3 I bambini di Anna sono allegr..........
4 Il professore corregge i compiti con la penna ross..........
5 Mi hanno detto che in Sardegna il cielo è sempre azzurr..........
6 Il mio piatto preferito sono le patatine fritt..........
7 La chiave dell'armadio è piccol..........
8 Il professor Bianchi è un insegnante alt.......... e magr..........

2 Fill in the correct endings. /15

1 Uomo ricc.......... e bell.......... cerca donn.......... alt.......... e snell..........

2 Sono una ragazza carin.......... ma anche molto timid.......... Vorrei un uomo buon.........., anche non bell.........., ma comprensiv..........

3 Sono una ragazza tedesc.......... e qui non conosco nessuno. Cerco amici allegr.......... e sportiv..........

4 Ci vuoi conoscere? Scrivici a questo indirizzo. Siamo due ragazze indian.......... e vorremmo conoscere ragazze e ragazzi italian..........

3 Complete the following Italian proverbs. /9

*Chi va piano va san***o** *e va lontano.*

1 La gatta frettolos.......... fa i gattini ciech..........
2 Lo scherzo è bell.......... quando è cort..........
3 Un ver.......... amico è un tesoro prezios..........
4 Le bugie hanno le gambe cort..........
5 Donne e uomini gelos.......... sono pericolos..........

4 Complete the sentences with the listed adjectives. /6

famoso • noioso • pieno • freddo • curioso • scuro

Mio fratello ha gli occhi ***chiari****.*

1 Io ho i capelli ....
2 Questa pizza è ....
3 Non amo i posti .... di gente.
4 Le mie amiche sono ...., vogliono sempre sapere tutto di tutti.
5 Il film è ....: non piace a nessuno!
6 Questi quadri sono molto ....

15 Dolce, dolci... Felice/triste...
Descriptive adjectives of the second group

Masculine	
Singular	**Plural**
ragazzo intelligent-**e** libro interessant-**e**	ragazzi intelligent-**i** libri interessant-**i**

Feminine	
Singular	**Plural**
ragazza intelligent-**e** donna elegant-**e**	ragazze intelligent-**i** donne elegant-**i**

Intelligente (clever), *dolce* (sweet), *divertente* (amusing) are descriptive adjectives of the 2nd group.
These adjectives ending in:

- ***-e***: are masculine and feminine singular;
- ***-i***: are masculine and feminine plural.
  *È un libro interessant**e** e molto util**e**.*
  It's an interesting and very useful book.
  *Adoro i profumi frances**i** e le camicie ingles**i**.*
  I love French perfume and English shirts.
  *Rita è una donna elegant**e** e affascinant**e**.*
  Rita is an elegant and attractive woman.

This is a list of the ***most common opposite adjectives*** of the 2nd group.

celibe/nubile single/married	***occidentale/orientale*** western/eastern
colpevole/innocente guilty/innocent	***orizzontale/verticale*** horizontal/vertical
debole/forte weak/strong	***possibile/impossibile*** possible/impossible
facile/difficile easy/difficult	***regolare/irregolare*** regular/irregular
felice/triste happy/sad	***settentrionale/meridionale*** northern/southern
femminile/maschile feminine/masculine	***utile/inutile*** useful/useless

Position of the adjective

Italian descriptive adjectives **are usually placed after the noun** they modify, with which they agree in gender and number.
When we need to give more emphasis to the adjective, we place it after the noun. If the adjective is placed before the noun, we are giving greater emphasis to the noun.

*Il mio fratellino frequenta la scuola **elementare**.*
My little brother attends the elementary school.
*Dobbiamo comprare **una nuova** bicicletta.*
We have to buy a new bicycle.

Exercises

1 Complete with the correct endings. /17

*Lucia è felic**e**.*

1 Il treno parte dalla stazione central..........
2 Il signor Corsini è un uomo gentil.......... e simpatic..........
3 La lezione di storia non è noios.........., ma è lung.......... e difficil..........
4 La signora Rossi è una donna ancora giovan.......... e bell..........
5 Questo libro è molto interessant.......... e divertent..........
6 Il signor Bianchi ama le auto sportiv.......... e veloc..........
7 Desidero un'enorm.......... porzione di pizza Margherita.
8 In Italia vivono molte persone che vengono dall'Europa Oriental..........
9 Carla, hai un vestito molto elegant.......... e costos..........!
10 L'esercizio di inglese non è semplic..........

2 Complete with the right adjective. /7

difficile • infelice • inutile • nubile • maschile • forte • meridionale

*Il tribunale lo ha dichiarato non colpevole, cioè **innocente**.*

1 Carla non è sposata: è ....
2 È un oggetto che non serve: è ....
3 Lucia non sorride mai: è ....
4 In quella classe non ci sono ragazze: è tutta ....
5 La Campania è una regione del Sud, cioè ....
6 Marta sa affrontare le difficoltà: è una ragazza ....
7 È un esame ...., ho paura di non superarlo.

3 Match noun and adjective. /9

1 autobus	☐ a) colorate
2 caffè	☐ b) freddo
3 feste	☐ c) interessante
4 latte	☐ d) lungo
5 libro	☐ e) puntuale
6 matite	☐ f) fitta
7 nebbia	☐ g) aperti
8 negozi	☐ h) verde
9 semaforo	☐ i) divertenti

4 Match the colour to the name. /5

1 sole	☐ a) bianco
2 luna	☐ b) giallo
3 speranza	☐ c) rosso
4 passione	☐ d) verde
5 dolore	☐ e) nero

16 Egoista/egoisti... Lungo/lunghi... Bello, buono, grande...
Irregular adjectives

Adjectives ending in *-a* and invariable adjectives

Adjectives ending in -***a***	masculine plural in -***i***	*egoista, ottimista, entusiasta*, etc.
Invariable adjectives	have only **one form**	• *pari, dispari* • the colours: *rosa, viola, blu*, etc.

*Paolo è ottimist**a**, suo fratello è pessimist**a**.* Paolo is optimistic, his brother is pessimistic.

Adjectives with an irregular plural

Adjectives ending in -***co*** ➞ -***chi***/-***ci*** (according to the accent)	*Siamo molto **stanchi**.* We're very tired. *I tuoi genitori sono **simpatici**.* Your parents are very nice.
Adjectives ending in -***go***, -***ga*** ➞ -***ghi***/-***ghe***	*Pietro porta i capelli **lunghi**.* Pietro has long hair.
Adjectives ending in -***io*** ➞ -***i***/-***ie***, -***i***/-***ie***	*Noi siamo uomini **pìi**.* We're religious men. *Marco e Thomas sembrano ragazzi **saggi**.* Marco and Thomas are considered wise men. *Le nuvole **grigie** portano pioggia.* Grey clouds carry rain.

Bello, buono, grande

These adjectives drop their final vowels when they precede the nouns they modify.

Bello, bell', bel	Buono, buon', buon	Grande, grand', gran
The adjective ***bello*** drops its final vowel when it precedes the noun it modifies. *bel* ➞ ***bel*** *cane!* ***Bello*** becomes ***bell'*** when it precedes a noun beginning with a vowel. The plural of ***bello*** is: *bello* ➞ **begli** *bella* ➞ **belle** *Avete un **bel** cane!* You've got a beautiful dog. *Che **bell'**albero!* What a beautiful tree! ***Bell'****amica!* Beautiful friend! *Maria ha dei **begli** occhi.* Maria has beautiful eyes.	The adjective ***buono*** follows the same rule. *Questo è un **buon** prodotto.* This is a good product. *Maria è una **buon'**amica.* Maria is a good friend. *È un **buono**.* He's a good man. *Ho dei **buoni** amici.* I've got some good friends. The plural of ***buono*** is: *buono* ➞ ***buoni*** *buona* ➞ ***buone***	The adjective ***grande*** follows the same rule. The only exception: it doesn't change when it precedes the noun beginning with -***z***, -***s*** + consonant. *Oggi fa un **gran** caldo.* Today it's very hot. *Ugo è un **grand'**uomo.* Ugo is a great person. *Serve un **grande** tavolo per questa sala.* We need a big table for this sitting room.

Exercises

1 Choose the right alternative. /6

1 Paolo è un *egoista/egoisto*.
2 Questo numero è *pari/paro*.
3 Questo divano è *rosa/roso*.
4 Invece questo muro è *blu/blo*.
5 Sei contento della tua promozione? Non contento, sono *entusiasta/entusiasto*!
6 Io e Clara siamo *ottimiste/ottimista* riguardo al futuro.

2 Correct the mistakes where necessary. /8

1 Non amo i numeri dispari. ....
2 I bambini sono stanci. ....
3 Avete degli amici simpatichi. ....
4 I tuoi amici sono impegnati e serii. ....
5 Non amo le gonne grigie. ....
6 Questi esercizi sono troppo lungi. ....
7 Non ci sono gli antinebbie qui. ....
8 A casa e in macchina ho degli antifurti. ....

3 Complete with *bello* or *buono*. /5

È un ***buon*** *cane. Obbedisce a tutti.*

1 Questo film non è .... È troppo noioso.
2 In questo bar la colazione è davvero .... Per questo ci torniamo sempre.
3 Quello è un .... attore. Infatti piace a tutte le donne.
4 Sei un .... amico. Ti voglio bene.
5 Che .... albergo! Voglio andarci.

4 Complete the sentences with the adjective *grande* in the correct form. /5

1 Gandhi è stato un .... uomo, secondo me.
2 Voglio delle porzioni .... Ho fame.
3 Fa un .... freddo.
4 Hai una casa ....!
5 I tuoi bambini sono diventati ....

5 Write the following sentences in the plural. /6

1 L'armadio è antico, il tavolo è recente. ....
2 Il bambino non mangia la verdura cruda. ....
3 Il problema di matematica è facile, l'esercizio di geometria è difficile.
....
4 Non c'è il formaggio fresco? ....
5 L'anziana signora è dolce e simpatica. ....
6 Perché bevi la birra analcolica? ....

17 Devo andare, puoi venire, vuole stare...
Modal verbs

Dovere (must/to have to), *potere* (can/to be able to), *volere* (will/to want)

Indicativo presente			
	DOVERE	**POTERE**	**VOLERE**
io	devo	posso	voglio
tu	devi	puoi	vuoi
lui/lei	deve	può	vuole
noi	dobbiamo	possiamo	vogliamo
voi	dovete	potete	volete
loro	devono	possono	vogliono

*Domani sera **voglio** andare a teatro, **volete** venire?*
Tomorrow evening I want to go to the theatre. Do you want to come? (Will you come? Would you like to come)?
*Oggi non **posso** uscire perché **devo** studiare.*
Today I cannot go out because I have to study.

Usage
In Italian like in English, modal verbs (*verbi servili*) **indicate an obligation**, **capability** or a **wish**. They are usually used **in conjunction with another verb in the infinitive tense**. In some cases they are used alone.
***Vuoi** una fetta di torta?* Do you want/Would you like a slice of cake?
***Devo** tre euro a Guido.* I owe Guido 3 euro.

Dovere	Potere	Volere
Indicates an **obligation**. ***Dobbiamo** mangiare meno perché siamo grassi.* We must eat less because we are fat.	1. Is used for **asking permission**. 2. Expresses **possibility**. *Oggi **posso** rimanere a casa.* Today I can stay at home.	Indicates a **wish** or **intention**. *Non **voglio** parlare con lui.* I don't want to talk to him. ***Volete** un caffè?* Will you have a cup of coffee?

Like in English, the verb ***vorrei*** (I'd like) and not **I want** is the polite way of asking for something
***Vorresti** uscire questa sera?*
Would you like to go out tonight?
***Vorrei** una fetta di torta.*
I'd like a slice of cake.

In Italian the verb **can**, indicating capability, is expressed by ***io so...*** + **infinitive**.
***So nuotare** molto bene.*
I can swim very well.

Exercises

1 Complete with the correct forms of the verb *volere.* /7

1 Nel pomeriggio Giorgio ***vuole*** andare in piscina. .... andare anche noi?
2 Luisa, ... venire a una festa domani?
3 E voi .... venire?
4 Oggi non .... fare niente. Sono stanco.
5 .... mangiare con noi, signora Franca?
6 I miei amici .... andare a una festa, ma io non vado perché mia mamma non ....

2 Complete with the correct forms of the verb *potere.* /8

1 ***Puoi*** dare la tua penna a Carlo? Sì, ... dargli la mia penna.
2 (Voi) .... venire a casa mia oggi pomeriggio? Sì, noi .... venire.
3 I tuoi amici .... portare una torta alla festa di Patrizia? Sì, loro .... portare una torta di mele.
4 Io non .... fare i compiti questo pomeriggio perché sono impegnato.
5 .... aiutarmi con questo esercizio, professore? Adesso non ...., mi dispiace.

3 Complete with the correct forms of the verb *dovere.* /7

1 Domani ***devo*** studiare. Anche voi .... studiare? Noi .... aiutare i nostri genitori a mettere in ordine la casa.
2 Lucia, ... fare la spesa?
3 Carla .... tornare a casa. Anche Luisa e Anna .... tornare a casa.
4 Tu non .... parlare ad alta voce. Anche voi non .... parlare ad alta voce.

4 Complete with the correct forms of the verbs *volere, dovere* and *potere*. /12

(Voi) ***volete*** *venire? Sì, noi* ***vogliamo*** *venire con voi, ma (noi) non* ***possiamo****.*

Stasera (io) 1) .... vedere il film in televisione, mamma? Sì, (tu) 2) .... vedere il film, ma non 3) .... andare a letto dopo le undici.

Oggi (voi) 4) .... lavorare fino a tardi?

Che cosa (lei) 5) .... fare stasera, signor Valle? (Io) 6) .... mangiare presto e andare a letto. Domani (io) 7) .... partire alle cinque di mattina. Ho un appuntamento alle sette in un'altra città.

8) .... (noi) fare qualcosa per te? Sì, 9) .... aiutarmi a pulire la macchina. È molto sporca e non riesco a fare tutto da solo.

10) .... (io) avere un bicchiere d'acqua? Sì, 11) .... un bicchiere d'acqua naturale o frizzante?

(Noi) 12) .... sposarci presto: ci amiamo!

18 Sto amando, stai vendendo, sta sentendo...
Present continuous (or present progressive)

The present progressive (or continuous)

Describes an action that is currently happening.
In Italian it is composed of two parts: the **present tense of the verb *to be* (*presente indicativo* of the verb *essere*)** + **the present participle** of the main verb.

Person	Auxiliar STARE	1st conjugation AMARE	2nd conjugation VENDERE	3rd conjugation SENTIRE
io	sto	amando	vendendo	sentendo
tu	stai	amando	vendendo	sentendo
lui/lei	sta	amando	vendendo	sentendo
noi	stiamo	amando	vendendo	sentendo
voi	state	amando	vendendo	sentendo
loro	stanno	amando	vendendo	sentendo

Carlo e Lucia ***stanno ascoltando*** *la radio.* Carlo and Lucia are listening to the radio.
Mario e Susanna ***stanno vendendo*** *la casa.* Mario and Susanna are selling their house.
Adesso non ti posso rispondere, ***sto leggendo*** *un libro.* Now I cannot answer you. I'm reading a book.

The gerund

It is equivalent to the English present participle. It is formed by adding a suffix ***-ando***, ***-endo***, ***-endo*** to the verb stem. The *gerundio* is **invariable** in form, and does not agree in gender or number with the subject of the verb.

The gerund of some verbs is **irregular**.

- ***Bere*** (to drink) ⟶ bevendo
- ***Fare*** (to do) ⟶ facendo
- ***Dire*** (to say) ⟶ dicendo
- ***Porre*** (to lay) ⟶ ponendo
  Bob ***sta facendo*** *i compiti.* Bob is doing his homework.

The compound gerund
Auxiliary verb + simple gerund

- With the auxiliary *avere*: *avendo amato* (having loved)
- With the auxiliary essere: *essendo partito* (having left)
- With reflexive verbs: *essendosi lavato* (having washed himself)
  Avendo perso *il suo numero di telefono, non ho potuto chiamare Chiara.*
  Having lost her telephone number, I couldn't call Chiara.

Exercises

1 Write the gerund of these verbs.

/8

Aiutare ⟶ ***aiutando***

1 Giocare ....

2 Leggere ....

3 Dire ....

4 Finire ....

5 Aspettare ....

6 Mettere ....

7 Fare ....

8 Partire ....

2 Build sentences with the present continuous.

/6

Il bambino/giocare/in giardino. ⟶ *Il bambino* ***sta giocando*** *in giardino.*

1 Noi/mandare/una mail.

....

2 I miei colleghi/leggere/il giornale.

....

3 Che cosa/pensare (tu)?

....

4 Giovanni/dire/una bugia.

....

5 (Voi) arrivare?

....

6 Dove/lavorare/adesso, signora Torti?

....

3 Complete the sentences with the present continuous of the following verbs.

/10

prendere • andare • fare (2) • guardare • bere • scrivere • telefonare • partire • studiare

(Io) ***Sto mangiando*** *una fetta di torta. È molto buona.*

1 Che cosa (voi) ....? .... una mail.

2 Perché (tu) ....? Perché domani ho un esame.

3 Signorina Martini, dove ....? In bagno, professore.

4 Carla .... la televisione. C'è un bel film.

5 Che cosa .... Fabio e Chiara? .... ai loro amici.

6 .... (voi) per Roma? No, ... il treno per Palermo.

7 Maria .... un tè con sua zia.

19 Io mi lavo, tu ti siedi, lui si veste...
Reflexive verbs

Paolo **lava la macchina**.

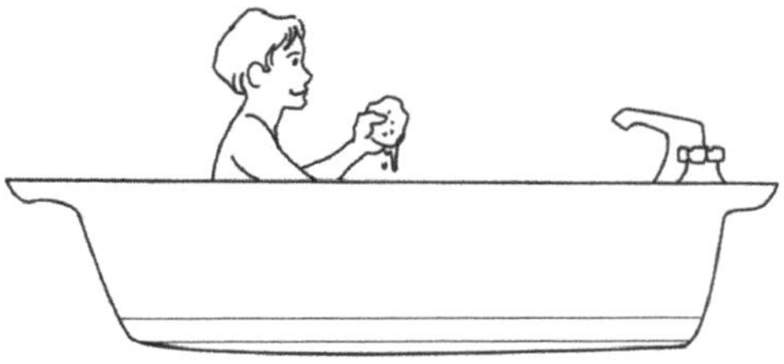

Paolo **si lava**.

In a reflexive sentence the action of the verb reverts to the subject. **Reflexive pronouns are placed before** a conjugated verb or attached to the infinitive.

		LAVARSI	SEDERSI	VESTIRSI
io	mi	lavo	siedo	vesto
tu	ti	lavi	siedi	vesti
lui/lei	si	lava	siede	veste
noi	ci	laviamo	sediamo	vestiamo
voi	vi	lavate	sedete	vestite
loro	si	lavano	siedono	vestono

*Mio padre **si alza** tutte le mattine alle 5.30.*
My father gets up every morning at 5:30.
***Si lava**, **si fa** la barba e **si veste**.*
He washes himself, he shaves and gets dressed.

Not all reflexive verbs in Italian are reflexive in English.
alzarsi ⟶ to get up/stand up
addormentarsi ⟶ to fall asleep etc.
***Mi alzo** alle otto di mattina.* I get up at eight in the morning.
*Quando **ti addormenti**?* When do you fall asleep?

The infinitive of reflexive verbs
In order to make an Italian verb reflexive, the ***-e*** of its infinitive ending **is dropped** and the pronoun ***si* is added**. For example *lavarsi*, *sedersi*, *vestirsi*.

Reflexive pronouns

io	tu	lui/lei/Lei	noi	voi	loro
mi	**ti**	**si/Si**	**ci**	**vi**	**si**

Reflexive pronouns **have only one form** both for the masculine and for feminine. They are always placed **before the verb**. They correspond to "myself", "yourself", "himself", etc.
*Come **ti** chiami? Mi chiamo Thomas. Come **vi** chiamate voi? Io **mi** chiamo Alberto e lei **si** chiama Anna. Loro **si** chiamano Giulia, Monica e Paolo.*
What is your name? My name is Thomas. What are your names? My name is Alberto and she is Anna. Their names are Giulia, Monica and Paolo.

Differently from English, reflexive pronouns are used in Italian also as **reciprocal pronouns**.
***Si amano**.* They love each other.

Exercises

1 Complete with the right form of the reflexive verb. /6

(Alzarsi) Carlo → ***si alza*** *tutte le mattine alle 6.15*

1 (*Farsi*) Daniele .... la doccia tutti i giorni.
2 (*Tagliarsi*) Domani io .... i capelli corti.
3 (*Arrabbiarsi*) Il direttore .... facilmente.
4 (*Trovarsi*) Ragazzi, ... bene in Italia?
5 (*Sentirsi*) Noi oggi non .... molto bene.
6 (*Divertirsi*) Quando giocano, i miei figli .... sempre.

2 Answer the questions using the reflexive verb. /5

A che ora ti alzi la mattina? → ***Mi alzo*** *alle 7.00*

1 Come si chiama tua madre? .... Giulia.
2 A che ora vi addormentate la sera? .... a mezzanotte.
3 Dove si trova Napoli? .... in Campania.
4 Quando vi rilassate un po'? .... dopo il lavoro.
5 Anna, perché ti preoccupi per Daniele? .... perché Daniele è molto distratto.

3 Complete the sentences with the verbs *rilassarsi, pettinarsi, alzarsi, sedersi, vestirsi.* /5

(Svegliarsi) Io → ***mi sveglio*** alle 7.00.

Tu .... alle 9.00.

Lui ....

Noi ....

Loro ....

Voi ....

4 Complete the text of the postcard. /9

Ciao Paolo,
qui io ***mi*** trovo benissimo, 1) .... riposo e 2) .... diverto un sacco. Alla mattina non 3) .... alzo prima delle 10.00. I miei genitori 4) .... dedicano allo sport e mia sorella Silvia 5) .... innamora ogni giorno di un ragazzo nuovo, poi 6) .... dispera quando lui parte! E tu, come 7) .... trovi in montagna? 8) .... annoi o 9) .... diverti come noi?
Ciao Davide

Units 11-19 Summary exercises

1 Complete with the irregular verbs. /11

(Morire, noi) ⟶ ***Moriamo*** *di fame.*

1 (*Dire, tu*) .... la verità? Certo! Io (*dire*) .... sempre la verità.
2 (*Uscire, noi*) ....? No, io non esco, (*rimanere*) .... a casa a studiare.
3 L'ascensore è rotto, (*salire, noi*) .... a piedi.
4 Scusa, Anna, oggi non (*venire, io*) .... perché (*fare*) .... troppo freddo.
5 (*Rimanere, io*) .... a casa e (*finire*) .... le pulizie.
6 (*Sapere, voi*) .... perché Giulio non (*dare*) .... retta a nessuno?

2 Complete with the irregular verbs. /8

(Fare, io) ⟶ *Io* ***faccio*** *l'infermiere.*

1 (*Pagare*) Pietro, quanto .... d'affitto?
2 (*Fare, voi*) .... silenzio quando parlo io.
3 (*Cercare, noi*) .... un appartamento più grande.
4 (*Fare, io*) .... attenzione sempre quando attraverso la strada.
5 (*Uscire*) Oggi i giornali non .... perché (*esserci*) .... sciopero.
6 (*Spegnere, io*) .... la luce perché c'è il sole.
7 (*Fare, noi*) .... la pace?

3 Complete with the verbs *potere, volere, dovere, preferire*. /14

Quando ***puoi*** *venire da me?*

1 Oggi (io) non .... uscire perché .... studiare.
2 Se (voi) non .... venire, ... telefonare.
3 (Tu) .... un po' d'acqua? Naturale o frizzante?
4 Scusa, (noi) non .... venire perché .... finire un lavoro.
5 (Voi) .... restare a casa o partecipare all'evento?
6 Nessuno .... fare quello che ...., tutti .... rispettare la legge.
7 Loro .... andare in vacanza all'estero ma non .... partire perché .... prima fare i documenti.

4 Complete with the right noun. /8

Giovedì faccio la ***spesa*** *al mercato*

squadre • estate • negozi • spesa • appuntamento • esami • affitto • occhiali • carne

1 Daniele è vegetariano, quindi non mangia la ....
2 L'................ è la mia stagione preferita perché fa caldo.
3 L'Inter e il Milan sono famose .... di calcio.
4 Senza gli .... non vedo bene.
5 Fabio paga poco per l'................ della sua casa.
6 In Italia i .... chiudono alle 19.30 circa.
7 Devo studiare se voglio superare gli .... di ammissione all'università.
8 Mi fa male un dente, devo prendere un .... dal dentista.

5 Choose the right adjective. /11

1 La nostra casa è *buia/luminosa* perché le finestre sono grandi.
2 Il caffè è *dolce/amaro*, posso avere ancora zucchero?
3 Daniela è *grassa/magra* perché mangia molti dolci.
4 Questo appartamento è troppo *caro/economico* per noi, non siamo così *poveri/ricchi*!
5 Nevica e la giornata è *calda/fredda*, mi metto i pantaloni *leggeri/pesanti.*
6 Martina è una ragazza *timida/socievole*: fa amicizia con tutti.
7 I tuoi amici sono *divertenti/noiosi*: fanno morire dal ridere.
8 Il vetro è *sporco/pulito*, devo lavarlo.
9 Palermo è una città dell'Italia *settentrionale/meridionale*.

6 Complete with the right adjectives. /12

Dobbiamo comprare una televisione ***nuova*** *perché la nostra non funziona.*

aperto • bollente • comodo • grande • interessante • intelligente • lungo • macchiato • piccolo • ricco • vecchio • verde

1 Mia sorella adora i bambini ....
2 Il mio gatto ha gli occhi .... e ....
3 Questa commedia è .... ma ....
4 Questa poltrona è .... ma ....
5 Vorremmo due caffè .... e ....
6 Non devi lasciare le finestre ...., altrimenti entra la pioggia.
7 Le persone .... riflettono prima di parlare.
8 La Sicilia è un'isola .... di arte e cultura.

7 Put the words in the right order to build sentences. /5

Leggere/noi/non/il giornale. → ***Noi non leggiamo il giornale.***

1 Amare/i bambini/i cibi/non/piccanti. ....
2 Fare/noi/una colazione/non/abbondante/mai. ....
3 Fare/volere/voi/una/passeggiata/bella/? ....
4 Preferire/voi/bionde/brune/le donne/o/? ....
5 Dovere/nuove/vestiti/noi/scarpe/e/comprare/pesanti. ....

8 Translate into Italian. /8

1 Marco is a clever man. ....
2 I've got interesting friends. ....
3 I speak slowly. ....
4 The magicians for the children's party are here.
....
5 Luca and Martina eat little, Sebastiano eats a lot.
....
6 What can I do for you? ....
7 Susanna wants to go to a party. ....
8 I still have to buy presents for Christmas. ....

20 Di sera, vado a, arrivo da...
Simple prepositions *di, a, da*

Simple prepositions are prepositions that aren't followed by articles. Here we present:

di	a	da	in

Di indicates:
- possession ⟶ *Questa è la giacca **di** Mattia.* This is Mattia's jacket.
- time ⟶ ***Di** sera faccio spesso una passeggiata.* In the evening I often go for a walk.
- cause ⟶ *Muoio **di** fame.* I'm starving.
- age ⟶ *È un bambino **di** tre anni.* He's a three-year-old child.
- a topic, theme ⟶ *Amo i libri **di** avventure.* I love adventure books.
- a material ⟶ *È una camicia **di** cotone.* It's a cotton shirt.

A indicates:
- location (in/at/to) ⟶ *Andiamo **a** Roma la prossima settimana.* We're going to Rome next week.
- age ⟶ ***A** 18 anni vado all'estero a lavorare.* At 18 I'll go to work abroad.
- time ⟶ ***A** Pasqua viene lo zio Guglielmo.* At Easter my uncle Guglielmo is coming over.
- means and manner ⟶ *Andiamo a scuola **a** piedi.* We go to school on foot.
- an indirect object (to) ⟶ *Diamo un libro **a** Maria.* We give Maria a book.

Da indicates:
- location (to/at/from) ⟶ *Vado **da** mia sorella ogni settimana.* I go to my sister's every week.
  *James viene **da** Londra.* James comes from London.
- time (since/for) ⟶ *Viviamo in Italia **da** tre anni.* We've been living in Italy for three years.
  *Lavoro qui **da** maggio.* I've been working here since May.
- manner ⟶ *Franco si comporta **da** stupido.* Franco behaves in a stupid way.
- the passive (by) ⟶ *Il cioccolato è amato **da** tutti.* Chocolate is loved by everybody.
- price (of/for) ⟶ *Vorrei una maglietta **da** 10 euro.* I'd like a T-shirt for 10 euros.

With the verbs ***andare, stare, abitare, vivere, essere*** you use the preposition:
- ***a*** + **town/city** ⟶ *Vado **a Firenze**.* I'm going to Florence.
- ***in*** + **countries, regions, continents** ⟶ *Vorremmo abitare **in Francia**.* We'd like to live in France.
- ***da*** + **people** ⟶ *Ceno sempre **da mia zia**.* I always have dinner at my aunt's.

With the verbs ***andare*** (to go), ***venire*** (to come) + **infinitive** you use the preposition ***a***.
***Vado a** fare le compere. **Io penso di** restare in campagna.*
I'm going shopping. I think I'll stay in the countryside.

With the verbs ***credere*** (to believe), ***sperare*** (to hope), ***pensare*** (to think), etc. you use the preposition ***di***.
***Spero di** partire domani. **Tu pensi di** restare in città?*
I hope to leave tomorrow. Do you think you'll stay in town?

Exercises

1 Complete with the right preposition: *di, d', a.* /15

*Abitiamo **a** Roma.*

1 Ogni domenica .... cena mangiamo dalla mamma .... Silvia.
2 C'è un po' .... acqua sul tavolo.
3 Oggi restiamo .... casa. Abbiamo mal .... pancia.
4 .... chi sono queste matite? Sono .... Claudio.
5 Stasera vediamo un film .... Fellini.
6 Il suo compleanno è nel mese .... ottobre
7 Vorremmo andare .... Firenze.
8 Andiamo con la macchina .... Giorgio.
9 Gli esercizi sono .... pagina 26.
10 Ti piacciono i film .... avventura? No, preferisco quelli .... amore.
11 Moriamo .... fame! Quando si mangia?

2 Choose the right alternative. /6

1 Vengo da te *di/a* sera.
2 Ho una figlia *di/a* sedici anni.
3 Nel mese *d'/a* agosto molti negozi sono chiusi.
4 Hai lezione *d'/a* italiano oggi?
5 *A/di* quarant'anni Giulio vuole smettere di lavorare.
6 Quando vengono i tuoi parenti? *A/di* Natale.

3 Match the question to the answer. /5

1 A chi date questo biglietto? ☐ a) Di lavoro.
2 Di che cosa parlate in ufficio? ☐ b) Di mia mamma.
3 Dove vai? ☐ c) Di Napoli.
4 Di dove sei? ☐ d) A Marina.
5 Di chi è questo borsellino? ☐ e) A Roma.

4 Complete with the right preposition: *in* or *da.* /10

*Ci sono delle birre **in** frigorifero.*

1 Vengo sub to .... te.
2 Preferiamo viaggiare .... treno.
3 Lei vive .... Sicilia, invece lui abita .... Lombardia.
4 Susanna viene .... Napoli.
5 Devi fare questo esercizio .... dieci minuti.
6 Quell'uomo è odiato .... tutti.
7 Posso avere un gelato .... un euro e trenta?
8 .... quanto vivete in Italia? .... vent'anni.

21 Vado in, passo per, vengo tra/fra...
Simple prepositions *in*, *per*, *tra/fra*

The preposition ***in*** indicates:

- location/lplace
  *Preferisco vivere **in** campagna.* I prefer to live in the countryside.
- time
  *Dobbiamo finire il lavoro **in** tre giorni.* We have to finish our work in three days.
- means
  *Andate al lavoro **in** macchina o in treno?* Do you go to work by car or by train?
- manner
  *Dovete fare **in** fretta.* You must be fast.

The preposition ***per*** indicates:

- location
  *Per andare a lavorare passo **per** un giardino.* I go through a garden to go to work.
- time
  *Ho aspettato l'autobus **per** venti minuti.* I waited for the bus for twenty minutes.
- purpose, ending
  *Studiamo **per** l'esame.* We're studying for the exam.
- cause, reason
  *Mary è a casa **per** una grave malattia.*
  Mary is at home because of a serious illness.
- means
  *Rispondo **per** posta.* I'm answering by mail.

***Tra/fra* (between/among)**
Can be used for:

- location
  ***Tra** il cinema e la scuola c'è una banca.*
  There is a bank between the cinema and the school.
- time
  *Arriviamo a casa **tra** le 8 e le 9.*
  We are getting home between 8 and 9 o'clock.
- relationship
  *Non ci sono segreti **tra** me e te.*
  There are no secrets between you and me.

Tra/fra are the equivalent of both **between** and **among**.

Exercises

1 Choose the right alternative. /6

1 Fa' .... fretta, per favore.	☐ a) in	☐ b) da	☐ c) a
2 Vengo subito .... voi.	☐ a) da	☐ b) di	☐ c) a
3 Siamo lontani .... Parma.	☐ a) in	☐ b) da	☐ c) di
4 Non vengo .... autobus.	☐ a) in	☐ b) da	☐ c) a
5 Finiamo tutto .... una settimana.	☐ a) in	☐ b) da	☐ c) a
6 L'Inter gioca la partita .... casa.	☐ a) da	☐ b) a	☐ c) in

2 Complete the dialogue with *per, tra/fra, in*. /6

Michele: Quando esci?
Vincenzo: 1) .... due minuti.
Michele: Con chi esci?
Vincenzo: Con Franco e Mario.
Michele: Ah, sono ancora qui? Quando partono 2) .... l'America?
Vincenzo: 3) .... tre giorni.
Michele: Adesso sono 4) .... casa?
Vincenzo: Sì.
Michele: Vai con loro?
Vincenzo: No, non posso. La mia ditta chiude 5) .... quattro giorni.
Michele: Ho comprato un regalo 6) .... Mario. Glielo dai tu?
Vincenzo: Volentieri.

3 Complete with *in, da, di,* or *a*. /14

1 Non parlo .... te. Non sono pettegolo.
2 Possiamo dormire .... voi?
3 Andiamo .... Roma .... Torino .... moto.
4 Siamo .... piscina. Venite anche voi?
5 Dove sei stato? .... Gianni.
6 Mangiamo ogni domenica .... Pino.
7 È un biglietto .... dieci euro.
8 Non trovo le scarpe .... ginnastica.
9 L'autore .... questo libro è molto famoso.

4 Complete with the correct preposition: *per* or *tra/fra*. /5

1 Che cosa posso fare .... te? Puoi aiutarmi.
2 Fabio ha molti esercizi .... domani.
3 Sono da te .... qualche giorno.
4 Hanno comprato un vestito .... me .... il mio compleanno.

5 Complete the sentence with the right ending. /4

1 Ti ho aspettato	☐ a) per restauri.
2 Vorrei un bel regalo	☐ b) per un'ora.
3 Il museo è chiuso	☐ c) tra poco.
4 Esco di casa	☐ d) per Natale.

22 Su quell'albero, con i miei amici, davanti/dietro al cinema...
Prepositions *su, con, davanti, dietro...*

Su (on, over, about) indicates:

- place
  Su *quell'albero ci sono dei fiori.* There are flowers on that tree.
- topic/theme
  È un film ***su*** *Leonardo da Vinci.* It's a film about Leonardo da Vinci.

Con (with) indicates:

- company
  Il sabato sera esco ***con*** *amici.* I go out with friends on Saturday evening.
- cause
  Non esco ***con*** *questo caldo.* I don't go out because of the heat.
- way, mode
  Franco lavora ***con*** *attenzione.* Franco works carefully.

Davanti → in front of /opposite
Ti aspettiamo ***davanti*** *al cinema.*
We'll wait for you in front of the cinema.

In Italian there is no difference between **in front of** and **opposite**. Both are translated with ***davanti***.

Dietro → behind
Il giardino è ***dietro*** *alla casa.*
The garden is behind the house.

Vicino a → near
Monza è ***vicino*** *a Milano.* Monza is near Milan.

Accanto → next to
Sono seduto ***accanto*** *alla ragazza che mi piace.*
I'm sitting next to the girl I like.

Fino a → until
Restiamo qui ***fino*** *alle cinque.*
We'll stay here until five o'clock.

Lontano da → far from
Londra è lontano ***da*** *Roma.* London is far from Rome.

Fuori da → out of
Il cane deve stare fuori ***da*** *qui.* The dog must stay out of here.

Exercises

1 Choose the right alternative. /5

1 .... che cosa hai scritto il tema?
☐ a) tra ☐ b) per ☐ c) su

2 Vorrei viaggiare .... la nave. Odio l'aereo.
☐ a) con ☐ b) su ☐ c) a

3 Devi fare le cose .... più impegno.
☐ a) di ☐ b) con ☐ c) per

4 Ho visto un film .... un famoso personaggio.
☐ a) su ☐ b) con ☐ c) a

5 Andiamo in vacanza .... i nostri amici.
☐ a) a ☐ b) con ☐ c) in

2 Complete the dialogue with *per, tra/fra, su, con.* /8

Marianna: Quando esci?
Paolo: ***tra*** due minuti.
Marianna: 1) .... chi esci?
Paolo: 2) .... Franco e Fabio.
Marianna: Ah, sono ancora qui! Quando partono 3) .... l'America?
Paolo: 4) .... tre giorni
Marianna: Perché non vai 5) .... loro?
Paolo: La mia ditta chiude solo 6) .... quattro giorni. Non posso partire prima.
Marianna: Resti qui 7) .... tuo fratello?
Paolo: No, vado a Parma. C'è una conferenza 8) .... Enzo Ferrari. Sai che sono appassionato di macchine!

3 Complete with *vicino, lontano, fuori, dietro, dentro, sotto.* /6

*Il libro è **sopra** il tavolo.*

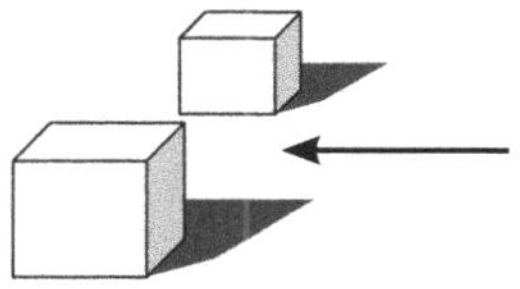

1 La scuola non è davanti, ma .... la chiesa.

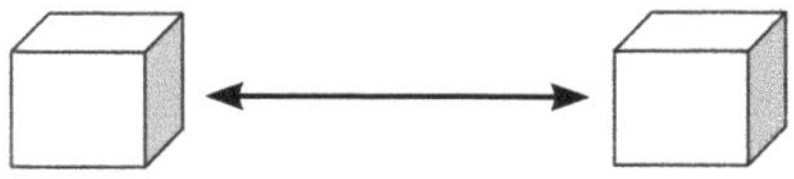

3 Tu lavori troppo .... da casa. Impieghi almeno un'ora a venire!

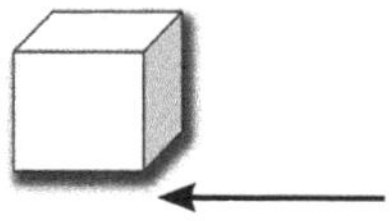

5 Il cane non è sopra il letto, ma .... il letto.

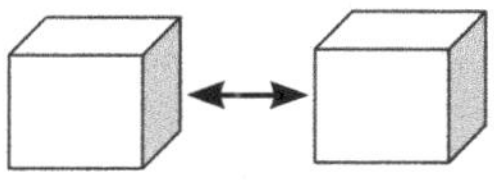

2 Susanna abita .... a me. La vedo sempre quando esco di casa.

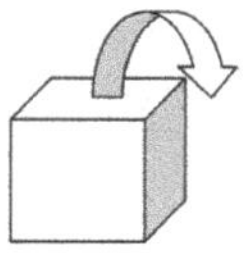

4 Il gatto non è dentro il cestino, ma .... dal cestino.

6 La collana è .... la scatola.

23 Mi-me, ti-te, lo, la...
Direct personal pronouns

Personal pronouns (subject)	Personal pronouns (object)
io	*me* (me)
tu	*te* (you)
lui	*lo* (him/it)
lei	*la* (her/it)
	La (formal)
noi	*ci* (us)
voi	*vi* (you)
loro	*li* (them)

Direct personal pronouns answer the question **what?** or **whom?**.
They replace **direct object nouns.**

Martino, ***ci*** *accompagni in macchina a scuola? Sì,* ***vi*** *accompagno a scuola.*
Martin, will you drive us to school? Yes, I'll drive you to school.
Inviti Paolo alla tua festa di compleanno? Sì, ***lo*** *invito alla mia festa di compleanno.*
Will you invite Paul to your birthday party? Yes, I'll invite him to my birthday party.
La mia amica si chiama Anna, ma io ***la*** *chiamo Titti.*
My friend's name is Anna, but I call her Titti.
I bambini sono a scuola. ***Li*** *vado a prendere più tardi.*
The children are at school. I'm going to pick them up later on.

Object pronouns precede the verb.

Il professore ***ci*** *aspetta.* The teacher is waiting for us.
Chi aspettate voi? Aspettiamo Stefania. ***La*** *aspettiamo da più di un'ora.*
Who are you waiting for? We're waiting for Stefania. We've been waiting for her for over an hour.

Other direct personal pronouns (*pronomi complemento forti*) are ***me/te/lui/lei/noi/voi/loro***. They are used to **give emphasis to a person**.

Giulia ama solo ***me****, non* ***te****.* Giulia loves only me, not you.
Marco, Patrizia, per questo lavoro ho scelto ***voi****.* Marco, Patrizia, I chose you for this job.

Exercises

1 Complete with *mi, ti, ci, vi.*

/13

Esco sempre alle otto, incontro Anna, ma lei non ***mi*** *saluta mai.*

1 .... vedi nello specchio? Sì, ... vedo. Sto proprio bene!
2 Mario, ... amo. E tu .... ami?
3 Non .... vedo più. Dove siete?
4 Se chiedete aiuto, io .... aiuto.
5 .... ringraziamo di cuore per il vostro regalo.
6 Marta .... aiuta a portare la mia valigia.
7 .... aspettate? Arrivo subito.
8 Giulia .... cerca, ma non .... trova mai: siamo sempre fuori!
9 Signori, ... ringrazio per la vostra attenzione.
10 Chi .... chiama da Palermo? Una mia amica.

2 Match the correct answer.

/6

1 Chi cercate?	☐ a) Perché non siamo a casa!
2 Perché non vi trovo?	☐ b) Non più di due minuti.
3 Mi aspetti?	☐ c) Cerchiamo te, come sempre.
4 Perché mi hai baciata?	☐ d) Sì, vi conosco bene.
5 Ci hai mai visti?	☐ e) Perché ti voglio bene.
6 Sei davvero maleducato.	☐ f) Per questo ti detesto!

3 Choose the right alternative.

/8

1 Scelgo .... e non Luisa.	☐ a) te	☐ b) ti	☐ c) vi
2 Dopo mesi di Facebook, finalmente .... conosco.	☐ a) te	☐ b) ti	☐ c) mi
3 Dove .... ho incontrato? Non mi ricordo... forse a Riccione.	☐ a) ti	☐ b) te	☐ c) mi
4 A questa festa ho invitato .... e non i vostri colleghi.	☐ a) voi	☐ b) ci	☐ c) vi
5 .... voglio con me in questo progetto.	☐ a) vi	☐ b) mi	☐ c) voi
6 Chi vuole vedere per prima, ... o lei?	☐ a) mi	☐ b) me	☐ c) voi
7 Non vuole .... ma soltanto	☐ a) noi/voi	☐ b) ci/vi	☐ c) noi/vi
8 Ha chiamato .... e non Anna.	☐ a) mi	☐ b) me	☐ c) vi

4 Answer the following questions using the pronouns.

/10

I tuoi figli amano gli animali? ⟶ *Sì,* ***li*** *amano.*

1 Conosci mia sorella Anna? No, ...
2 Preferite il tè con il limone? Sì, ...
3 Chi prepara la pasta oggi? .... noi!
4 Guardi spesso la televisione? No, ... raramente.
5 Usi i mezzi pubblici per andare a lavorare? Sì, ...
6 Compri le patate per stasera? Va bene, ...
7 Mangi il pesce crudo? Sì, ...
8 Sapete a che ora parte il treno per Genova? Sì, ...
9 Facciamo anche noi una partita a carte? No, ...
10 Dite sempre la verità? Certo, noi ....

24 Mi-a me, ti-a te, gli-a lui...
Direct and indirect personal pronouns

mi = a me **ti** = a te **gli** = a lui **le** = a lei **ci** = a noi **vi** = a voi **loro** = a loro (gli) **Le** = forma di cortesia

These pronouns are used when the verb answers the question **to whom?** or **for whom?**. They always **precede the verb.**

*Scrivi una lettera a tuo padre? Sì, **gli** scrivo.*
Will you write a letter to your father? Yes, I'll write him.
*Telefoni a Paola? Sì, **le** telefono.*
Will you phone Paola? Yes, I'll phone her.
*Parli a Carlo e a Mario? Sì, **gli** parlo/parlo loro.*
Will you talk to Carlo and Mario? Yes, I'll talk to them.

As you see, the preposition ***a*** always **precedes the noun**. If the preposition is not *a*, the pronouns (***pronomi forti***) ***me***, ***te***, ***lui***, ***lei***, ***noi***, ***voi***, ***loro*** are used.

*Esci con **me**?*
Will you go out with me?
*Questo libro è per **lui**.*
This book is for him.

The construction of the verb "to like" (*piacere*)

io piaccio	tu piaci	lui piace	noi piacciamo	voi piacete	loro piacciono

The construction of the verb *piacere* (to like) is different than in English. The **verb agrees with the object**, which is the thing or the person that is liked, as you can see in the example.

***Ci piace** il cioccolato.*
We like chocolate.

Other verbs

The verbs ***servire*** (to need), ***sembrare*** (to seem), ***bastare*** (to be sufficient/enough), ***interessare*** (to interest), ***dispiacere*** (to be sorry) have a similar construction.

***Ci serve** una persona per rispondere al telefono.*
We need a person who answers the phone.
*Questo libro **gli interessa** molto.*
He's very interested in this book.

Exercises

1 Replace the underlined words with *mi, ti, ci, vi.* /7

A te Carlo non sembra pallido? → *Carlo non **ti** sembra pallido?*

1 A noi serve una pallina da tennis.

....

2 A te piace giocare a carte?

....

3 A voi occorre un foglio di carta.

....

4 A noi dispiace il tuo comportamento.

....

5 A voi bastano i fogli?

....

6 A te servono le scarpe da tennis.

....

7 A me non interessano le chiacchiere della gente.

....

2 Answer the questions with direct and indirect pronouns. /5

Il vostro medico vi visita spesso? → *Sì, il nostro medico **ci** visita spesso.*

1 Ci date una mano a finire il lavoro?
Sì, ...

2 Arriviamo tardi, ci aspettate per la cena?
Sì, ...

3 Paolo, ti scrivono spesso i tuoi amici?
Sì, ...

4 Mi accompagni in biblioteca?
No, ...

5 Carlo vi chiama a casa?
Sì, ...

3 Rewrite the sentences using the pronouns. /5

Io amo viaggiare in treno, infatti prendo il treno tutti i giorni. → *Infatti **lo** prendo tutti i giorni.*

1 Stai mangiando le verdure? Sì, anche se non amo le verdure.

....

2 Quella signora dà da mangiare ai gatti randagi, perché ama i gatti.

....

3 Dove passi le vacanze? Passo le vacanze al mare.

....

4 Conosci le amiche di Carlo? No, non conosco le amiche di Carlo.

....

5 Paolo conosce l'inglese? Sì, parla l'inglese abbastanza correttamente.

....

25 Ne voglio, non ce ne sono, non ce n'è
The pronoun *ne* and *ce + ne*

In Italian, the pronoun ***ne*** indicates **a part, a quantity** and it can mean "about", "any", "some", "of it", "of them", etc. It is used with:

- **numbers**
  Quanti anni ha tuo nonno? ***Ne*** *compie 86 domani!*
  How old is your grandfather? He's turning 86 tomorrow.
  Avete 10 euro? No, ***ne*** *abbiamo solo 5.*
  Have you got 10 euros? No, we've got only 5.
- ***nessuno*** **(nobody)**
  Quante amiche di Carlo conosci? Non ***ne*** *conosco nessuna.*
  How many of Carlo's friends do you know? I don't know any of them.
  Hai dei libri di Umberto Eco? No, non **ne** *ho nessuno.*
  Have you got any books by Eco? No, I haven't any.
- ***metà*** (half), ***mezzo/a*** (half), ***un po'*** (a little bit), ***un pezzo*** (a piece, a slice), ***etto***, ***chilo*** etc. (100 grams, kilo)
  Vuoi una fetta di torta? ***Ne*** *prendo solo una fettina, grazie.*
  Will you have a slice of cake? I'll have only a small slice, thank you.
  Comprate delle mele? Sì, ***ne*** *compriamo un paio di chili.*
  Will you buy some apples? Yes, we'll buy a couple of kilos.

Ce ne/ce n'è

When the "ne" is followed by the verb *to be*, you use ***ce n'è*** if the subject is singular, ***ce ne sono*** if the subject is plural.

C'è un po' di torta? Mi dispiace non ***ce n'è*** *più.*
Is there any cake? I'm sorry. There isn't any more.
Ci sono dei biscotti? Non ***ce ne*** *sono più.*
Are there any biscuits? There aren't any more.
C'è del caffè? Sì, ma non ***ce n'è*** *per tutti.*
Is there some coffee? Yes, but it's not enough for everyone.

Exercises

1 Complete the sentences with *lo, li, la, le, l'* or with *ce* or *ce ne*. /8

Che belle mele: me ***ne*** *dà una, per favore?*

1 Quanti panini porti in gita? .... porto due al formaggio e uno con il salame.
2 Conosci la ragazza di Aldo? Sì, ... conosco.
3 Quanti fratelli avete? .... abbiamo tre, due maschi e una femmina.
4 Ora ho sedici anni, quando .... ho diciotto posso prendere la patente.
5 Avete un lavoro? No, non .... abbiamo.
6 Vuoi ancora un po' di zuppa? No, grazie, non .... voglio più.
7 Mi scusi, sa dov'è un meccanico? Mi dispiace, non .... conosco nessuno.
8 Perché hai gli occhiali se poi non .... usi?

2 Complete the description with the correct pronouns. /6

Questa è Rossana. Noi 1) .... conosciamo bene perché abita vicino a noi da anni. Nella foto ha i capelli rossi, ma non sono veramente rossi. Lei 2) .... tinge perché così le piacciono di più. La sua casa è bella e grande, 3) .... ha in affitto da quindici anni. Dice sempre che 4) .... vuole comprare, ma non guadagna abbastanza soldi per comprar- 5) .... E comunque i soldi lei 6) .... spende tutti per vestiti e prodotti di bellezza!

3 Complete the dialogue with the formal form. /6

Vuole parlare con il direttore? Sì ***lo*** *cerco da ieri mattina.*

- Pronto, posso parlare con il dottor Magrini?
- Chi 1) .... desidera?
- Sono Fabio Fiocchi.
- 2) .... avviso, attenda in linea.
- Il dottor Magrini al momento è occupato. 3) .... richiama lui più tardi.
- Va bene, 4) .... ringrazio, arriveder- 5) ....
- Non c'è di che, 6) .... saluto.

4 Rewrite the sentences in the plural form. /14

1 La camicia? La lascio dentro il cassetto.
....
2 Non saluto quella ragazza perché non la conosco.
....
3 Il collega di mia sorella è simpatico.
....
4 Sopra il tavolo c'è la tovaglia con il piatto, il bicchiere, la forchetta e il cucchiaio.
....
5 Non mangio il formaggio fresco perché lo detesto.
....

26 Me lo, te li, ce ne, ve la
Combined pronouns

Combined pronouns are the result of the combination of an **indirect object pronoun** + **a direct object pronoun** or + **the partitive *ne***. They are used to replace people or things named before.

Mi, ti, ci, vi + direct object pronoun or *ne*

	lo	**la**	**li**	**le**	**ne**
mi	me lo	me la	me li	me le	me ne
ti	te lo	te la	te li	te le	te ne
ci	ce lo	ce la	ce li	ce le	ce ne
vi	ve lo	ve la	ve li	ve le	ve ne

Paolo presta una penna a me. → *Paolo* ***me la*** *presta.*
Paolo lends me a pen. → Paolo lends it to me.
La nonna raccontava le favole a voi. → *La nonna* ***ve le*** *raccontava.*
Grandma used to tell you fairy tales. → Grandma used to tell them to you.
Che bel pallone! ***Me lo*** *presti?*
What a beautiful ball! Will you lend it to me?

Gli, le + direct object pronoun or *ne*

	lo	**la**	**li**	**le**	**ne**
gli	glielo	gliela	glieli	gliele	gliene
le	glielo	gliela	glieli	gliele	gliene
Le	Glielo	Gliela	Glieli	Gliele	Gliene
loro	glielo	gliela	glieli	gliele	gliene

Paolo presta una penna a Giulio. → ***Gliela*** *presta.*
Paolo lends Giulio a pen. → He lends it to him.
Marta regala molti fiori alla nonna. → ***Glieli*** *regala al compleanno.*
Marta gives her grandma many flowers. → She gives them to her for her birthday.
Quando restituisci i libri ai tuoi amici? → ***Glieli*** *restituisco la prossima settimana.*
When will you return the books to your friends? → I'll return them to them next week.
Se hai delle caramelle, perché non ***gliene*** *dai un po'?*
If you've got some toffees, why don't you give him some?

Exercises

1 Answer these questions using the combined pronouns. /6

Dai il regalo a Maria? ⟶ *Sì,* ***glielo*** *do.*

1 Professore, spiega le regole ai ragazzi? ....
2 Consigliate ai nonni un buon libro? ....
3 Mostri il tuo appartamento ai conoscenti? ....
4 Gli fai vedere la tua borsa? ....
5 Regalate un cappello a Marta? ....
6 Hai dato i soldi a tuo padre? ....

2 Complete using the combined pronouns. /7

Mamma, mi compri le caramelle? ⟶ *No, non* ***te le*** *compro.*

1 Paola, invii pacco ai tuoi amici? Sì, ... invio.
2 Hai dato al dottore le analisi? Sì, ... ho date.
3 Avete portato gli appunti ai vostri compagni? No, non .... abbiamo ancora portati.
4 Hai scritto una mail alle tue amiche? Sì, ... ho scritta ieri.
5 Hai dato dei dolci ai bambini? No, non .... ho dati. La zia .... ha già dati ieri.
6 Ha spedito le lettere ai fornitori, signorina? Sì, ... ho spedite.

3 Answer the questions with the *passato prossimo*, or the "*ne* combined pronouns". /8

Mi avete portato la carta d'identità? ⟶ *Sì,* ***te l'abbiamo portata****.*

1 Hai chiesto a Paolo la sua moto? Sì, ...
2 Vi hanno dato il permesso di soggiorno? Sì, ...
3 Hanno spedito gli inviti ai parenti? No, ...
4 Hai fatto gli auguri a Maria per il suo compleanno? Sì, ...
5 Quanti anni ha compiuto? .... 23.
6 Mi hai chiesto il permesso? No, ...
7 Quanti biglietti mi avete comprato? .... 7.
8 Ci avete consegnato quanto vi abbiamo chiesto? No, ...

4 Correct the mistake where necessary. /5

1 Avete il permesso di entrare? No, non glielo abbiamo.
....
2 Datemi il vostro documento, per favore. No, non ne diamo.
....
3 Vuoi parlare con me dei tuoi problemi? No, non te ne voglio parlare.
....
4 Consegnate a lui il vostro zaino? Sì, gliene consegniamo.
....
5 Hai delle idee per il progetto? Sì, ce le ho molte!
....

27 Si sente, ci si sente... Si devono usare...
Impersonal form with *si*

Nell'Italia del Sud **si cena** tardi.

Si

We use the pronoun ***si*** + 3rd person singular of the **verb** when we don't express the subject of the action.

*Quando **si mangia** non si parla.*
When you eat you don't speak.

Uno

We can also use the form ***uno*** + **3rd person singular**.

*Su questo letto **uno** dorme bene.*
On this bed one sleeps well.

Other cases

With **reflexive verbs** the construction of the impersonal form is the following:

uno + **pronoun *si*** + **verb** in the **third person singular**

*Con gli amici **uno** si diverte sempre.* One always has fun with friends.

- With: *ci* + *si* + verb in the 3rd person singular
  *Dopo le vacanze ci **si** sente sempre in forma.* After a holiday one always feels fit.

The impersonal form can be translated in English as "they", "you", "it", "one".

Usage

You use the impersonal form in different cases:

- when you want to make **generalizations**
  *Nell'Italia del sud **si** mangia tardi.* In southern Italy they eat late.
- to ask **less direct and intrusive questions**.
  *Quando **si** va al cinema stasera?* When shall we go the cinema tonight?

Si passivante/Si used in passive sentences

It is the Italian **equivalent of the passive** (see at pg. 122: the passive form).
Only verbs that are **transitive** (answer to the question what? whom?) can have this form. It is formed with **subject singular + 3rd person singular/subject plural + 3rd person plural**

*Per questo dipinto **si** devono usare colori particolari.*
For this painting particular colours must be used.
*Dal mio albergo **si** vedevano le montagne.*
From my hotel mountains could be seen.

Exercises

1 Write the following sentences in the impersonal form. /5

La gente in Italia viaggia tanto in macchina. → *In Italia* ***si viaggia*** *tanto in macchina.*

1 La gente guida troppo velocemente la sera.

....

2 La gente va in vacanza per lo più in agosto.

....

3 Molta gente non fa un'abbondante colazione.

....

4 La gente non lavora la domenica.

....

5 La gente si alza presto alla mattina e va a lavorare.

....

2 Write sentences with *si*. /6

Che cosa si fa in vacanza? Divertirsi. → ***Ci si diverte.***

1 Rilassarsi. ....
2 Dormire molto. ....
3 Mangiare in spiaggia. ....
4 Tenersi in forma. ....
5 Leggere. ....
6 Innamorarsi. ....

3 Rewrite these sentences using the impersonal form. /5

In questo negozio compri bene. → *In questo negozio* ***si compra*** *bene.*
In vacanza ci si alza tardi (noi). → *In estate* ***ci alziamo*** *tardi.*

1 In Italia a Natale si gioca a tombola (noi). ....
2 In questo mercatino si compra bene (tu). ....
3 Partiamo alle nove (si). ....
4 In questo negozio si paga due e si compra tre (tu). ....
5 Nei giorni di festa ci vestiamo bene (si). ....

4 Answer these questions about your country. /5

1 A che ora si comincia a lavorare?

....

2 A che ora si finisce di lavorare in genere?

....

3 Si va spesso fuori a mangiare (ristorante o altro)?

....

4 Si fa shopping nel centro della città?

....

5 Ci si alza tardi nei giorni di festa?

....

28 Il mio gatto, i tuoi gatti, i suoi gatti...
Possessive adjectives and pronouns

Buon giorno signor Rossi, come sta **Sua moglie**? E **i Suoi figli**?

I miei stanno bene. Grazie.

Masculine		Feminine	
Singular	**Plural**	**Singular**	**Plural**
mio	miei	mia	mie
tuo	tuoi	tua	tue
suo/Suo	suoi/Suoi	sua/Sua	sue/Sue
nostro	nostri	nostra	nostre
vostro	vostri	vostra	vostre
loro	loro	loro	loro

Possessive adjectives indicate **possession** (*il **mio** gatto* my cat).
Possessive adjectives **agree in gender and number** with the name to which they refer.

La casa di Aldo è piccola. ⟶ *La **sua** casa è piccola.*
Aldo's house is small. ⟶ His house is small.
Le poesie di Marco sono belle. ⟶ *Le **sue** poesie sono belle.*
Marco's poems are beautiful. ⟶ His poems are beautiful.
I quaderni di Maria sono nuovi. ⟶ *I **suoi** quaderni sono nuovi.*
Maria's exercise books are new. ⟶ Her exercise books are new.
Questo è il cane di Anna. ⟶ *Il **suo** cane si chiama Fido.*
This is Anna's dog. ⟶ His dog is Fido.

The adjective ***loro*** is used for the feminine, masculine, singular and plural.

I bambini hanno una bicicletta. ⟶ *Quella è la **loro** bicicletta.*
The children have got a bicycle. ⟶ That is their bicycle.
Cerchi i documenti di Rita e Vincenzo? ⟶ *Ecco i **loro** documenti.*
Are you looking for Rita and Vincenzo's documents? ⟶ Here are their documents.

Differently from English, the Italian possessive adjectives are **usually preceded by definite articles** (my friend ***il mio** amico/**la mia** amica*).

Exception: with the names of **family members** we use the article only in the plural form.

*Tua nonna vive con voi? E i **tuoi** zii?* Does your grandmother live with you? What about your uncles?
*I **suoi** fratelli sono simpatici, invece **sua** sorella non mi piace.*
Her brothers are nice, but I don't like her sister.

The possessive pronouns

Possessive pronouns have the **same form as possessive adjectives**. They are **used alone** in place of nouns. They are always preceded by the article.

*I **miei** pantaloni sono nuovi, e i tuoi?* My trousers are new, what about yours?
***Tua** sorella lavora, la mia studia.* Your sister works, mine studies.

Exercises

1 Change the sentences using the possessive adjective.

/10

La bicicletta di Aldo ⟶ *La **sua** bicicletta.*

1 Il fidanzato di Carla ....
2 La proposta di voi due ....
3 I CD di Carlo e Marta ....
4 Lo zaino di Marta ....
5 Il numero di telefono di Mario ....
6 La sorellina di Francesco ....
7 Gli occhi di Federica ....
8 I cugini degli amici ....
9 Il quadro di Picasso ....
10 I genitori di Anna e Paolo ....

2 Answer with the possessive adjective.

/5

Qual è il nome della città più grande d'Italia? ⟶ *Il **suo** nome è Roma.*

1 Qual è il titolo di questi telefilm italiani? Il .... titolo è "Il commissario Montalbano".
2 Dove sono i tuoi amici? I .... amici sono all'università.
3 Qual è l'indirizzo della ragazza? Il .... indirizzo è scritto su questo foglio.
4 La nostra abitazione è bella e la vostra? La .... casa è piccola ma carina.
5 I nostri dolci sono molto buoni e il .... prezzo non è alto.

3 Complete with the possessive adjective + article.

/5

*Anna è contenta perché oggi è **il suo** compleanno.*

1 Anna è bellissima: .... occhi sono molto espressivi.
2 Paolo, ... idea è davvero originale!
3 Signora Bianchi, come stanno .... figli?
4 Noi studiamo molto, perché .... professori sono molto severi.
5 Non mi sento sola, perché .... amiche mi vogliono bene.

4 Answer with the possessive pronoun.

/8

Questa è la casa di Patrizio? ⟶ *No, non è **la sua**.*

1 Mi presti la tua macchina? .... sicuramente no. Prendi quella della mamma!
2 Questa è la vostra borsa? No, non è ....
3 I nostri amici sono molto colti e intelligenti. Come sono ....?
4 Ci date il vostro indirizzo mail? Sì, noi vi diamo .... e voi ci date ....
5 Mio padre è qui, anche ....? No, mio padre arriva alle otto.
6 Queste sono le nostre biciclette, ma dove sono quelle di Mario e Lucia? .... sono ancora nel box.
7 Vedo una moto. È la moto di Silvia? No, non è ...., ne sono sicuro.

29 Questo libro, quella zia, quei ragazzi...
Demonstrative adjectives

Questo cane si chiama Oliver.
Quei gatti si chiamano Luna e Sole.

Singular: ***questo/questa*** (this)
Plural: ***questi/queste*** (these)
They indicate closeness to the speaker or listener, or both.

Singular: ***quello/quella*** (that)
Plural: ***quelli/quelle*** (those)
They indicate people or things far from the speaker and listener.

Singular: ***stesso/a*** – ***medesimo/a*** (the same)
Plural: ***stessi/e – medesimi/e*** (the same)
They indicate the same identity.

Leggi **questo** *libro! È interessante.*
Read this book. It is interesting.
Guarda **quella** *ragazza. È Jane!*
Look at that girl. It's Jane.
Io e Mario abbiamo lo **stesso** *carattere.*
Mario and I have the same personality.

Demonstrative adjectives **agree in gender and number** with the name to which they refer.

Quello

The adjective ***quello*** follows the rules of the **determinative article.**

masculine nouns beginning with a **consonant**	singular → **quel**	plural → **quei**
masculine nouns beginning with ***z-***, ***gn-***, ***ps-***, ***s-*** + consonant	singular → **quello**	plural → **quegli**
masculine nouns beginning with a **vowel**	singular → **quell'**	plural → **quegli**
feminine nouns beginning with a **consonant**	singular → **quella**	plural → **quelle**
feminine nouns beginning with a **vowel**	singular → **quell'**	plural → **quelle**

Quei *ragazzi e* ***quell'****insegnante stanno lavorando a un progetto.*
Those boys and that teacher are working on a project.
Quello *zio di mio padre abita a Firenze.*
That uncle of my father's lives in Florence.

Exercises

1 Complete with *questo*. /6

*Vuoi **questi** fogli? No, non mi servono.*

1 I pantaloni in vetrina sono carini, ma .... gonna è più bella.
2 Di solito non mi piacciono le torte salate, ma .... torta è davvero buona!
3 .... è il quaderno di Giorgio, quello è di Maria.
4 .... albero è molto vecchio.
5 .... anno voglio imparare bene l'italiano.
6 .... poesie d'amore sono molto romantiche e tristi.

2 Complete with *quel/quello/quella/quei/quegli/quelle*. /7

1 .... studenti sono francesi.
2 Non trovo più le mie calze, ... rosse.
3 Preferisci la pasta con il sugo di carne o .... con il sugo di pesce?
4 .... persone non mi piacciono perché sono maleducate.
5 Non conosco .... uomo e nemmeno .... ragazzi.
6 .... cane è molto dolce e affettuoso.

3 Complete with *questo* e *quello* in the singular and plural form. /10

1 .... ristorante è economico, ma .... è più elegante.
2 .... uomini alla fermata dell'autobus sono dei poliziotti.
3 Preferisci .... abito a quadretti o .... a righe?
4 .... isola vicino alla Sardegna si chiama Sicilia; .... più a Nord si chiama Corsica e appartiene alla Francia.
5 .... sono giraffe, ma non conosco il nome di .... animali.
6 Andiamo da un'altra parte, ... negozio è troppo caro!

4 Write these sentences in the singular or plural. Pay attention: verbs and adjectives also change! /6

Questa torta è molto buona. → ***Queste** tort**e** **sono** molto buon**e**.*

1 Desidero quel maglione, per favore.

....

2 Quegli animali sono malati.

....

3 Quell'albero ha più di 100 anni.

....

4 Questi amici abitano a Genova.

....

5 Quelle ore di lezione sono divertenti.

....

6 Quella ragazza è molto carina.

....

Units 20-29 Summary exercises

1 Complete with the simple prepositions. /18

*Vieni **a** cena **a** casa mia?*

1 Marco abita .... Roma, ... via Garibaldi .... i genitori.
2 Lucia abita .... sette anni .... Spagna.
3 Andiamo .... biblioteca .... piedi o .... bicicletta?
4 Possiamo contare .... di te?
5 Vieni tu .... me o vengo io?
6 .... i miei genitori c'è un bel rapporto: si vogliono bene.
7 Nonna, prepari la crostata .... fragole .... domani?
8 La domenica gioca .... calcio .... i figli.
9 Prima .... uscire .... casa devi mettere .... ordine!

2 Choose the right alternative. /11

*È un uomo **di** circa settant'anni.*

1 *Da/Per/Su* due mesi *di/per/a* notte non riesco a dormire.
2 Salite *da/in/a* piedi o *da/in/a* ascensore?
3 Vorrei un quaderno *per/in/a* righe e una cartelletta *su/di/a* plastica.
4 *Da/In/A* luglio rimani *da/in/a* città? Penso di sì.
5 Quando discutono *di/su/a* politica, i miei genitori litigano.
6 *Per/In/A* estate indosso solo magliette.
7 Sei giovane. Sei già *per/in/a* pensione?

3 Answer with direct or indirect pronouns. /8

*Scrivete spesso ai vostri genitori? ⟶ Sì, **gli scriviamo** tutte le settimane.*

1 Ti piacciono le patatine fritte? Sì, ... molto.
2 Quando telefonate a Martina? .... domani.
3 Leggi spesso il giornale? No, non .... spesso.
4 Cerchi i tuoi occhiali? Sì, ...
5 Avete il libro? No, non ....
6 Sapete a che ora torna Alfredo? No, non ....
7 Perché non parli a Filippo? Non .... perché sono arrabbiato con lui.
8 A Carlo racconti tutto? Sì .... tutto.

4 Complete with *si*/*ci* using the verbs below. /8

capire • cenare • diventare • leggere • alzarsi • fumare • vestirsi • parlare

*D'estate **ci si lava** spesso.*

1 In Italia .... maggiorenni a 18 anni.
2 Con questa confusione non .... niente.
3 Per andare a un matrimonio non .... di nero.
4 Nel mio Paese .... molto e si vendono molti libri.
5 A casa mia la sera .... presto.
6 Nella mia famiglia .... poco.
7 Nei locali pubblici non ....
8 Quando entra il preside .... in piedi.

5 Answer the questions with the verb *piacere* and with the expressions *molto, poco, per niente, abbastanza.* /5

Ti piacciono gli spinaci? → *Sì, gli spinaci* ***mi piacciono molto****.*

1 A te piace cucinare?

....

2 Ti piacciono i dolci?

....

3 Ti basta un caffè di mattina per svegliarti?

....

4 Ti interessa l'arte moderna?

....

5 Ti serve una casa più grande?

....

6 Complete with "*di* + article". /5

Questo è il libro ***del*** *professore.*

1 Ho lasciato il cellulare nella macchina .... zia.
2 Sono allergico al pelo .... gatti.
3 Di cosa state parlando? .... situazione politica in Austria.
4 Di chi sono questi computer? .... nostri colleghi.
5 Di chi è quella moto? .... ragazzo di Diana.

7 Translate into Italian. /8

1 This is my book. What is that?

....

2 My friends are here.

....

3 Do you want some milk? Yes, I want some.

....

4 Will you tell me the truth? I'll tell it to you.

....

5 I'm going to my uncle's.

....

6 Lily's staying at my house.

....

7 The school is near the station.

....

8 The trees are behind the university.

....

30 1 mese, 2 cani, 3 studenti...
Cardinal numbers

0 zero	**8** otto	**16** sedici
1 uno	**9** nove	**17** diciassette
2 due	**10** dieci	**18** diciotto
3 tre	**11** undici	**19** diciannove
4 quattro	**12** dodici	**20** venti
5 cinque	**13** tredici	**21** ventuno
6 sei	**14** quattordici	**22** ventidue
7 sette	**15** quindici	**23** ventitré, etc.

30 trenta
40 quaranta
50 cinquanta
60 sessanta
70 settanta
80 ottanta
90 novanta
100 cento

1000	mille
10.000	diecimila
100.000	centomila
1.000.000	un milione
1.000.000.000	un miliardo

*Per il nostro appartamento spendiamo **milleduecentocinquanta** (1250) euro al mese.*
For our flat we spend 1250 euro a month.
*Ho pagato questo vestito **45** euro.*
I paid 45 euros for this dress.

Cardinal numbers ***do not change in gender or number***.
Exception: if they are **composed with *uno*** (one), they **agree**, like the indeterminative article, **with the noun**.

*Martina ha **sessantun** anni. Nella mia classe ci sono **trentuno** student.*
Martina is sixty one years old. In my class there are thirty one students.

Milione/miliardo

Milione and *miliardo* have the **plural form** in ***-i*** for both the masculine and the feminine and they are **followed by the preposition *di*.**

*In Italia vivono più di sessanta **milioni** di persone.*
Over 60 million people live in Italy.
*Sulla terra vivono più di sei **miliardi** di persone.*
Over six billion people/human beings live on earth.

Exercises

1 Write the numbers in letters.

/16

*20 = **venti***

1 7 ....
2 9 ....
3 17 ....
4 19 ....
5 4 ....
6 15 ....
7 10 ....
8 18 ....
9 14 ....
10 2 ....
11 5 ....
12 16 ....
13 12 ....
14 0 ....
15 13 ....
16 11 ....

2 Write the numbers in letters.

/5

*842 = **ottocentoquarantadue***

1 745 ....
2 578 ....
3 116 ....
4 1396 ....
5 5668 ....

3 Write these telephone numbers in letters. Write your telephone number on line 4 (the last line).

/4

*02 8438745: **zero due otto quattro tre otto sette quattro cinque***

1 338 543 765 0 ....
2 034 786543 ....
3 440 66 789 43 ....
4 ....

4 Look at these famous people. Write how old they are.

/5

1 Sofia Loren, attrice (1934)

....

2 Roberto Baggio, calciatore (1967)

....

3 Roberto Benigni, attore (1952)

....

4 Riccardo Muti, direttore d'orchestra (1941)

....

5 Rita Levi Montalcini, scienziata (1909)

....

31 Primo piano, secondo anno, settimo livello...
Ordinal numbers

I *primo* first	**XI** *undicesimo* eleventh	**XL** *quarantesimo* fortieth
II *secondo* second	**XII** *dodicesimo* twelfth	**L** *cinquantesimo* fiftieth
III *terzo* third	**XIII** *tredicesimo* thirteenth	**LX** *sessantesimo* sixtieth
IV *quarto* fourth	**XIV** *quattordicesimo* fourteenth	**XC** *novantesimo* ninetieth
V *quinto* fifth	**XV** *quindicesimo* fifteenth	**C** *centesimo* hundredth
VI *sesto* sixth	**XVI** *sedicesimo* sixteenth	**D** *cinquecentesimo* five hundredth
VII *settimo* seventh	**XVII** *diciassettesimo* seventeenth	**M** *millesimo* thousandth
VIII *ottavo* eighth	**XVII** *diciottesimo* eighteenth	
IX *nono* ninth	**XIX** *diciannovesimo* nineteenth	
X *decimo* tenth	**XX** *ventesimo* twentieth	

Oggi è la ***prima*** *domenica di dicembre.*
Today is the first Sunday of December.
È il ***secondo*** *volume dell'enciclopedia.*
It is the second volume of the encyclopedia.

As you can see, starting from the number 11, to form the ordinal number, the suffix ***-esimo*** is added to the cardinal numbers **by dropping the final vowel** of the cardinal number (with the **exception of 3: *tre***).
13° = *tredic-**esimo*** ⟶ tredicesimo

Ordinal numbers may also be written:

- with the **symbol °** for the masculine and **ª** for the feminine: 1°/1ª.
- with **Roman numbers**/numerals I, II, III, IV

The **ordinal numbers** are **usually preceded by the definite article** and since they are adjectives they must **agree in gender and number** with the nouns they modify.
Mercoledì è il ***terzo*** *giorno della settimana.*
Wednesday is the third day of the week.
È la sua ***ottava*** *festa di compleanno.*
It is his eighth birthday party.
Vivo al ***6°*** *piano, mentre i miei genitori vivono all'****ottavo*** *piano.*
I live on the 6th floor, while my parents live on the 8th floor.

Exercises

1 Convert the ordinal numbers to their cardinal equivalent. /10

quarantaquattro ⟶ ***quarantaquattresimo***

1 sei ....
2 dieci ....
3 quattordici ....
4 novantanove ....
5 mille ....
6 sessanta ....
7 cinquantacinque ....
8 uno ....
9 duecentotrenta ....
10 cinque ....

2 Convert the cardinal numbers to their ordinal equivalent. /6

trentesimo ⟶ ***trenta***

1 decimo ....
2 centotredicesimo ....
3 terzo ....
4 cinquantunesimo ....
5 primo ....
6 ottataduesimo ....

3 Write the numbers in letters. /8

Enrico IV ⟶ *Enrico* ***quarto***

1 Paolo VI ....
2 Filippo III ....
3 Carlo V ....
4 Vittorio Emanuele I ....
5 Luigi XIV ....
6 Enrico VIII ....
7 Elisabetta II ....
8 Benedetto XVI ....

4 Correct the mistakes where necessary. /8

Gira alla secondo ⟶ ***seconda*** *strada a destra.*

1 Questa è la nove volta che ti vedo qui. ....
2 Sei il primo di una lunga serie. ....
3 Non siete i primo, siete i terzo. ....
4 Beviamo la nostra quattra tazza di tè. ....
5 Fabio abita al piano tre. ....
6 Abbiamo milli euro. ....
7 Beviamo il nostro settimio caffè oggi. ....
8 Domani è centesimo compleanno di nonno Giorgio. ....

32 Ho amato, hai venduto, ha sentito...
Present perfect and past participle

Past participle (*participio passato*)

The **past participle** is formed **by dropping** the **infinitive ending** -***are***, -***ere***, or -***ire*** and **adding the ending:** -***ato***, -***uto***, **or** -***ito*** (see tables below).

	Infinite	Past participle
1st conjugation	am-are	am-**ato**
2nd conjugation	vend-ere	vend-**uto**
3rd conjugation	sent-ire	sent-**ito**

Present perfect (*passato prossimo*)

The ***passato prossimo*** is formed with: **the present indicative of the verb *avere* or *essere* + past participle of the verb**.

In English it can be translated with the present perfect or the simple past. It is used to ***describe past events that are now completed***.

Ho mangiato *una mela.* (= I've eaten an apple/I ate an apple.)

Person	Auxiliary *avere*	Past participle 1st conjugation	Past participle 2nd conjugation	Past participle 3rd conjugation
io	ho	amato	venduto	sentito
tu	hai	amato	venduto	sentito
lui/lei	ha	amato	venduto	sentito
noi	abbiamo	amato	venduto	sentito
voi	avete	amato	venduto	sentito
loro	hanno	amato	venduto	sentito

Oggi mangio solo frutta perché ieri ***ho mangiato*** *troppo.*
Today I'll eat only fruit because yesterday I ate too much.
Avete incontrato *Luca in discoteca?*
Did you meet Luca in the disco?
La notte scorsa non ***abbiamo dormito*** *per il caldo.*
Last night we didn't sleep due to the heat.

Remember that in Italian there are other past tenses: the *imperfetto* (see pg. 78) and the *passato remoto* (see pg. 102).

Exercises

1 Write the past participle. /12

mangiare ⟶ ***mangiato***

1 pulire ....
2 potere ....
3 telefonare ....
4 disegnare ....
5 cantare ....
6 volere ....
7 sapere ....
8 pagare ....
9 credere ....
10 dovere ....
11 contare ....
12 parlare ....

2 Rewrite the following sentences in the plural form. /6

Noi abbiamo mangiato troppo. ⟶ ***Io ho mangiato** troppo.*
Ho parlato inglese. ⟶ ***Abbiamo parlato** inglese.*

1 Che cosa hai comprato al mercato?
....
2 Prima di cena ho finito i compiti.
....
3 A Capodanno ha ballato tutta la notte.
....
4 Hai sentito le brutte notizie?
....
5 Hai dato i regali a Emma?
....
6 Non ho avuto tempo di fare i compiti.
....

3 Match the two columns. /5

1 Voglio preparare una torta,
2 Oggi sono stanco morto,
3 Dovete fare gli auguri a tutti gli amici,
4 Carla non ha legato la sua bicicletta,
5 Sai perché Lea e Aldo non si parlano?

☐ a) Sì, ieri hanno litigato!
☐ b) così qualcuno l'ha rubata.
☐ c) perché ieri ho pulito la mia stanza.
☐ d) così ho comprato farina e uova.
☐ e) così avete spedito 50 biglietti di auguri.

4 Complete the letter with the *passato prossimo*. /12

Caro Dario,
scusami se non ***ho potuto*** scriverti fino a oggi, ma (*avere*) 1) .... un sacco di cose da fare. Come stai? Io sto piuttosto bene, (*trovare*) 2) .... lavoro in un negozio di dischi. Ieri un collega (*invitare*) 3) .... tutti alla sua festa di compleanno. Così (*io, incontrare*) 4) .... una ragazza meravigliosa: Emma! Prima (*noi, ballare*) 5) .... insieme, poi (*mangiare*) 6) .... la torta che (*noi, portare*) 7) .... e (*noi, chiacchierare*) 8) .... di cinema e di sport per tutta la sera. Così (*io, capire*) 9) .... che Emma è proprio una ragazza simpatica. Alla fine della serata (*io, domandare*) 10) .... a Emma il suo indirizzo e lei mi (*dare*) 11) .... il suo numero di telefono. Così, questa mattina io (*telefonare*) 12) .... a Emma. Ho un appuntamento con lei domani!

33 Ho fatto, hai letto, ha scritto...
Irregular forms of the present perfect

Many verbs in Italian have **irregular past participles**.

Infinitive	Past participle	Examples
accendere to switch on	**acceso**	***Ho acceso*** *la luce perché è buio.* I've switched on the light because it's dark.
aprire to open	**aperto**	***Hanno aperto*** *la porta.* They opened the door.
bere to drink	**bevuto**	***Ho*** *già* ***bevuto*** *un litro d'acqua.* I've already drunk a litre of water.
chiedere to ask	**chiesto**	***Ho chiesto*** *dei soldi a un mio amico.* I asked my friend for some money.
chiudere to close	**chiuso**	***Abbiamo chiuso*** *la porta perché fa freddo.* We closed the door because it's cold.
conoscere to know/to meet	**conosciuto**	***Ho conosciuto*** *Paul a una festa.* I met Paul at a party.
dire to say	**detto**	*Chi* ***ha detto*** *questo?* Who said this?
fare to do	**fatto**	***Ho fatto*** *i compiti.* I did my homework.
mettere to put	**messo**	*Dove* ***hai messo*** *il mio borsellino?* Where did you put my purse?
offrire to offer	**offerto**	*Cosa ti* ***hanno offerto*** *da bere?* What did they offer you to drink?
perdere to lose	**perso**	***Abbiamo perso*** *peso nelle ultime settimane.* We have lost weight in the last few weeks.
prendere to take	**preso**	***Ho preso*** *l'autobus ieri.* I took the bus yesterday.
rimanere to stay	**rimasto**	*Non* ***sono rimasto*** *a scuola nel pomeriggio.* I didn't stay at school in the afternoon.
rompere to break	**rotto**	*Il bambino* ***ha rotto*** *il suo giocattolo.* The child broke his toy.
scegliere to choose	**scelto**	***Avete scelto*** *la pizza?* Did you choose the pizza?
scrivere to write	**scritto**	***Ho*** *appena* ***scritto*** *una mail al mio amico.* I've just written an email to my friend.
spegnere to switch off	**spento**	*Non* ***ho spento*** *la luce in camera da letto.* I haven't switched off the light in the bedroom.
succedere to happen	**successo**	*Cosa* ***è successo*** *laggiù?* What happened over there?
vedere to see	**visto**	***Avete visto*** *l'ultimo film con Brad Pitt?* Have you seen the latest film with Brad Pitt?
vincere to win	**vinto**	*La mia squadra* ***ha vinto*** *questa partita.* My team has won this match.

The adverbs ***sempre*** (always), ***mai*** (never), ***ancora*** (still/yet), ***già*** (already), etc are placed between the auxiliary and the past participle.

Exercises

1 Complete with the *passato prossimo* of the following verbs. /8

giocare • leggere • perdere • piangere • rispondere • scrivere • vedere • vincere

Oggi sono molto nervoso perché ***ho bevuto*** *troppi caffè.*

1 Io .... a carte con i miei zii: loro .... e io ....! Sono stato sfortunato.

2 Noi .... una lettera a Maia, ma lei non ci ....

3 Ragazzi, ... la pagina dello sport sul giornale di oggi?

4 Ieri noi .... un film così triste che .... per tutta la sera!

2 Complete with the present and with the *passato prossimo* of the verbs in brackets. /8

(Litigare, mai) Mio fratello e io non ***litighiamo*** *mai.* → *non* ***abbiamo*** *mai* ***litigato****.*

1 (*Capire, sempre*) Noi .... le regole di grammatica.

....

2 (*Tu, mandare*) A chi .... la cartolina?

....

3 (*Avere*) Loro .... mal di denti.

....

4 (*Raccontare, sempre*) Mia nonna mi .... le favole.

....

3 Find the twelve past participles of the following verbs. /12

P	R	E	S	**T**	**R**	**A**	**D**	**O**	**T**	**T**	**O**	A	R
R	A	T	R	E	I	T	I	T	R	U	Y	F	I
I	A	G	F	E	R	R	G	T	I	T	A	F	S
A	C	H	I	U	S	O	G	O	S	I	L	I	P
S	H	I	N	B	E	V	A	A	P	E	R	T	O
T	I	R	I	M	M	V	C	C	E	S	O	E	S
L	E	T	T	O	I	T	I	U	S	E	T	T	T
A	S	H	O	U	V	I	N	T	O	R	T	E	O
R	T	C	F	A	I	P	E	O	I	A	O	V	E
E	O	C	M	E	S	S	O	L	P	T	O	L	R
I	N	V	E	T	T	E	S	T	R	A	D	A	R
S	C	E	L	T	O	T	A	O	L	M	A	N	I

tradurre • chiudere • aprire • leggere • vincere • scegliere • chiedere • finire • vedere • togliere • spendere • rompere • rispondere

4 Build sentences using the *passato prossimo*. /5

Noi/mangiare/pizza/squisita. → ***Noi abbiamo mangiato una pizza squisita.***

1 Voi/mettere/bottiglie/in frigorifero? ....

2 Lui/bere/tazza di tè. ....

3 Lei/ridere/perché/lui/raccontare/barzelletta.

....

4 Tu/chiedere/Claudia/se/portare/piatti di plastica?

....

5 Quando/io/perdere/orecchini d'oro/piangere/come una fontana!

....

34 Sono andato, sei tornata, siamo uscite...
Present perfect of the verbs with the auxiliary *essere*

The *passato prossimo* of some verbs is formed with the verb ***essere*** (auxiliary verb) **in the present** + **past participle**. These verbs are called **intransitive** because they do not have a direct object. When the *passato prossimo* is formed with the auxiliary ***essere***, the past participle changes and **agrees with the subject like an adjective** (for the first group).

Person	Auxiliary *essere*	Past participle 1st conjugation	Past participle 2nd conjugation	Past participle 3rd conjugation
io	sono	andato/a	venuto/a	partito/a
tu	sei	andato/a	venuto/a	partito/a
lui/lei	è	andato/a	venuto/a	partito/a
noi	siamo	andati/e	venuti/e	partiti/e
voi	siete	andati/e	venuti/e	partiti/e
loro	sono	andati/e	venuti/e	partiti/e

*Filippo **è restato** a casa tutta la sera.* Filippo stayed home all evening.
*Mia sorella **è partita** qualche giorno fa.* My sister left a few days ago.
*I miei amici **sono andati** al cinema.* My friends have gone to the cinema.
*Le mie amiche non **sono venute** al cinema.* My friends haven't come to the cinema.
*Giorgia e Filippo **sono partiti** ieri.* Giorgia and Filippo left yesterday.

The verb ***essere*** uses the **auxiliary *essere***. The past participle of the verb *essere* is ***è stato/a***, the same as the verb ***stare***.

essere	**io sono stato/a**	**tu sei stato/a**	**lui/lei è stato/a**	**noi siamo stati/e, etc.**

*Durante l'inverno mia figlia **è stata** malata, ha avuto la febbre per due settimane.*
During the winter my daughter was ill, she had fever for two weeks.
*Dove **sei stato** lo scorso fine settimana?* Where were you last weekend?

Exercises

1 Rewrite these sentences in the singular or in the plural. /5

I nonni mi sono sembrati un po' stanchi. ⟶ ***Il nonno** mi **è sembrato** un po' **stanco**.*

1 Il mio pesce rosso è diventato grande. ....

2 I nonni di Paul sono tornati in Scozia. ....

3 Siamo arrivate tardi perché non siamo state bene. ....

4 Dove siete state tutto il pomeriggio? ....

5 Ieri le mie amiche sono andate al cinema a vedere un film giallo. ....

2 Complete these sentences with the present, then with the *passato prossimo*. /11

*(Costare) Questa sciarpa **costa** molto, i guanti invece non **costano** niente!*

⟶ *Questa sciarpa **è costata** molto, i guanti invece non **sono costati** niente!*

1 (*Andare*) Mia nonna .... al mercato a fare la spesa.

....

2 (*Uscire*) Chiara, con chi .... sabato pomeriggio?

....

3 (*Salire*) L'ascensore .... fino al terzo piano.

....

4 (*Essere*, *venire*) Carla .... malata, per questo non .... a scuola.

....

5 (*Alzarsi*) Mio fratello domenica .... alle 12.30.

....

3 Complete Anna's letter about an excursion to Genoa. /7

(*Noi, partire*) ***Noi siamo partiti*** in orario e dopo circa due ore di viaggio (*arrivare*) 1) .... a Genova. Dopo una breve passeggiata a piedi (*entrare*) 2) .... nel famoso acquario: che meraviglia! Mi (*piacere*) 3) .... molto i pesci tropicali. Belli anche i delfini, ma i pinguini mi (*sembrare*) 4) .... i più simpatici di tutti. Devo dire che (*essere*) 5) .... fortunata perché (*potere*) 6) .... assistere al loro pasto. Purtroppo (*dimenticare*) 7) .... di mandarti una cartolina: scusami tanto!

4 Complete the dialogue with the present or the *passato prossimo* of the following verbs. /9

andare • avere (2) • dare • fare • stare (2) • tornare • venire

Carla: Ciao, Paola, come ***stai***?

Paola: Ora 1) .... bene ma 2) .... malata per una settimana.

Carla: Poverina! 3) .... l'influenza?

Paola: Sì, 4) .... la febbre e la tosse

Carla: Ma 5) .... dal dottore?

Paola: Il dottore 6) .... a casa mia e mi 7) .... delle medicine. Ora mi 8) .... solo un po' male la testa; così domani forse 9) .... in ufficio.

35 Sono andato, si è rotta, siamo partiti...
Usage of the auxiliary with the present perfect

The auxiliary *essere*

We use the **auxiliary *essere*** in the following cases:

- with verbs that indicate **staying in one place** like: *stare* (to stay), *restare* (to remain), *rimanere* (to remain);
  *Ieri era vacanza e gli studenti **sono rimasti** a casa.*
  Yesterday was a holiday and the students stayed at home.
- with verbs that indicate **movement** like: *andare* (to go), *venire* (to come), *tornare* (to come back), *partire* (to leave), *entrare* (to enter);
  *Sabato scorso le mie amiche **sono andate** al cinema.*
  Last Saturday my friends went to the cinema.
- with verbs that indicate **changes** like: *nascere* (to be born), *diventare* (to become), *succedere* (to happen), *dimagrire* (to lose weight).
  *Tua figlia Ive **è diventata** davvero alta.* Your daughter Ive has become really tall.

Reflexive verbs

*Ieri Paola **si è svegliata** alle 5 ma si è alzata alle 6.*
Yesterday Paola woke up at five but she got up at six.

Direct pronouns with the *passato prossimo*

When the *passato prossimo* is formed **with** the auxiliary verb ***essere***, we must have **agreement in number and gender with the personal pronoun**.

*Hai la patente? No, **l'ho dimenticata**.*
Have you got your driving license? No, I've forgotten it.
*Dove sono le chiavi? **Le ho messe** sul tavolo.*
Where are the keys? I put them on the table.
*Quanto costano questi occhiali? **Li ho pagati** 120 euro.*
How much do these glasses cost? I paid 120 euros for them.

With the **indirect object pronouns** the past participle doesn't change.

*Ho perso l'indirizzo di Anna, così **le ho telefonato**.* I lost Anna's address, so I phoned her.
***Vi hanno detto** tutta la verità.* They told you the whole truth.

Exercises

1 Complete with the right ending. /10

*La settimana scorsa Paola è andat***a** *in Francia a trovare sua zia.*

1 Pochi giorni fa il mio cane è mort......... di vecchiaia.
2 Che peccato! La tazzina è cadut......... e si è rott.........
3 Paolo e io siamo nat......... a Bologna.
4 La commedia non è piaciut......... a Paola, così non è rimast......... fino alla fine ma è uscit......... mezz'ora prima.
5 I bambini si sono alzat........., si sono lavat........., poi sono uscit......... per andare a scuola.

2 Complete the sentences with the *passato prossimo*. Choose the right verb. /8

chiedere • avere • perdere • cadere • piacere • spendere • alzarsi • suonare

Non ***ho letto*** *il messaggio che Paolo* ***ha mandato****.*

1 Non ***abbiamo telefonato*** a Pietro perché .... il suo numero di telefono.
2 Ci .... il film di ieri.
3 Maia .... un incidente: .... dalle scale.
4 Anna .... tutti i soldi, così .... un prestito ai suoi genitori.
5 Noi .... quando .... la sveglia.

3 *Avere* or *essere*? Underline the correct form of the verb. /20

Cara Alina,
scusami se fino a oggi non ***ti ho scritto****/è scritto*, ma 1) *sono successe/hanno successo* così tante cose che non 2) *è avuto/ho avuto* un attimo di tempo. Da quando 3) *sono arrivata/ho arrivato* in Italia 4) *ho passati/sono passati* quattro mesi. Prima con i miei genitori 5) *abbiamo vissuto/siamo vissuti* a Napoli, una città che mi 6) *è piaciuta/ha piaciuto* moltissimo. Poi mio padre 7) *è trovato/ha trovato* lavoro a Milano e 8) ci *abbiamo trasferito/siamo trasferiti* lì. 9) *Ho dovuto/sono dovuta* cambiare scuola, ma 10) *ho conosciuto/sono conosciuta* molte persone simpatiche e 11) mi *sono trovata/ho trovato* subito bene. 12) *Ho fatto/sono fatta* molti progressi con la lingua e 13) *sono capito/ho capito* che l'italiano non è così difficile. Ma non 14) ti *ho ancora raccontato/sono ancora raccontata* la cosa più importante: 15) *ho incontrato/sono incontrata* un ragazzo molto carino che si chiama Mohammed. 16) *L'ho conosciuta/l'ho conosciuto* a una festa e appena 17) l'*ho visto/ho vista* 18) mi *ha piaciuto/è piaciuto* subito.
Per il momento siamo solo amici, però, chissà!
Ora devo salutarti perché non 19) *ho ancora finito/sono finita* i compiti.
Scrivimi presto, voglio avere tue notizie e sapere che cosa 20) *ha successo/è successo* a Casablanca in questi quattro mesi.
Un abbraccio
Fatima

36 Io amavo, tu vendevi, lui sentiva...
Imperfect tense

The ***imperfetto*** (imperfect tense) can be translated in English with the simple past or the past continuous. When the action is repeated in the past, it can also be translated with **used to** or **would**.
It is formed by dropping the -***re*** of the infinitive and adding the vowel:

- -***a*** for the first conjugation;
- -***e*** for the second conjugation;
- -***i*** for the third conjugation.

Verb stem	Vowel	Ending
am-	-a-	**-vo**

Person	1st conjugation	1nd conjugation	1rd conjugation
io	am-**a**-**vo**	vend-**e**-**vo**	sent-**i**-**vo**
tu	am-**a**-**vi**	vend-**e**-**vi**	sent-**i**-**vi**
lui/lei	am-**a**-**va**	vend-**e**-**va**	sent-**i**-**va**
noi	am-**a**-**vamo**	vend-**e**-**vamo**	sent-**i**-**vamo**
voi	am-**a**-**vate**	vend-**e**-**vate**	sent-**i**-**vate**
loro	am-**a**-**vano**	vend-**e**-**vano**	sent-**i**-**vano**

Usage

The *imperfetto* is used to:

- describe **actions that lasted for an indefinite time in the past or that were repeated in the past**;
  In Grecia mia padre ***lavorava*** *in un ospedale.*
  In Greece my father worked/used to work in a hospital.
- describe **longer actions in relation to shorter actions**;
  Mentre ***stirava guardava*** *la televisione.*
  While he was ironing, he was watching television.
- describe **people, objects and situations in the past**;
  Da ragazzo Aldo ***aveva*** *i capelli lunghi.*
  When he was a boy Aldo had long hair.

It is also used to **translate the form *I used to*** in English.

Exercises

1 Write the *imperfetto* of the following verbs. /10

mangio ⟶ ***mangiavo***

1 parlano ....
2 vedi ....
3 finisce ....
4 crede ....
5 cantate ....
6 studia ....
7 sentono ....
8 vado ....
9 lavora ....
10 piangono ....

2 Complete the sentences with the *imperfetto*. /14

Quando (essere) ⟶ ***ero*** *piccola mi (piacere)* ⟶ ***piacevano*** *i palloncini.*

1 Mentre Carlo (*disegnare*) ...., sua sorella (*ascoltare*) .... la musica e (*cantare*) ....
2 Durante l'estate (*noi, divertirsi*) .... ad andare al mare tutti i giorni, mentre i nostri amici (*preparare*) .... gli esami.
3 Quando (*tu, vivere*) .... a Casablanca, (*mangiare*) .... tutti i giorni il cous-cous?
4 Due anni fa mio padre (*lavorare*) .... in una fabbrica, mia madre invece (*occuparsi*) .... di una bambina che (*abitare*) .... vicino a noi.
5 Il professore ci ha spiegato che gli antichi Romani (*costruire*) .... acquedotti e terme dove (*andare*) .... a rilassarsi.
6 Da ragazza mia madre (*uscire*) .... tutte le sere: le (*piacere*) .... andare al cinema o a ballare con i suoi amici.

3 Complete the description with the present and with the *imperfetto*. /28

Il mio cane (*chiamarsi*) ***si chiama/si chiamava*** Oro. (*essere*) 1) .... un cucciolo simpatico e curioso, (*avere*) 2) .... il pelo nero con delle macchie bianche. Quando mi (*vedere*) 3) .... mi 4) (*venire*) .... incontro festoso e mi (*leccare*) 5) .... tutta. Purtroppo, spesso (*abbaiare*) 6) .... e i nostri vicini di casa non (*essere*) 7) .... contenti. Tutti noi lo (*amare*) 8) ...., lo (*io – coccolare*) 9) .... e lo (*viziare*) 10) .... Mia madre addirittura (*dire*) 11) .... che non (*essere*) 12) .... un animale, ma il suo bambino peloso. Anche io gli (*volere*) 13) .... molto bene e mi (*piacere*) 14) .... molto giocare con lui.

37 Io ero, voi eravate... Tu facevi, lui diceva, loro bevevano...
Imperfect of irregular verbs
Usage of the imperfect and present perfect

The imperfect (*imperfetto*) of the verb "to be" (*essere*)

essere	io ero	tu eri	lui/lei era	noi eravamo	voi eravate	loro erano

Era *molto triste perché non poteva vederla.*
He was very sad because he couldn't see her.

The most common verbs with an irregular *imperfetto*

bere	bevevo	bevevi	beveva	bevevamo	bevevate	bevevano
dire	dicevo	dicevi	diceva	dicevamo	dicevate	dicevano
fare	facevo	facevi	faceva	facevamo	facevate	facevano

Ogni sera mia nonna ***beveva*** *una tazza di camomilla.*
Every evening my grandma drank (used to drink) a cup of chamomile tea.
Da bambino mio fratello ***diceva*** *un sacco di bugie.*
When he was a child, my brother used to tell a lot of lies.

Verbs ending with *-urre*

Verbs ending with *-urre* **drop *-rre* and add *-c* to the ending.**

tradurre	tradu**c**evo	tradu**c**evi	tradu**c**eva	tradu**c**evamo	tradu**c**evate	tradu**c**evano

Imperfetto or *passato prossimo*?

The ***imperfetto*** and the ***passato prossimo*** can be found together in the same sentence. Look at the example.

Dormivamo *ancora quando Giulia* ***ha telefonato.***
We were still sleeping when Giulia phoned.
Quando era ragazza mia madre era molto timida.
When she was a girl, my mother was very shy.

Here the ***imperfetto*** **gives the setting**, and the ***passato prossimo*** **describes the main action.**
The *imperfetto* is used when the dependent clause is introduced by ***mentre***.

Mentre parlava *scriveva messaggi.*
While he was talking he was texting.

Exercises

1 Write the correct forms of the *imperfetto* of the following verbs. /10

bevo ⟶ ***bevevo***

1 dici ....
2 facciamo ....
3 traducete ....
4 siamo ....
5 dobbiamo ....
6 posso ....
7 sei ....
8 beve ....
9 fate ....
10 dicono ....

2 Complete with the *imperfetto* of these verbs. /8

essere • dire • fare (2) • bere • abitare • mangiare • volere

Quell'estate noi ***eravamo*** al mare e 1) .... davvero molto caldo. Per fortuna 2) .... in una casetta molto vicino a mare. Io 3) .... ogni giorno tre o quattro litri di acqua. Mia sorella non 4) .... bere. 5) .... che bere tanto 6) .... male. E invece di bere, 7) .... tanta frutta. Un giorno si è sentita male: aveva mangiato due chili di pesche. Mia sorella 8) .... proprio una ragazza strana!

3 Imperfetto or *passato prossimo*? Choose the right form. /12

*Marco **ha vissuto**/viveva per sette anni a Napoli.*

1 Da piccolo, mio padre è *andato/andava* tutti i giorni a scuola.
2 Martedì *vedevo/ho visto* un film di fantascienza che mi è *piaciuto/piaceva* molto.
3 Mentre *leggeva/ha letto* il giornale, mio padre per sbaglio *ha messo/metteva* il sale nel caffè: *abbiamo riso/ridevamo* tutti come dei matti!
4 Mia nonna mi racconta che quando *c'era/è stata* la guerra le persone non *hanno avuto/avevano* niente da mangiare e *sono morte/morivano* di freddo.
5 A ottant'anni mio nonno *leggeva/ha letto* il giornale senza occhiali.
6 Nel Medioevo le persone *abitavano/hanno abitato* nei castelli perché *avevano/hanno avuto* paura delle invasioni dei barbari.

4 Correct the mistake where necessary. /5

1 Da piccolo dormo tanto. ....
2 Ieri guardavo la televisione mentre ho mangiato.
....
3 C'era una volta una principessa che viveva in un castello.
....
4 Per anni studiava l'inglese ma non riusciva a impararlo bene.
....
5 Ha cominciato la scuola quando aveva sei anni.
....

38 Ascolta!, Vendete!, Non sentire!...
Imperative

The imperative has **only one tense**: the **present**. The imperative in the **second person singular and plural** is called ***diretto*** (direct).
The imperative has the **same form as the indicative present** with the exception of the 2nd person singular of the verbs of the first conjugation which end in -***a***.

	1st conjugation	2nd conjugation	3rd conjugation	Reflexive form
	ASCOLTARE	**VENDERE**	**SENTIRE**	**ALZARSI**
tu	ascolt-**a**!	vend-**i**!	sent-**i**!	alz**a**ti!
voi	ascolt-**ate**	vend-**ete**!	sent-**ite**!	alz**ate**vi!

Usage

It is used to **give orders** or **advice or to urge someone**.

*Aldo, parl**a** più chiaramente per favore.*
Aldo, talk more clearly, please.
*Veronica, vedo che non stai bene. **Vai** dal dottore!*
Veronica, I see you aren't well. Go to the doctor!

The imperative in the negative form

	1st conjugation	2nd conjugation	3rd conjugation	Reflexive form	
	ASCOLTARE	**VENDERE**	**SENTIRE**	**ALZARSI**	
tu	**non** ascolt-**are**!	**non** vend-**ere**!	**non** sent-**ire**!	**non ti** alzare!	**non** alzar**ti**!
voi	**non** ascolt-**ate**!	**non** vend-**ete**!	**non** sent-**ite**!	**non vi** alzate!	**non** alzate**vi**!

For the **second person singular**, the negative imperative is formed with ***non*** + **the infinitive of the verb**.
For the **second person plural the form is the same (=) as the present indicative**.

With the **reflexive verbs the pronoun can be placed before** or **after the verb**.

*Gina, Silvia, **non sedetevi/non vi sedete**!*
Gina, Silvia, don't sit down!
*Pietro, **non addormentarti/non ti addormentare**!*
Pietro, don't fall asleep!

Exercises

1 Write these verbs in the imperative.

/20

restare ⟶ ***Resta! Restate!***

1 mangiare ....
2 dormire ....
3 scrivere ....
4 parlare ....
5 correre ....
6 giocare ....
7 ascoltare ....
8 finire ....
9 tradurre ....
10 usare ....

2 Write these sentences in the imperative.

/6

Non andare (2ª pers. plur.) ⟶ ***Non andate!***
Mangiare la frutta (2ª pers. sing.) ⟶ ***Mangia la frutta!***

1 Prendere l'autobus (2ª persona sing.) ....
2 Aspettare a casa (2ª persona sing.) ....
3 Non studiare di più (2ª persona plur.) ....
4 Pulire la stanza (2ª persona plur.) ....
5 Lavare i piatti (2ª persona sing.) ....
6 Non guardare la televisione (2ª persona plur.) ....

3 Build sentences with the imperative.

/4

Chiedi a un amico di non fumare nella stanza. ⟶ ***Non fumare qui per favore!***

1 Invita i tuoi colleghi a parlare a bassa voce.
....
2 Chiedi a tua sorella di spegnere la televisione.
....
3 Chiedi al tuo amico Gianni di apparecchiare la tavola.
....
4 Chiedi ai tuoi colleghi di non aprire la finestra.
....

4 Choose the right alternative.

/6

1 Ragazzi, *non voi sedete/non sedetevi* vicino al calorifero!
2 Gianna, è tardi. *Svegliati/Ti svegli*!
3 Bambini, *vi lavate/lavatevi* le mani!
4 Carla, non *torni/tornare* tardi!
5 Ragazzi, qui è pericoloso, *vi spostate/spostatevi*!
6 Fa freddo. Fabio, non *uscire/esci*!

39 Sii!, Va'!, Dimmi!...
Indirect imperative and imperative with pronouns

Imperative form of irregular verbs

	ESSERE (positive)	AVERE (positive)
tu	**sii!**	**abbi!**
voi	**siate!**	**abbiate!**

	tu	voi
andare	va'!	andate!
dare	da'!	date!
dire	di'!	dite!

	tu	voi
fare	fa'!	fate!
sapere	**sappi**!	**sappiate**!
stare	sta'!	state!

Negative imperative form of the verbs "to be/to have" (*essere/avere*)

	ESSERE (negative)	AVERE (negative)
tu	**non** essere!	**non** avere!
voi	**non siate!**	**non abbiate!**

Imperative with pronouns

With the imperative in the positive form the **pronouns are usually placed after the verb**.

Lucia, ecco le lettere. ***Spediscile****!* Lucia, here are the letters. Send them, please!
A Marco servono dei guanti. ***Regaliamoglieli****!* Marco needs gloves. Why don't we give them to him?

Negative imperative with pronouns

With the imperative in the negative form the **pronouns are placed before or after the verb. In the second person singular the verb drops the -e** like in the example: ***Non aprirlo***! (Don't open it!).
But you can also say: *Non **lo** aprire!*
For the second person plural: ***Non dateglielo/non glielo date***! (Don't give it to him!).

The form of the **irregular verbs doubles the consonant of the pronoun**, as you can see in these tables.

di' + lo = **dillo!** (say it!)	fa' + le = **falle!** (do them!)	sta' + mi (vicino) = **stammi** (vicino)**!** (stay next to me!)
da' + me lo = **dammelo!** (give it to me)	di' + ce + lo = **diccelo!** (say it to us!)	va' + ci = **vacci!** (go there!)

Che cosa ti ha detto Giulio di me? ***Dimmelo****!* What did Giulio tell you about me? Tell me!
Luca non sa cosa è successo: ***diglielo****!* Luca doesn't know what happened: tell him!

Exercises

1 Complete with the correct imperative forms of the verbs *essere* and *avere*. /6

Per favore, (tu, essere) gentile con i parenti in visita! ⟶ *Per favore,* ***sii*** *gentile con i parenti in visita!*

1 (*Tu, avere*) .... il coraggio di dire quello che pensi!
2 Vi prego, (*avere*) .... pazienza!
3 (*Tu, essere*) .... buono!
4 (*Tu, non avere*) .... paura!
5 (*Voi, non essere*) .... indisciplinati e seguite le regole!
6 (*Voi, non avere*) .... fretta! C'è tempo.

2 Write these verbs in the imperative. /8

(Fare) ⟶ ***Fa'*** *quello che ti dico.*

1 (*Andare*) subito a casa! ....
2 (*Dire*) delle parole in italiano! ....
3 (*Dare*) al tuo amico il suo dizionario! ....
4 (*Fare*) le faccende di casa! ....
5 (*Essere*) più buono con tutti! ....
6 (*Stare*) tranquillo! ....
7 (*Avere*) coraggio. ....
8 (*Sapere*) dominare la tua rabbia! ....

3 Choose the right alternative. /6

1 *Va'/anda* lì!
2 *State/stiate* qui un attimo, per favore!
3 *Abbi/hai* un po' di tolleranza per i bambini!
4 *Non abbiate/avete* timore di lui! Non è così cattivo.
5 *Sia/sii* intelligente e non sfidare il tuo capo!
6 Hai scritto a Lucia? No? Allora *scrivile/scriverle* adesso!

4 Build sentences with the imperative forms and the pronouns. /5

Devi dire la verità a Paolo: ⟶ ***digliela****!*

1 Dovete dare la penna a Giulio: ....!
2 Non devi telefonare a Martina: ....!
3 Devi comperare il pane: ....!
4 Non dovete riferire la notizia: ....!
5 Devi scrivere alla nonna: ....!

5 Correct the verbs. /6

1 <u>Dici</u> a lui quello che hai detto a me! ....
2 Paolo, vogliamo sapere le novità, <u>dicele</u>! ....
3 Il pesce, <u>falo</u> al forno! ....
4 <u>Anda</u> a posto e non parlare! ....
5 <u>Di lo</u> anche agli altri! ....
6 Giuseppe, non <u>fa</u> lo sciocco! ....

Units 30-39 Summary exercises

1 Complete with numeral or ordinal adjectives in number or in letters. /9

Marzo è il ***quarto (IV)*** *mese dell'anno. Le stagioni sono* ***quattro (4)****.*

1 Mercoledì è il .... giorno della settimana.
2 Se ottieni il .... posto vinci la medaglia d'argento.
3 .... metri corrisponde a un chilometro.
4 In Italia porta sfortuna il numero .... o il numero ....?
5 Maggio è il .... mese dell'anno.
6 .... centimetri corrispondono a un metro.
7 La maratona conta più di .... chilometri.
8 Quando compio .... anni divento maggiorenne.

2 Complete with the present and then rewrite the following sentences in the *passato prossimo*. /10

(Mangiare) Io non ***mangio*** *mai il pesce crudo. ⟶ Io non* ***ho mai mangiato*** *il pesce crudo.*

1 (*Brindare, noi*) A Capodanno .... sempre con gli amici.
A Capodanno .... con gli amici.
2 (*Pulire, tu*) Non .... mai il pavimento.
Non .... il pavimento.
3 (*Potere, io*) A causa del rumore non .... mai dormire.
A causa del rumore non .... dormire.
4 (*Litigare*) Io e mio fratello non .... mai.
Io e mio fratello non ....
5 (*Capire*) Tu non .... ancora bene le regole di grammatica.
Tu non .... bene le regole di grammatica.

3 Complete with the present and then rewrite the following sentences in the *passato prossimo*. /12

(Venire) Paola, ***vieni*** *da sola? ⟶ Paola* ***sei venuta*** *da sola?*

1 (*Entrare*) Gli operai .... in fabbrica alle 8.00.
Gli operai .... in fabbrica alle 8.00.
2 (*Addormentarsi*) A che ora .... i tuoi bambini?
A che ora .... i tuoi bambini?
3 (*Uscire*) A che ora (tu) .... da casa?
A che ora .... da casa?
4 (*Alzarsi*) I miei genitori .... sempre presto.
I miei genitori .... sempre .... presto.
5 (*Spedire*) Io .... sempre gli auguri ai miei parenti per Pasqua.
Io .... sempre .... gli auguri ai miei parenti per Pasqua.

4 Complete with the *passato prossimo* of the irregular verbs. /10

(Prendere) Chi ***ha preso*** *il giornale?*

1 (*Essere*) Carla, dove .... fino adesso?
2 (*Bere*) Oggi Luca è molto nervoso perché .... troppi caffè.

3 (*Accendere*) Perché (voi) .... la luce?
4 (*Leggere, scrivere*) Non (noi) .... ancora ....
la lettera che (voi) ci ....
5 (*Sciogliere, rimanere, venire*) Il sole .... la neve così (noi)
.... a casa e non .... da te in montagna.
6 (*Spendere, chiedere*) (*voi*) .... troppi soldi. Per questo
.... un prestito?

5 Complete with the *passato prossimo* and with the *imperfetto*. /12

(Bere, vedere, uscire) Mentre ***bevevamo*** *qualcosa insieme,* ***abbiamo visto*** *Daniele che* ***usciva*** *dal bar.*

1 (*Essere, aiutare, stare*) Quando .... piccoli, mia nonna ci ....
sempre a fare i compiti e .... sempre con noi.
2 (*Dire, rompere, giocare*) (*loro*) Mi .... che mio figlio .... per sbaglio
gli occhiali di un compagno mentre .... nel cortile.
3 (*Perdere, parcheggiare*) Che sbadato! (Io) .... le chiavi di casa mentre
.... la macchina.
4 (*Togliere, fare*) Il dentista mi .... il dente del giudizio perché mi .... male.
5 (*Fare, essere*) Ieri la nonna .... la torta di fragole perché ....
il mio compleanno.

6 Translate these sentences. /8

1 Monday is the first day of the week.

....

2 Yesterday we went to a party.

....

3 Where did you go last week, Roxana?

....

4 On Saturday night Adriano didn't sleep at home.

....

5 Fred has gone out with Paul.

....

6 Come here and listen to me!

....

7 Go home! It's late.

....

8 I was washing the dishes when the phone rang.

....

40 Del cielo, degli altri... Al cinema, alle otto...
Prepositional articles with *di* and *a* + article

The ***preposizioni articolate*** (prepositional articles) are formed by **simple prepositions** (***di*, *a*, *da***, etc.) + **the determinative article** (***il*, *lo*, *la***, etc.).

The preposition *di* + article

Amo il colore ***del*** *cielo di sera.* I love the colour of the sky in the evening.	di + il = **del**
Lo zaino ***dello*** *studente è vicino alla porta.* The student's rucksack is next to the door.	di + lo = **dello**
Mi piace il calore ***dell'****estate.* I like the heat of summer.	di + l' = **dell'**
La matita è ***della*** *professoressa.* The pencil belongs to the teacher.	di + la = **della**
Quali sono i nomi ***delle*** *tue amiche?* What are the names of your friends?	di + le = **delle**
Sono le foto ***dei*** *colleghi di Mario.* They're the photos of Mario's colleagues.	di + i = **dei**
Mi piacciono le foto ***degli*** *animali.* I like photos of the animals.	di + gli = **degli**

Partitive articles (*articoli partitivi*)

The prepositional articles can also be used as **partitive articles**.

- ***Di*** + ***il*** → *Ho comprato* ***del*** *pane.* I bought some bread.
- ***Di*** + ***le*** → *Vuoi* ***delle*** *fragole?* Do you want some strawberries?
- ***Di*** + ***la*** → *Mi serve* ***della*** *frutta.* I need some fruit.

They can be considered the **plural form of the indeterminative articles *un*, *uno*, *una***.

In Italian the partitive article is less common than in English. In many cases in fact it is not expressed.
Ho bisogno ~~dei~~ soldi. → *Ho bisogno di soldi.* I need some money.

The preposition *a* + article

Sabato sera andiamo ***al*** *cinema.* On Saturday evening we're going to the cinema.	a + il = **al**
La domenica vado sempre ***allo*** *stadio.* On Sunday I always go to the stadium.	a + lo = **allo**
Mia mamma prepara spesso il tè ***all'****arancia.* Mia mother often prepares orange tea.	a + l' = **all'**
Alle cinque devo andare ***alla*** *stazione.* At five I have to go to the station.	a + la = **alla**
Il treno parte ***alle*** *19.45.* The train leaves at 19.45.	a + le = **alle**
Ho cucinato i maccheroni ***ai*** *quattro formaggi. I cooked maccheroni ai quattro formaggi.*	a + i = **ai**
Ho chiesto ***agli*** *amici di venire con me.* I asked my friends to come with me.	a + gli = **agli**

Exercises

1 Write the *preposizione articolata* in the singular. /12

bambino ⟶ ***del*** *bambino*

1 .... uomo	4 .... casa	7 .... zaino	10 .... pomeriggio
2 .... donna	5 .... aeroplano	8 .... amore	11 .... studente
3 .... libro	6 .... zio	9 .... telefono	12 .... impiegata

2 Write the *preposizione articolata* in the plural. /8

1 .... uomini	3 .... libri	5 .... aeroplani	7 .... zaini
2 .... donne	4 .... case	6 .... zii	8 .... pomeriggi

3 Complete the dialogue with *del, dello, dell', della, dei, degli, delle.* /20

Carlo: Buongiorno, vorrei organizzare una festa e mi servono molte cose. Può aiutarmi?
Negoziante: Certamente. Cominciamo con ***delle*** bibite. Per esempio 1) .... aranciate e 2) .... aperitivi analcolici e poi 3) .... acqua liscia e gassata. Se non ci sono minorenni, anche 4) .... birra.
Carlo: Bene. Poi mi serve 5) .... cibo.
Negoziante: Certo. Ecco 6) .... patatine, 7) .... salatini e 8) .... pane per fare 9) .... tartine.
Carlo: Ma con che cosa le faccio le tartine?
Negoziante: Puoi usare 10) .... burro o 11) .... maionese, con 12) .... olive, o 13) .... affettati, per esempio 14) .... prosciutto crudo o cotto e 15) .... salame. Ma se hai 16) .... amici vegetariani, puoi usare 17) .... formaggio.
Carlo: Benissimo. Ah, non devo dimenticarmi di comprare 18) .... bicchieri di plastica e 19) .... tovaglioli di carta...
Negoziante: Eccoli qua! Abbiamo 20) .... pacchi in offerta!

4 Answer with "*di* + article". /6

1 Di chi è quella moto? .... ragazzo di Diana.
2 Di dove siete? Siamo .... Sud della Germania.
3 Di cosa state parlando? .... situazione politica in Austria.
4 Di chi sono questi computer? .... nostri colleghi.
5 Di cosa discuti sempre con Raimondo? .... importanza dell'amore.

5 Complete with "*a* + article". /10

Andiamo ***al*** *cinema?*

1 In estate vado .... mare .... isole Eolie.
2 Siamo andati .... ristorante e abbiamo ordinato un filetto .... pepe verde.
3 Stasera .... TV c'è un film storico.
4 Carlo lavora nella pizzeria dietro .... stazione.
5 .... nove cominciano le lezioni .... università.
6 Ho regalato .... nonna un bagnoschiuma .... mandorle.

41 Dal medico... Nella casa... Sugli scogli...
Prepositional articles with *da*, *in* and *su* + article

The preposition *da* + article

Devo andare ***dal*** *medico.* I must go to the doctor's.	da + il = **dal**
Stanno uscendo ***dallo*** *stadio.* They're leaving the stadium.	da + lo = **dallo**
Siamo appena scesi ***dall'****autobus.* We have just got off the bus.	da + l' = **dall'**
Anna è andata ***dalla*** *parrucchiera.* Anna went to the hairdresser's.	da + la = **dalla**
I negozi sono chiusi ***dalle*** *13.00 alle 16.00.* Shops are closed from 13.00 to 16.00.	da + le = **dalle**
Stasera vado a mangiare ***dai*** *nonni.* Tonight I'm going to eat at my grandparents'.	da + i = **dai**
Carla vive ***dagli*** *zii.* Carla lives at her uncles'.	da + gli = **dagli**

Differently from English, to indicate the **time** you use the **prepositional articles in the plural form**.
Frequento il corso d'inglese ***dalle*** *8* ***alle*** *11.* I attend the English course from 8 to 11.

But with expressions like **noon** (*mezzogiorno*) and **midnight** (*mezzanotte*) you use the simple preposition.
Ho lavorato ***da*** *mezzogiorno* ***alle*** *16.00.* I worked from noon to 4 p.m.

The preposition *in* + article

C'è della carta ***nel*** *cestino.* There is some paper in the bin.	in + il = **nel**
Ci sono delle rane ***nello*** *stagno.* There are some frogs in the pond.	in + lo = **nello**
Metti i pantaloni ***nell'****armadio.* Put the trousers in the wardrobe.	in + l' = **nell'**
Ho messo dell'olio ***nella*** *minestra.* I put some oil in the soup.	in + la = **nella**
Ho una casa ***nelle*** *Alpi.* I've got a house in the Alps.	in + le = **nelle**
Non trovo informazioni ***nei*** *tuoi appunti.* I can't find any information in your notes.	in + i = **nei**
Ci sono dei fiori ***negli*** *stagni.* There are some flowers in the ponds.	in + gli = **negli**

The preposition *su* + article

Sul *tavolo c'è una tazza di tè.* On the table there is a cup of tea.	su + il = **sul**
Hai riflettuto ***sullo*** *sbaglio che hai fatto?* Have you reflected upon the mistake you made?	su + lo = **sullo**
Vedo una barchetta ***sull'****acqua.* I see a little boat on the water.	su + l' = **sull'**
La matita è ***sulla*** *sedia.* The pencil is on the chair.	su + la = **sulla**
C'è neve ***sulle*** *cime delle montagne.* There is snow on the peaks of the mountains.	su + le = **sulle**
Hai un ragno ***sui*** *capelli.* You've got a spider on your hair.	su + i = **sui**
Non metto mai formaggio ***sugli*** *spaghetti.* I never put any cheese on the spaghetti.	su + gli = **sugli**

Exercises

1 Complete with "*da* + article". /7

Ho finito le mele: devo andare ***dal*** *fruttivendolo.*

1 Quando sto .... zia, mangio sempre troppo.
2 .... zoo a casa possiamo prendere l'autobus.
3 Il fiume che passa .... mia città è l'Arno.
4 Quando la mia cuginetta è lontana .... sua mamma è triste.
5 È .... anno scorso che non vedo Veronica.
6 Nada viene .... Marocco, è in Italia .... mese di dicembre.

2 Where do you go? Complete the sentence with "preposition + noun". /6

Dal macellaio *a comprare la carne.*

1 .... a comprare la frutta.
2 .... perché ho mal di denti.
3 .... per prendere il treno.
4 .... a vedere un film.
5 .... per fare la spesa.
6 .... a comprare il pane.

3 Complete with "*in* + article". /6

Entriamo ***nel*** *castello delle fate?*

1 Ho messo le monete .... portafoglio.
2 .... ultimo anno ho visitato posti molto belli.
3 Carla è .... guai, dobbiamo aiutarla!
4 Chi ha messo il formaggio .... mio panino!?
5 Non parlare al professore con le mani .... tasche!
6 Metti i maglioni .... cassetti!

4 Complete with "*su* + article". /6

Sulle *montagne è già caduta la neve.*

1 .... spaghetti non metto mai il formaggio grattugiato.
2 Gli uccellini hanno fatto il nido .... albero del mio giardino.
3 Siamo arrivati .... cima della collina dopo due ore.
4 Ho incontrato un mio ex collega .... treno.
5 Dovete mettere in ordine quei libri .... scaffali della libreria.
6 Hai una macchia .... maglietta.

5 Paola has written a short essay about her room. Complete with the right preposition. /10

Nella nostra stanza 1) .... pareti sono appesi molti poster 2) .... nostri attori preferiti. 3) .... la porta e la finestra c'è una scrivania 4) .... tre cassetti. 5) .... scrivania ci sono due computer portatili, 6) .... cassetti ci sono i quaderni e 7) .... scaffale 8) .... libreria io ho messo i miei libri e mia sorella i suoi pupazzi. C'è sempre un po' 9) .... disordine, ma se qualcuno guarda 10) .... armadio, c'è davvero un grande caos!

42 Io amerò, lui venderà, voi sentirete... Noi saremo stati, loro avranno visto...

Simple future and future perfect tense

The simple future is formed **by dropping the end of the infinitive and adding the endings**:

- *-e* for the **1st and 2nd conjugation**;
- *-i* for the **3rd conjugation**.

	1st conjugation	2nd conjugation	3rd conjugation
	AMARE	**VENDERE**	**SENTIRE**
io	am-**e**-**rò**	vend-**e**-**rò**	sent-**i**-**rò**
tu	am-**e**-**rai**	vend-**e**-**rai**	sent-**i**-**rai**
lui/lei	am-**e**-**rà**	vend-**e**-**rà**	sent-**i**-**rà**
noi	am-**e**-**remo**	vend-**e**-**remo**	sent-**i**-**remo**
voi	am-**e**-**rete**	vend-**e**-**rete**	sent-**i**-**rete**
loro	am-**e**-**ranno**	vend-**e**-**ranno**	sent-**i**-**ranno**

It is used:

- for **actions that will take place in the future**;
  *Domani **visiteremo** la Cappella Sistina.* Tomorrow we'll visit the Cappella Sistina.
- to express **uncertainty in the present**.
  *Credo che **pioverà**.* I think it will rain.

Like in English, in spoken language the **present is often used in the place of the future**.
*Quest'estate **vado** in vacanza in luglio.* This year I'm going on holiday in July.

Future perfect tense

The ***futuro anteriore*** (future perfect tense) is formed with the **future of the auxiliary verb *avere/essere* + the past participle of the verb**, as you can see in the table.

	io	tu	lui/lei	noi	voi	loro
amare	avrò amato	avrai amato	avrà amato	avremo amato	avrete amato	avranno amato
andare	sarò andato/a	sarai andato/a	sarà andato/a	saremo andati/e	sarete andati/e	saranno andati/e
essere	sarò stato/a	sarai stato/a	sarà stato/a	saremo stati/e	sarete stati/e	saranno stati/e
avere	avrò avuto	avrai avuto	avrà avuto	avremo avuto	avrete avuto	avranno avuto

It is used in **dependent clauses if the main clause has a verb in the future tense**. It can also be used **in independent clauses** when **it expresses uncertainty and doubt**.

*Maria **avrà avuto** un incidente?* Will Maria have had an accident?
*Che cosa **sarà successo** a Daniele? È in ritardo.* What will have happened to Daniele? He is late.

As you can see in the example, the ***futuro anteriore*** is translated in English with the **present perfect in temporal clauses.**

*Usciremo **dopo che avremo lavato** i piatti.* We'll leave after we've washed the dishes.

Pay attention: in **spoken language** this tense is less and less used. The simple future is used instead.

Exercises

1 Complete the sentences with the future forms of the verbs. /10

Adesso telefono a Cristina. → *Poi* ***telefonerò*** *a Giulio.*

1 Gianni parte in treno. Maria e Anna .... domani in macchina.
2 Ieri ho scritto una cartolina a Marina. Domani .... una lettera ad Anna.
3 Oggi i negozi aprono alle nove. Lunedì prossimo .... nel pomeriggio.
4 Franco arriva oggi da Milano. Patrizia, invece, ... dopodomani sera.
5 Di solito passiamo le vacanze al mare. L'anno prossimo .... un mese in montagna.
6 Guido finisce di studiare alle tre. Io .... alle cinque.
7 Oggi mio padre smette di lavorare tardi. Domani .... un po' prima.
8 Ieri abbiamo lavato i pavimenti. La settimana prossima .... i vetri.
9 L'anno scorso ho comprato la bicicletta. L'anno prossimo .... il computer.
10 Ieri mio fratello è uscito con un amico. Tra due giorni .... con la sua ragazza.

2 Giorgio has great plans for his future. Write what he will do. /5

(frequentare) →
Frequenterò *l'università.*

1 *(diventare)*
....

2 *(comperare)*
....

3 *(sposarsi)*
....

4 *(abitare)*
....

5 *(viaggiare)*
....

3 What are you going to do on holiday? Answer the questions. /6

Viaggerai in macchina? → ***No, non viaggerò*** *in macchina/****Sì, viaggerò*** *in macchina.*

1 Partirai da solo o con altre persone? ....
2 Passerai dei giorni in montagna? ....
3 Visiterai delle città? ....
4 Ti divertirai? ....
5 Leggerai molto? ....
6 Mangerai al ristorante? ....

43 Io sarò, tu avrai... Lui verrà, noi terremo... Irregular forms of the future

The simple future of the verbs "to be" (*essere*) and "to have" (*avere*)

essere	sarò	sarai	sarà	saremo	sarete	saranno
avere	avrò	avrai	avrà	avremo	avrete	avranno

Che ore sono? Non so, ***saranno*** *le dieci.* What time is it? I don't know. It may be 10.
Se ***avremo*** *sete, berremo qualcosa.* If we're thirsty, we'll drink something.

Differently from English, the future can be expressed with **may**. As you can see in the first example.

The simple future of the irregular verbs

dovere	dovrò	dovrai	dovrà	dovremo	dovrete	dovranno
potere	potrò	potrai	potrà	potremo	potrete	potranno
andare	andrò	andrai	andrà	andremo	andrete	andranno
sapere	saprò	saprai	saprà	sapremo	saprete	sapranno
vedere	vedrò	vedrai	vedrà	vedremo	vedrete	vedranno
vivere	vivrò	vivrai	vivrà	vivremo	vivrete	vivranno

volere	vorrò	vorrai	vorrà	vorremo	vorrete	vorranno
venire	verrò	verrai	verrà	verremo	verrete	verranno
rimanere	rimarrò	rimarrai	rimarrà	rimarremo	rimarrete	rimarranno
tenere	terrò	terrai	terrà	terremo	terrete	terranno
bere	berrò	berrai	berrà	berremo	berrete	berranno

dare	darò	darai	darà	daremo	darete	daranno
fare	farò	farai	farà	faremo	farete	faranno
stare	starò	starai	starà	staremo	starete	staranno

Other verbs

The verbs ending with ***-ciare/-giare*** in the future **drop the -*i*.**

mangiare	mangerò	mangerai	mangerà	mangeremo	mangerete	mangeranno

Sono a dieta. Prometto che non ***mangerò*** *troppo.* I'm on a diet. I promise I won't eat too much.

The verbs ending with ***-care/-gare*** in the future **add an -*h*.**

giocare	giocherò	giocherai	giocherà	giocheremo	giocherete	giocheranno

La mia squadra ***giocherà*** *stasera.* My team will play tonight.

The form **to be going to...** (*futuro intenzionale*) can be expressed in Italian with the future or with the expression *avere intenzione di*.

I'm going to leave soon. ***Partirò*** *presto/****Ho intenzione di*** *partire presto.*

Exercises

1 Complete the sentences with the future forms of the verbs. /8

*Oggi fanno sciopero gli autobus. Domani **faranno** sciopero i treni.*

1 La settimana scorsa tu sei stato malato. Per domani .... guarito?
2 Ieri ho avuto mal di testa. Domani non .... più niente.
3 Il 10 dicembre è stato il compleanno di Anna. Il 5 aprile .... il compleanno di Sara.
4 Ieri ho mangiato una fetta di torta di mele. A Natale .... il panettone.
5 Oggi fa bel tempo e non piove. Domani .... brutto tempo e ....
6 Mi dispiace ma stasera non possiamo uscire insieme. .... la prossima settimana.
7 Carlo, quando vedi i tuoi amici? Li .... sabato in pizzeria.

2 Augusto, the magician. What does he foresee for the future? Complete with the future forms of the verbs. /5

*Ci (essere) ⟶ **saranno** computer e robot dappertutto.*

Sempre più persone (*lavorare*) 1) .... da casa. In tanti (*parlare*) 2) .... molte lingue. Molti (*vivere*) 3) .... fino a centoventi anni. L'inglese (*essere*) 4) .... la lingua nazionale della maggior parte dei Paesi del mondo. Tutti (*avere*) 5) .... abbastanza soldi per andare in vacanza.

3 Choose the right alternative. /7

1 Ieri *andremo/siamo andati/andiamo* al cinema.
2 Oggi in pizzeria *pagando/pagherò/pago* io. Domani *stai pagando/pagherai/hai pagato* tu.
3 La prossima settimana *partiremo/siamo partiti/stiamo partendo* tutti.
4 Non *dimenticherò/ho dimenticato/sto dimenticando* mai quello che stai facendo per me.
5 Quando *saprete/state sapendo/avete saputo* se potete venire con noi?
6 Lo scorso mese *siamo stati/staremo/stiamo* tutto il tempo a casa.

4 Giulia asked you to go out with her, but you're very busy these days. Read what you have to do and report to her. /6

- **Lunedì**: andare in palestra
- **Martedì**: invitare la mamma a cena
- **Mercoledì**: rimanere in ufficio fino alle otto
- **Giovedì**: prendere un aperitivo con colleghi
- **Venerdì**: giocare a tennis con Stefania
- **Sabato**: uscire con gli amici
- **Domenica**: dormire tutto il giorno

*Lunedì **andrò in palestra**.*

1 Martedì ....
....
2 Mercoledì ....
....
3 Giovedì ....
....
4 Venerdì ....
....
5 Sabato ....
....
6 Domenica ....
....

44 Più alto di, meno bello di, basso come...
Comparative of adjectives and adverbs

There are three comparatives in Italian:

- the comparative of **majority** (*comparativo di maggioranza*);
  *Paolo è **più alto di** Mario.* Paolo is taller than Mario.
- the comparative of **minority** (*comparativo di minoranza*);
  *Paolo è **meno alto di** Mario.* Paolo is less tall than Mario.
- the comparative of **equality** (*comparativo di uguaglianza*).
  *Paolo è **alto come** Mario.* Paolo is as tall as Mario.

The comparative of majority

The comparative of majority is formed with the adjective preceded by ***più* (more)** + **preposition *di*** (with or without the article).

*La mia casa è **più** bella **della** tua.* My house is more beautiful than yours.

Differently from English, in Italian there is no difference between short or long adjectives. All comparisons are formed in the same way.

*Paolo è **più alto** di Mario.* Paolo is tall**er** than Mario.

The comparative of minority

The comparative of minority is formed with the **adjective preceded by *meno* (less)** + **preposition *di*** (with or without the article).

*Queste scarpe sono **meno** care **delle** tue.* These shoes are less expensive than yours.

The comparative of equality

The comparative of equality is formed with the **adjective** (that can be preceded by ***tanto* or *così*** (as much or as) + by ***come/quanto* (as/as much)**.

*Il mio gatto è **magro come** il tuo.* My cat is as thin as yours.
*La mia casa è **tanto grande quanto** la tua.* My house is as big as yours.

The comparative of the adverb

Adverbs form the comparative **like adjectives**.

*Ho guidato **più velocemente**.* I've driven more quickly.
*Siamo arrivati **meno tardi di** te.* We've arrived less late than you.
*Giochiamo **bene come** te a pallone.* We play football as well as you.

In the comparison ***che*** (instead of *di*) is used if the comparison is **between two verbs, adjectives, or names preceded by preposition**.

*Giacomo è **più bello che** intelligente.* Giacomo is more handsome than clever.
*Le vacanze sono **più rilassanti** in montagna che al mare.*
Holidays are more relaxing in the mountains than at the seaside.

Exercises

1 Build sentences with the comparative form. /6

La tua macchina/veloce/la nostra macchina. → *La tua macchina è* ***più veloce della*** *nostra macchina. La tua macchina è* ***veloce quanto/come*** *la nostra macchina. La tua macchina è* ***meno veloce della*** *nostra macchina.*

1 Il mare/vicino/montagna. ....
2 Mio fratello/alto/Claudio. ....
3 Questa camera/bella/nostra. ....
4 Noi/ricchi/voi. ....
5 Il vino/costoso/birra. ....
6 Inglese/difficile/francese. ....

2 Answer the question with the comparative form. /6

Quale è più costosa? La frutta o la verdura? → *Secondo me* ***la frutta è più costosa della verdura****.*

1 Quale dei due è più lungo? Il fiume Po o il fiume Tevere?
....
2 Che cosa mangiano più volentieri i bambini? Cioccolato o carne?
....
3 Che cosa costa di più? Una vacanza in Italia o alle Bahamas?
....
4 Che cos'è più comodo? Una sedia o una poltrona?
....
5 Quale città è più grande? Milano o Bologna?
....
6 Che cos'è più antico? Il Colosseo o le Piramidi?
....

3 Complete with the right comparative: *maggioranza* (+), *minoranza* (–), *uguaglianza* (=). /5

In Italia fa ***meno*** *freddo* ***che*** *in Germania. (–)*

1 L'acqua è .... salutare .... vino. (+)
2 Sabrina Ferilli è .... famosa .... Madonna. (–)
3 Umberto Eco è .... famoso .... Roberto Benigni. (=)
4 In Italia il caffè è .... lungo .... in Inghilterra. (–)
5 In Italia il mare è .... caldo .... in Spagna. (=)

4 Complete with *di* or *che*. /5

Fa ancora meno ***di*** *me. Da non crederci!*

1 Siamo più poveri .... nostro zio.
2 Le tasse qui sono più alte .... in Germania.
3 È più grosso .... alto.
4 È più magro .... un grissino.
5 Sembrano meno preparati .... Gianna.

45 La più grande di, intelligentissima, molto simpatica, pessimo...
Superlative (relative and absolute)

The superlative of the adjective

The superlative is formed with the adjective preceded by the **determinative article** (the most) and followed by the preposition ***di*** or ***fra*** (with or without the article).

*Nella mia classe Giorgio è **il più alto** di tutti.*
In my class Giorgio is the tallest.
*Roma è **la città più grande** d'Italia.*
Roma is the biggest city in Italy.

Superlative of the adverb

Adverbs form the superlative with:

- article + comparative of the adverb + possibile
- comparative of the adjective + -***mente*** + ***possibile***
  *Veronica guida in città **più prudentemente possibile**.*
  In the city, Veronica drives as carefully as possible.

The absolute superlative

It is the form of the adjective that indicates that the quality is possessed in the highest degree without any comparison.

It is formed:

- with **molto** + adjective whose ending changes according to the gender and number of the noun;
  *Una tazza **molto piccola**.* A very small cup.
- by changing the ending of the adjective with ***-issimo/-a/-i/-e***;
  *Una tazza **piccolissima**.* A very small cup.
- by repeating the adjective.
  *Una tazza **piccola piccola**.* A very small cup.

Adjectives with irregular forms

Aggettivo	**buono** (good)	**migliore**	**ottimo/a/i/e**
Avverbio	**bene** (well)	**meglio**	**ottimamente (benissimo)**
Aggettivo	**cattivo** (bad)	**peggiore**	**pessimo/a/i/e**
Avverbio	**male** (badly)	**peggio**	**pessimamente (malissimo)**

Exercises

1 Build sentences with the superlative form. /10

Anna/brava/a scuola. → *Anna è **la più brava** a scuola.*

1 Paolo/alto/famiglia. ....
2 Il nostro appartamento/pulito/tutti. ....
3 Questa città/ricca/Italia. ....
4 I musei di Firenze/interessanti/Toscana. ....
5 L'aeroplano/mezzo/veloce/tutti. ....
6 Questo quartiere/elegante/città. ....
7 Il tuo caffè/buono/tutti. ....
8 Questo locale/brutto/quartiere. ....
9 Il tempo di questa settimana/cattivo/tutta l'estate. ....
10 Sergio/piccolo/miei fratelli. ....

2 Write the sentences with the absolute superlative form. Use the form that you prefer. /5

Fabio è simpatico. → *Fabio è **molto simpatico/simpaticissimo**.*

1 Vorrei piatti raffinati per la mia cucina. ....
2 Il mio amico è veloce. ....
3 Mi piace una casa luminosa. ....
4 Questo gioco è divertente. ....
5 Mio fratello è magro. ....

3 Build sentences with the adverbs in the absolute superlative form. /5

Marina scrivere/bene/italiano. → *Marina scrive **molto bene/benissimo** in italiano.*

1 Si viaggia/velocemente/in aereo. ....
2 Costa/molto. ....
3 Ha parlato/lentamente. ....
4 È arrivata/presto. ....
5 Scrive/male. ....

4 Build sentences with the comparative or the superlative form. /10

È la persona/gentile/palazzo. → *È la persona **più gentile del palazzo**.*

1 Il fiume Reno/lungo/Po. ....
2 Il Po è il fiume/lungo/Italia. ....
3 Qual è il monte/alto/d'Italia? Il Monte Bianco. ....
4 Il Monte Rosa/alto/Cervino? Sì, è/alto/Cervino. ....
5 Abbiamo mangiato piatti/buoni/ristorante. ....
6 La mia auto/veloce/tua. Però l'auto del signor Rossi/veloce/tutte.
....
7 Ho visto il quadro/interessante/della mostra. ....
8 I dipinti di Raffaello sono secondo me/belli/quelli di Michelangelo.
....
9 Franco/lo studente/pigro/classe. Non credo. Maria/ancora/pigra/Franco.
....
10 I vestiti di marca/cari/tutti. ....

46 Qualcuno, qualsiasi, niente...
Indefinite pronouns and adjectives

Indefinite pronouns and adjectives indicate things or persons without specifying the quantity or the quality. The pronouns replace the nouns.

Indefinite pronouns

- ***Ognuno***: everybody/everyone
- ***Qualcuno***: someone/somebody
- ***Qualcosa***: something
- ***Chiunque***: everybody/everyone
- ***Nulla/niente***: nothing/anything

  *Posso fare **qualcosa** per voi?*
  Can I do something for you?

Qualcuno, ***chiunque***, ***nulla*** only have a singular form.

  ***Qualcuno** ci spiega cosa è successo?*
  Can anyone explain to us what happened?

Indefinite adjectives

- ***Ogni***: every/each
- ***Qualche***: some/any
- ***Qualsiasi/qualunque***: any

  ***Ogni** sera leggo **qualche** pagina prima di dormire.*
  Every evening I read some pages before going to sleep.

Remember that, differently from English, with ***niente/nulla/nessuno*** you must use the negative word ***non*** (**double negative**).

  *Non capisco **niente**.*
  I don't understand anything.
  *Non vedo **nessuno**.*
  I cannot see anyone.

Like in English, when the indefinite (pronouns or adjectives) refer to a group, they are followed by *di*.

  ***Ognuno di** noi sa quello che bisogna fare.*
  Each of us knows what they have to do.
  ***Nessuno di** voi ha visto cosa è successo?*
  None of you has seen what happened?

Exercises

1 Complete with the indefinite adjectives and pronouns. /12

qualcuno • qualcosa (2) • niente (2) • nessuno • tutti (2) • ciascuno • ogni • qualsiasi (2)

Cesare, c'è ***qualcuno*** *che ti vuole parlare.*

1 Sono diventati famosi: .... parlano di loro.
2 Abbiamo sete. Avete .... da bere? No, non abbiamo ....,
ci dispiace. Non siamo ancora andati a fare la spesa.
3 .... di noi deve fare il proprio dovere. Invece ci stiamo annoiando e non abbiamo .... da fare.
4 Questo compito è davvero facile. Lo può fare .... persona.
5 In questo periodo non abbiamo visto .... Abbiamo lavorato e basta.
6 Alla festa .... ragazzo deve portare una cravatta rossa.
7 .... vogliono vedere questo monumento, noi però ne vogliamo vedere un altro.
8 Serena, ... bussa alla porta. Puoi andare ad aprire?
9 Perché non potete venire alla festa? Avete .... di meglio da fare?
10 Come vuoi il tè? Uno .... mi va bene.

2 Choose the right alternative in this dialogue. /8

Susan: Cerco una nuova casa.
Agente immobiliare: Che tipo di casa?
Susan: Mi va bene 1) *qualunque/qualche* tipo purché abbia 2) *alcune/qualche* caratteristiche.
Agente immobiliare: Quali caratteristiche?
Susan: Può essere anche piccola, ma non deve avere 3) *nessun/niente* armadio o letto.
Agente immobiliare: Cioè non la vuole ammobiliata?
Susan: Già, voglio una casa non ammobiliata o con 4) *pochi/poco* mobili.
Agente immobiliare: D'accordo, signorina. Adesso però vorrei io 5) *qualcuno/qualcosa* da lei. Ha 6) *qualche/qualsiasi* garanzia?

Susan: Garanzia?
Agente immobiliare: Sì, voglio dire... ha uno stipendio, ha 7) *qualcuno/qualche* lavoro?
Susan: No, ma i miei genitori mi spediscono soldi 8) *ognuno/ogni* mese.

3 Correct the mistakes in the letter that Ivan writes to his parents. /6

Cari mamma e papà,
sono qui da *qualsiasi* → **qualche** mese, ma ancora non mi sono ambientato.
Ho 1) *poco* .... amici anche se nel mio corso conosco proprio 2) *tutto* .... Invece nel posto in cui abito 3) *niente* .... mi parla.
Forse perché quando parlo in italiano ancora faccio 4) *molto* .... errori.
E voi come state? Papà ha trovato 5) *qualcosa* .... lavoro? Spero di sì.
Il tempo qui è molto bello anche se spesso ci sono 6) *qualche* .... temporali.
Adesso vi saluto. A presto.
Ivan.

47 Io amai, noi scrivemmo, loro sentirono... Tu fosti, lui ebbe, noi dovemmo...
Regular and irregular forms of the *passato remoto*

The *passato remoto* is formed by **replacing the end of the infinitive with the endings for the *passato remoto*** as you can see in the table.

	1st conjugation	2nd conjugation	3rd conjugation
	AMARE	**VENDERE**	**SENTIRE**
io	am-**a**-**i**	vend-**e**-**tti/ei**	sent-**i**-**i**
tu	am-**a**-**sti**	vend-**e**-**sti**	sent-**i**-**sti**
lui/lei	am-**ò**	vend-**e**-**tte/é**	sent-**ì**
noi	am-**a**-**mmo**	vend-**e**-**mmo**	sent-**i**-**mmo**
voi	am-**a**-**ste**	vend-**e**-**ste**	sent-**i**-**ste**
loro	am-**a**-**rono**	vend-**e**-**ttero/erono**	sent-**i**-**rono**

The *passato remoto* is **rarely used in conversation** (except for some regions). It is used **in the written language** to express an **action completed in the past**. It is also used to **tell fairy tales or report historical facts.**

Passato remoto of the **verbs *essere*, *avere*** and of the ***verbi servili***.

	io	**tu**	**lui/lei**	**noi**	**voi**	**loro**
essere (to be)	fui	fosti	fu	fummo	foste	furono
avere (to have)	ebbi	avesti	ebbe	avemmo	aveste	ebbero
dovere (to have to)	dov-ei/-etti	dovesti	dov-é/-ette	dovemmo	doveste	dov-erono/-ettero
potere (to be able to)	pot-ei/-etti	potesti	pot-é/-ette	potemmo	poteste	pot-erono/-ettero
volere (to want to)	volli	volesti	volle	volemmo	voleste	vollero

Verbs with an irregular *passato remoto*

bere	bevvi	bevesti	bevve	bevemmo	beveste	bevvero
chiedere	chiesi	chiedesti	chiese	chiedemmo	chiedeste	chiesero
conoscere	conobbi	conoscesti	conobbe	conoscemmo	conosceste	conobbero
dare	diedi	desti	diede	demmo	deste	diedero
dire	dissi	dicesti	disse	dicemmo	diceste	dissero
fare	feci	facesti	fece	facemmo	faceste	fecero
leggere	lessi	leggesti	lesse	leggemmo	leggeste	lessero
mettere	misi	mettesti	mise	mettemmo	metteste	misero
nascere	nacqui	nascesti	nacque	nascemmo	nasceste	nacquero
perdere	persi	perdesti	perse	perdemmo	perdeste	persero
prendere	presi	prendesti	prese	prendemmo	prendeste	presero
rispondere	risposi	rispondesti	rispose	rispondemmo	rispondeste	risposero
sapere	seppi	sapesti	seppe	sapemmo	sapeste	seppero
scrivere	scrissi	scrivesti	scrisse	scrivemmo	scriveste	scrissero
venire	venni	venisti	venne	venimmo	veniste	vennero
vivere	vissi	vivesti	visse	vivemmo	viveste	vissero

Exercises

1 Write these verbs in the *passato remoto.* /32

- Due anni fa, noi (*partire*) 1) .... a Natale e (*tornare*) 2) .... per l'Epifania. Noi (*divertirsi*) 3) .... molto.
- La prima guerra mondiale (*cominciare*) 4) .... nel 1914 e (*finire*) 5) .... nel 1918; (*morire*) 6) .... molti milioni di persone.
- Alla fine dell'800, molti Europei (*emigrare*) 7) .... in America dove (*trovare*) 8) .... lavoro.
- Ricordo che quella (*essere*) 9) .... una notte terribile: (*io, dormire*) 10) .... molto male, (*avere*) 11) .... un incubo e (*svegliarsi*) 12) .... più volte. Al mattino (*alzarsi*) 13) .... distrutto.
- Quando noi lo (*incontrare*) 14) .... non (*capire*) 15) .... il suo nome.
- A che ora (*voi, andare*) 16) .... a casa quella sera?
- La prima volta che i miei genitori mi (*portare*) 17) .... a Roma (*essere*) 18) .... oltre 10 anni fa. Poi ci (*noi, tornare*) 19) .... altre volte finché mio padre (*trovare*) 20) .... lavoro lì.
- (*Essere*) 21) .... un'impresa eccezionale: (*tu, viaggiare*) 22) .... per tutta la notte e (*arrivare*) 23) .... in tempo.
- (*Voi, spedire*) 24) .... il materiale all'inizio della settimana, ma noi lo (*ricevere*) 25) .... un mese dopo.
- Tre anni fa mio nonno (*avere*) 26) .... un infarto. Il chirurgo che lo (*operare*) 27) .... (*essere*) 28) .... molto bravo e lui (*guarire*) 29) .... perfettamente.
- Le automobili (*passare*) 30) .... con il rosso e non (*rallentare*) 31) .... nemmeno quando (*essere*) 32) .... vicino alle strisce pedonali.

2 Change the tense of the verbs in the *passato prossimo* to the *passato remoto.* /12

- Sabato sera *siamo andati* → ***andammo*** alla festa di Lucia. 1) Abbiamo bevuto .... 2) abbiamo mangiato .... e 3) abbiamo ballato .... Due ragazzi 4) hanno letto .... delle poesie. Io 5) ho conosciuto .... molte ragazze e ragazzi. 6) È stato .... molto divertente.
- Il mese scorso 7) è accaduto .... un brutto incidente all'incrocio tra via Roma e via Napoli. Due automobili 8) si sono scontrate .... e uno dei guidatori 9) è rimasto .... ferito.
- Il dottor Paoli 10) è venuto .... qui per eliminare un problema, ma non 11) è riuscito .... a risolverlo. Per questo 12) abbiamo chiamato .... un'altra persona. Speriamo più competente!

48 Avevo amato, ero stato... Ebbi amato, fossi stato... Past perfect and past perfect of the *passato remoto*

The *trapassato prossimo* (plusperfect) is formed with the *imperfetto* of the auxiliary verb ***avere/ essere*** + the **past participle** of the verb, as you can see in the table.

	io	tu	lui/lei	noi	voi	loro
amare	avevo amato	avevi amato	aveva amato	avevamo amato	avevate amato	avevano amato
andare	ero andato/a	eri andato/a	era andato/a	eravamo andati/e	eravate andati/e	erano andati/e
essere	ero stato/a	eri stato/a	era stato/a	eravamo stati/e	eravate stati/e	erano stati/e
avere	avevo avuto	avevi avuto	aveva avuto	avevamo avuto	avevate avuto	avevano avuto

With the verb ***essere*** as auxiliary the **past participle agrees with the subject**.

*La mamm**a** era uscit**a** da poco e i bambini si erano appena addormentat**i** quando cominciò a piovere.*
Mum had gone out a short time before and the children had just fallen asleep when it started raining.

It is used to express an **action or event that precedes a past action**. It is the **equivalent of the English past perfect**. It is frequently used in sentences like those in the examples.

*Ho visto il film di cui mi **avevi parlato**.*
I saw the film you had told me about.

It can also be used alone in sentences when the other verb is not present (but is implied).

*Non **avevo** mai **mangiato** degli gnocchi così buoni.* I had never eaten such delicious gnocchi.
*Non **avevano** mai **viaggiato** in treno!* They had never travelled by train!

Trapassato remoto

The *trapassato remoto* is formed with the ***passato remoto* of the auxiliary verb *avere/essere*** + ***participio passato*** of the verb, as you can see in the table.

	io	tu	lui/lei	noi	voi	loro
amare	ebbi amato	avesti amato	ebbe amato	avemmo amato	aveste amato	ebbero amato
andare	fui andato/a	fosti andato/a	fu andato/a	fummo andati/e	foste andati/e	furono andati/e
essere	fui stato/a	fosti stato/a	fu stato/a	fummo stati/e	foste stati/e	furono stati/e
avere	ebbi avuto	avesti avuto	ebbe avuto	avemmo avuto	aveste avuto	ebbero avuto

It is used **in dependent clauses to refer to actions and events that happened before a point of reference in the past**. It is very rarely used.

*Giulia capì quello che era successo dopo che Carlo le **ebbe raccontato** la verità.*
Giulia realized what had happened after Carlo had told her the truth.

Exercises

1 Write these verbs in the *trapassato prossimo*. /10

Penso a te. → ***Avevo pensato** a te.*

1 Succede un incidente. ....

2 Guardo un film. ....

3 Scrivi un messaggio. ....

4 Vedono una persona. ....

5 Offriamo aiuto. ....

6 Capisco bene il consiglio. ....

7 Mangiate molto. ....

8 Consiglia una soluzione. ....

9 Escono di casa. ....

10 Ordinano una bistecca. ....

2 Complete with the verbs in the *trapassato prossimo*. /5

1 Scusami se non ti ho salutato. Non ti (*vedere*) ....

2 Quando Filippo era in Germania, (*trovare*) .... lavoro facilmente.

3 Prima di allora io non (*stare, mai*) .... al mare.

4 Gli ho dato il lavoro dopo che (*sentire*) .... come parlava italiano.

5 Ho letto il libro che (*tu, regalare*) .... a mia sorella. Bellissimo!

3 Complete with the *passato prossimo* or *trapassato prossimo*. /12

1 Moglie: Dove (*essere*) 1) .... fino adesso?
Marito: (*essere*) 2) .... in ufficio.
Moglie: Non è vero. Ti (*telefonare*) 3) .... e i tuoi colleghi (*dire*) 4) .... che tu (*uscire*) 5) .... due ore prima.
Marito: Non è così. (*essere*) 6) .... nell'ufficio del capo, però loro non mi hanno visto.

2 Quando il film (*uscire*) 7) .... nel 1998, (*avere*) 8) .... un grande successo anche se i critici ne (*parlare*) 9) .... molto male.

3 Stavo leggendo il libro che mi (*prestare*) 10) .... quando (*suonare*) 11) .... il telefono. Io non (*rispondere*) 12) ....

4 Complete with the *passato prossimo* and *trapassato prossimo*. /9

1 Ieri ero stanca perché il giorno precedente (*lavorare*) .... fino a tardi, così (*rimanere*) .... a casa.

2 Noi (*finire*) .... appena .... di mangiare, quando (*entrare*) .... Carlo.

3 Questa mattina (*noi, alzarsi*) .... tardi perché ieri sera (*addormentarsi*) .... a mezzanotte.

4 (*Tu, conoscere*) .... mai .... una ragazza così simpatica, prima di Marina?

5 (*Voi, uscire*) .... appena ...., quando (*arrivare*) .... la zia con i cuginetti.

49 Io amerei, tu venderesti, lui sentirebbe...
Present conditional

The present conditional is formed **by dropping the *-e* of the infinitive and add the ending.**

	1st conjugation (AMARE)	2nd conjugation (VENDERE)	3rd conjugation (SENTIRE)
io	am-**e**-**rei**	vend-**e**-**rei**	sent-**i**-**rei**
tu	am-**e**-**resti**	vend-**e**-**resti**	sent-**i**-**resti**
lui/lei	am-**e**-**rebbe**	vend-**e**-**rebbe**	sent-**i**-**rebbe**
noi	am-**e**-**remmo**	vend-**e**-**remmo**	sent-**i**-**remmo**
voi	am-**e**-**reste**	vend-**e**-**reste**	sent-**i**-**reste**
loro	am-**e**-**rebbero**	vend-**e**-**rebbero**	sent-**i**-**rebbero**

The mode conditional has only **two tenses**: the **present** and the **past**.

The present conditional is used **in independent clauses to express in the present or in the future**:

- **wish or intentions**: ***Prenderei*** *volentieri bere.* I'd like to drink something.
  Vorremmo *una pizza.* We'd like a pizza.
- **doubt**: *Che cosa* ***regaleresti*** *a Maria per il suo compleanno?*
  What would you give Maria for her birthday?
- **personal opinion**: ***Dovresti*** *guidare con più prudenza.* You should drive more carefully.
  Secondo me ***impareresti*** *l'inglese meglio con l'aiuto di un insegnante.*
  In my opinion you'd learn English better with the help of a teacher.
- **request or invitation**: *Cosa ne* ***direste*** *di andare al cinema?* What about going to the cinema?
  Sareste *così gentili da prestarmi una penna?* Would you be so kind as to lend me a pen?

It is the **equivalent** of the English construction **would** + **verb**, although, as you have seen in the examples, the use is in some cases different.

Irregular *condizionale presente*

The conjugation of the present conditional of the verbs ***essere*** **(to be)**, ***avere*** **(to have)** and of the ***verbi servili*** **(*dovere*, *potere*, *volere*)** is as follows in the table below.

	io	**tu**	**lui/lei**	**noi**	**voi**	**loro**
essere	sarei	saresti	sarebbe	saremmo	sareste	sarebbero
avere	avrei	avresti	avrebbe	avremmo	avreste	avrebbero

dovere	dovrei	dovresti	dovrebbe	dovremmo	dovreste	dovrebbero
potere	potrei	potresti	potrebbe	potremmo	potreste	potrebbero
volere	vorrei	vorresti	vorrebbe	vorremmo	vorreste	vorrebbero

Irregular verbs

The verbs in -***care*** and -***gare*** take the ***h***.

cercare	cerc**h**erei	cerc**h**eresti	cerc**h**erebbe	cerc**h**eremmo	cerc**h**ereste	cerc**h**erebbero

The verbs in -***ciare*** and -***giare*** drop the ***i***.

mangiare	mangerei	mangeresti	mangerebbe	mangeremmo	mangereste	mangerebbero

Exercises

1 Write the verbs in the conditional.

/10

dormo → ***dormirei***

1 parlo ....
2 piove ....
3 regaliamo ....
4 prendete ....
5 credono ....
6 camminano ....
7 finisci ....
8 seguite ....
9 lavoro ....
10 si sveglia ....

2 What would I do with one million euro?

/4

Comprare una casa bella e grande. → ***Comprerei una casa bella e grande.***

1 Spendere tutto per i miei animali.
....
....

2 Lasciare subito il lavoro.
....
....

3 Lavorare due mesi all'anno.
....
....

4 Investire in titoli e azioni.
....
....

3 Write the verbs in the conditional.

/20

sono → ***sarei***

1 date ....
2 vogliono ....
3 puoi ....
4 sappiamo ....
5 sei ....
6 siamo ....
7 posso ....
8 vuole ....
9 potete ....
10 vogliono ....
11 mangi ....
12 beve ....
13 traduco ....
14 traducete ....
15 fai ....
16 fanno ....
17 ho ....
18 hanno ....
19 bevono ....
20 mangiamo ....

4 Correct the mistake where necessary.

/5

1 Vorrò un caffè, per favore. ....
2 Potrei dirmi dove si trova la stazione? ....
3 Mi piacerebbe avere un gatto. ....
4 Beveremmo tutto il tempo. ....
5 Mi piacerei lasciare il lavoro. ....

Units 40-49 Summary exercises

1 Complete with the prepositional articles. /18

*I ragazzi **delle** mie amiche si mettono sempre **nei** guai.*

1 Paul torna .... Stati Uniti per trascorrere le vacanze di Natale in Italia.
2 L'appuntamento è .... 17.30 davanti .... pizzeria "Sole mio".
3 Hai una macchia .... jeans.
4 Mi piacciono i colori .... estate e adoro il profumo .... mare e .... fiori.
5 Hai già messo i vestiti .... valigie o sono ancora .... armadio?
6 .... mensola .... cucina ho lasciato gli avanzi .... pranzo.
7 Ho il sole .... occhi: non ci vedo!
8 L'ufficio è aperto .... 10.00 .... 12.00.
9 Domani andiamo .... mare .... nostri zii.
10 Lo sciopero .... lavoratori è stato molto lungo.

2 Complete with the correct forms of the future. /10

*Sabato prossimo (fare, noi) ⟶ **faremo** una festa in giardino.*

1 Domani (*venire*) .... a cena dei colleghi di mio padre.
2 Quando (*essere, io*) .... grande, (*viaggiare, io*) .... in molti Paesi.
3 Voi che cosa (*fare*) .... durante le vacanze? Se (*avere*) .... i soldi (*andare*) .... in vacanza al mare.
4 I miei amici mi hanno promesso che mi (*scrivere*) .... durante le vacanze.
5 Se Luca (*potere*) ...., ti telefonerà.
6 Purtroppo domani tu (*dovere*) .... andare dal dentista.
7 Sabato i miei nonni (*partire*) .... per il mare.

3 Complete with the correct forms of the *passato remoto*. /10

*L'uomo (scrivere) ⟶ **scrisse** molte lettere alla famiglia.*

1 L'uomo non (*dire*) .... il suo nome.
2 Il principe (*vedere*) .... la fanciulla che dormiva.
3 Dante Alighieri (*essere*) .... un grande poeta.
4 Alle 8.00 la donna (*uscire*) .... di casa.
5 I nonni (*dare*) .... a Mara un vecchio libro.
6 Il ragazzo (*fare*) .... tutto di nascosto.
7 La madre (*leggere*) .... una favola al figlio.
8 I medici (*andare*) .... dall'ammalato.
9 I soldati (*dormire*) .... a lungo.
10 I tre porcellini (*avere*) .... paura del lupo cattivo.

4 Complete with the right forms of the *passato prossimo* and the *trapassato prossimo*. /15

*(Finire) ⟶ **Ho** già **finito** di leggere il libro. Lo (prendere) ⟶ **avevo preso** in biblioteca due giorni fa.*

1 Il film che (*andare, voi*) .... a vedere ieri Paola (*vedere*) l'............ già .... e non le (*piacere*) ....
2 Suo marito le (*comprare*) .... lo stesso regalo che le (*fare*) .... l'anno scorso, e che non (*trovare*) .... bello.

3 Noi non (*rispondere*) .... alla domanda perché nessuno (*capire*) l'................................ .
4 La mamma (*sgridare*) .... Carla perché (*prendere*) .... i giocattoli del suo fratellino.
5 L'ambulanza (*arrivare*) .... quando l'uomo (*morire*) .... già .... a causa delle ferite.
6 Che bontà! (*mangiare, voi*) .... mai .... della frutta così dolce?
7 (*Andare, io*) .... al supermercato perché (*finire, io*) .... il detersivo per la lavatrice.

5 Complete with adjectives in the comparative or in the superlative form. /5

prezioso • popoloso • lungo • piccolo • grande • alto

Oggi il tempo è ***migliore*** *di ieri, infatti non fa freddo e c'è il sole.*
1 Roma è la .... città d'Italia, infatti conta più di due milioni di abitanti.
2 Il Po è il fiume .... d'Italia.
3 Il Kilimangiaro è .... dell'Everest.
4 La mia casa è .... la tua, infatti hanno entrambe due locali più servizi.
6 Ugo è il mio fratellino ...., dopo di lui i miei genitori non hanno avuto altri figli.

6 Complete with *meno, più, come* and with the article when necessary. /5

Cesare è ***il più*** *simpatico dei miei colleghi.*
1 Il legno è .... fragile del vetro.
2 Paola è altissima, è .... alta della famiglia.
3 Il miele è dolce .... lo zucchero? Sì sono dolci uguali.
4 Carlo è .... taciturno del solito: oggi non ha ancora detto una parola.
5 Per questa salsa servono dei pomodori molto maturi, ... maturi che trovi.

7 Translate into Italian. /8

1 I'll buy some clothes for your birthday.
....
2 Will you come to my party in the disco?
....
3 Ben is taller than his brother.
....
4 I don't want anything for me.
....
5 Is anybody at home?
....
6 Somebody is always at home.
....
7 Could you phone me tomorrow?
....
8 I'd like to sell my house as soon as possible.
....

50 Io ami, tu venda, lui senta... Io vada, tu dica, lui finisca... Present subjunctive tense

The present subjunctive is formed **by dropping the *-e* of the infinitive and add the ending**.

	1st conjugation (AMARE)	2nd conjugation (VENDERE)	3rd conjugation (SENTIRE)
io	am-**i**	vend-**a**	sent-**a**
tu	am-**i**	vend-**a**	sent-**a**
lui/lei	am-**i**	vend-**a**	sent-**a**
noi	am-**iamo**	vend-**iamo**	sent-**iamo**
voi	am-**iate**	vend-**iate**	sent-**iate**
loro	am-**ino**	vend-**ano**	sent-**ano**

It is used **in dependent clauses if the verb of the main clause doesn't express certainty**, for example *credere* (to believe), *pensare* (to think), *immaginare* (to imagine), *temere* (to be afraid).

__Speriamo__ che domani __arrivino__ i nostri amici e restino con noi durante le feste.
Hopefully tomorrow our friends will come and stay with us during the holidays.

Main clause	Dependent clause with the subjunctive
So *che Paolo* ***detesta*** *Clara.*	***Credo*** *che Paolo* ***detesti*** *Clara.*
I know that Paolo hates Clara.	I think/believe that Paolo hates Clara.
Il maestro ***dice*** *che Aldo non* ***scrive*** *bene.*	*Il maestro* ***pensa*** *che Aldo non* ***scriva*** *bene.*
The teacher says that Aldo doesn't write well.	The teacher thinks that Aldo doesn't write well.

The present subjunctive is used to express **an action which happens at the same time as the one of the main clause** in which **the verb** is in the **present and** in the **future**.

Present subjunctive of the verbs *essere, avere* and of the *verbi servili*

Remember that the subjunctive is used as the **imperative in the *forma di cortesia* (formal imperative)**.

Entri*, signor Bianchi!* Come in, Mr Bianchi!
Signor Villa, ***sia*** *gentile e* ***abbia*** *pazienza.* Mr Villa, be kind and patient, please.

Negative form: ***Non*** *lavori troppo, signor Rossi.* Don't work too hard, Mr Rossi.

Subjunctive of irregular verbs

	io	tu	lui/lei	noi	voi	loro
dire	dica	dica	dica	diciamo	diciate	dicano
fare	faccia	faccia	faccia	facciamo	facciate	facciano
tradurre	traduca	traduca	traduca	traduciamo	traduciate	traducano
finire	finisca	finisca	finisca	finiamo	finiate	finiscano
andare	vada	vada	vada	andiamo	andiate	vadano
venire	venga	venga	venga	veniamo	veniate	vengano

For the forms of other irregular verbs see Appendix on pg. 156.

Exercises

1 Complete with the correct forms of the verbs in the *congiuntivo presente*. /7

Mi sembra che Giulio non (studiare) → ***studi*** *per niente.*

1 È difficile che Carlo (*accettare*) .... di cambiare programma.
2 Credo che mio marito (*dormire*) .... ancora
3 Preferisco che voi mi (*aspettare*) .... sotto casa.
4 Spero che tu (*partire*) .... prima di Pasqua.
5 È importante che voi (*prendere*) .... quello che serve.
6 È meglio che voi (*scendere*) .... alla prossima fermata.
7 Speriamo che le varie nazioni (*impegnarsi*) .... di più per l'ambiente.

2 *Indicativo* or *congiuntivo*? Complete with the verbs in the correct form. /7

parlare • pensare • scrivere • tornare • sentirsi • lavorare • partire

1 Temi che tua nonna non .... bene?
2 So che Anna .... bene l'inglese.
3 Sappiamo che Pietro .... per le vacanze a fine mese.
4 Desidero che voi .... il vostro nome in modo leggibile.
5 È chiaro che quelle persone .... solo alla carriera.
6 Dubito che Marco .... prima di sera.
7 Vedo che voi .... con impegno.

3 Choose the correct form of the verb. /7

1 Bisogna che uno di noi si *informa/si informi* sugli orari dei treni.
2 Spero che loro *accettino/accettono* il nostro invito.
3 Il medico dice che le mie condizioni *migliorino/migliorano*.
4 Occorre che tutti *si mettono/si mettano* al lavoro.
5 Devo cercare casa perché il contratto d'affitto *scada/scade* tra un mese.
6 Sappiamo che finalmente Carlo *lavora/lavori* con soddisfazione.
7 È necessario che loro *prendono/prendano* delle precauzioni.

4 Write the verbs in the *congiuntivo presente* and *imperfetto*. /30

io faccio → ***io faccia, facessi***

1 noi diamo ....
2 tu dai ....
3 voi sapete ....
4 loro sanno ....
5 voi state ....
6 io sto ....
7 loro traducono ....
8 lui traduce ....
9 voi bevete ....
10 lui beve ....
11 noi beviamo ....
12 loro dicono ....
13 loro vanno ....
14 tu vai ....
15 tu vieni ....

51 Io amassi, tu vendessi, lui sentisse...
Imperfect of the subjunctive tense

	1st conjugation AMARE	2nd conjugation VENDERE	3rd conjugation SENTIRE
io	am-**a**-**ssi**	vend-**e**-**ssi**	sent-**i**-**ssi**
tu	am-**a**-**ssi**	vend-**e**-**ssi**	sent-**i**-**ssi**
lui/lei	am-**a**-**sse**	vend-**e**-**sse**	sent-**i**-**sse**
noi	am-**a**-**ssimo**	vend-**e**-**ssimo**	sent-**i**-**ssimo**
voi	am-**a**-**ste**	vend-**e**-**ste**	sent-**i**-**ste**
loro	am-**a**-**ssero**	vend-**e**-**ssero**	sent-**i**-**ssero**

The imperfect of subjunctive tense is used when the verb **in the dependent clause** is in a **past tense or** in the **conditional** and **the action in the dependent clause happens at the same time as the one in the main clause**.

Main clause	Dependent clause
Non sapevo I didn't know	*che Carlo* ***parlasse*** *il francese.* that Charles spoke French. *che* ***veniste*** *anche voi.* you would come too.
Non ero sicuro I wasn't sure	*che i nostri amici* ***arrivassero*** *oggi.* that our friends would come today. *che tu* ***fossi*** *così bravo in italiano.* you where so good at Italian.
Era probabile It was likely	*che Maria e Angelo* ***si sposassero*** *a settembre.* that Maria and Angelo would have got married in September.
Mi era sembrato I believed	*che il negozio all'angolo* ***vendesse*** *le cartoline.* that the shop on the corner sold postcards. *che la tua casa* ***fosse*** *più buia.* that your house was darker.

For the forms of the irregular verbs see Appendix on pg. 156.

Exercises

1 Write these verbs in the congiuntivo *imperfetto*. /12

io gioco → ***io giocassi***

1 tu vedi ....
2 loro mangiano ....
3 noi crediamo ....
4 io telefono ....
5 lui guarda ....
6 voi pensate ....
7 io abito ....
8 io esco ....
9 loro mettono ....
10 voi vendete ....
11 tu menti ....
12 io parto ....

2 Write these sentences with the *congiuntivo imperfetto*. /4

Penso che Davide sia un vero Don Giovanni. → ***Pensavo** che Davide **fosse** un vero Don Giovanni.*

1 Temo che Luca perda il suo tempo con quella ragazza.
....
2 Speriamo che Sergio abbia tempo per noi.
....
3 È meglio che tu decida che cosa fare.
....
4 Credete che Lucia possa venire alla festa?
....

3 Transform these verbs in the *congiuntivo imperfetto*. /6

Credevo che Marco (tornare) → ***tornasse** in ufficio.*

1 Speravo che ieri (*arrivare*) .... la lettera che aspettavo da tanti giorni.
2 Pensavo che in autunno i prezzi (*salire*) ....
3 Vorrei che tu (*ascoltare*) .... questo discorso.
4 Ci sembrava che spesso Anna (*comportarsi*) .... male.
5 Preferirei che voi mi (*aspettare*) .... sotto casa.
6 Ero sicuro che tuo padre (*sapere*) .... già tutto.

4 Choose the right alternative. /6

1 Matteo credeva che lei *cucinasse/cucinerasse* meglio.
2 È probabile che loro *recitassero/recitino* nello spettacolo.
3 Mi era sembrato che *partisse/partesse* da solo.
4 Speravamo che Emma e Bernardo *capessero/capissero* l'italiano.
5 Pensavamo che tu non ti *arrabbiassi/arrabbiesse* facilmente.
6 Preferirei che voi *venissero/veniste*.

52 Io abbia amato, tu sia stato...
Io avessi fatto, tu fossi partito...
Past and past perfect of the subjunctive tense

Past of the subjunctive (*congiuntivo passato*)

	io	tu	lui/lei	noi	voi	loro
amare	abbia amato	abbia amato	abbia amato	abbiamo amato	abbiate amato	abbiano amato
essere	sia stato/a	sia stato/a	sia stato/a	siamo stati/e	siate stati/e	siano stati/e
partire	sia partito/a	sia partito/a	sia partito/a	siamo partiti/e	siate partiti/e	siano partiti/e

Paolo è in ritardo; temo che non ***si sia svegliato*** *e* ***abbia perso*** *il treno.*
Paolo is late. I'm afraid he hasn't woken up and has missed the train.
Non sappiamo se Carla ***sia*** *già* ***arrivata*** *a casa.*
We don't know if Carla has arrived home yet.

The past subjunctive is used to express an **action that happens before the one expressed in the main clause** when the tense of the verb in **main clause** is **present or future**.

Main clause	Dependent clause
Credo I believe *Pensiamo* We think	*che Paolo* ***abbia litigato*** *con sua sorella.* that Paolo has quarreled with his sister.

Past perfect of the subjunctive (*congiuntivo trapassato*)

	io	tu	lui/lei	noi	voi	loro
amare	avessi amato	avessi amato	avesse amato	avessimo amato	aveste amato	avessero amato
partire	fossi partito/a	fossi partito/a	fosse partito/a	fossimo partiti/e	foste partiti/e	fossero partiti/e
essere	fossi stato/a	fossi stato/a	fosse stato/a	fossimo stati/e	foste stati/e	fossero stati/e

The past perfect of the subjunctive is formed with the **auxiliary verb *avere* or *essere* + past participle**.

It is used when the verb **in the dependent clause** expresses an **action that happens before the one in the main clause when the tense of the verb in the main clause is in the past tense or the future perfect tense**.

Paolo era in ritardo; temevo che non si ***fosse svegliato*** *e* ***avesse perso*** *il treno.*
Paolo was late. I was afraid that he hadn't woken up and had missed the train.
Non sapevamo se Carla ***fosse*** *già* ***arrivata*** *a casa.*
We didn't know if Carla had arrived home yet.

Exercises

1 Write these verbs in the *congiuntivo passato* and *trapassato*. /20

io amo ⟶ *io* ***abbia amato/avessi amato***

1 tu credi ....
2 noi usciamo ....
3 loro tornano ....
4 io sono ....
5 lui dice ....
6 voi sapete ....
7 voi ricevete ....
8 tu parti ....
9 loro fanno ....
10 loro vogliono ....

2 *Indicativo* or *congiuntivo*? Choose the right alternative. /4

1 Ho pensato che *era/fosse* tardi. ....
2 Ha confessato che mi *abbia/aveva* amato profondamente. ....
3 Hanno scritto che non *fosse/era* successo niente. ....
4 Hanno paura che non *dicono/dicano* la verità. ....

3 Complete the sentences with the correct form of the *congiuntivo imperfetto* or *trapassato*. /8

Immaginavamo che Luisa (dormire) ⟶ ***dormisse*** *ancora.*

1 Maria voleva che i figli (*tenere*) .... in ordine le loro camere.
2 Noi temevamo che nostro figlio non (*riuscire*) .... a prendere dei bei voti.
3 Ci sembrava strano che a quell'ora Giorgio non (*telefonare*) .... ancora.
4 Quando vidi che Carlo non era ancora arrivato, pensai che (*avere*) .... un incidente.
5 Non eravamo sicuri che gli studenti (*prepararsi*) .... per quell'esame.
6 Pensammo che loro (*sbagliarsi*) .... quando ti avevano dato quella informazione.
7 Ero felice che Laura e Marco (*sposarsi*) .... pochi mesi prima.
8 Mi sembrava che Giovanna (*prendere*) .... il diploma nel 1992.

4 Transform the sentences in the past. /5

Luca pensa che Giorgio abbia commesso un errore. ⟶ *Luca pensava che Giorgio* ***avesse commesso*** *un errore.*

1 Anna pensa che il marito sia andato al cinema.
Anna pensava che ....
2 Carla crede che Luca le abbia nascosto qualcosa.
Carla credeva che ....
3 Questi uomini pensano che le ragazze non debbano indossare i pantaloni.
Questi uomini pensavano che ....
4 Non so se Andrea sappia giocare a scacchi.
Non sapevo se ....
5 Spero che tutti abbiano finito il lavoro.
Speravo che ....

53 Alzare, vendere, dormire... Avere amato, avere corso, essere partiti...
Present and past infinitive

The infinitive mode has two tenses: **present infinitive** and **past infinitive**.
The present infinitive of the reflexive verbs is formed by adding -***a*** , -***e***, -***i*** + -***re*** or -***rsi***.
*am-**a**-**re**, vend-**e**-**re**, sent-**i**-**re**, alz-**a**-**rsi**, alz-**a**-**rsi**, etc.*

The present infinitive (*infinito presente*)

The present infinitive is used **after** the prepositions ***per*** or ***a*** to express the **aim/goal of an action**.
It is also used with the expression ***stare per*** + **infinitive** which is the equivalent of the English expression **"to be going to"**.

The past infinitive (*infinito passato*)

The past infinitive is formed with ***avere/essere*** + **past participle**: *avere amato, avere venduto, essere partito/a/i/e*.
For **reflexive verbs** it is formed with ***essersi*** + **past participle**: *essersi alzato/a/i/e, essersi lavato/a/i/e.*

Like in English, the infinitive in Italian doesn't conjugate, but while in English the infinitive is formed by **to** + the verb, in Italian it **is composed of only one word**.

The present and the past infinitive are used:

- as a noun;
  *Marina adora **cucinare**.* Marina loves cooking.
  ***Aver controllato** l'orario è stata un'ottima idea.*
  Checking the time was an excellent idea.
- in dependent clauses;
  *Penso di **tornare** in Spagna la prossima settimana.*
  I think I'll go back to Spain next year.
  *Credeva di **aver superato** gli esami.*
  He thought he had passed his exams.
- when the main clause is impersonal;
  *È necessario **accendere** il computer.*
  It's necessary to switch on the computer.
- with ***senza*** (without), ***prima di*** (before), ***in modo da*** (so as to) and other similar expressions.
  *Non uscire **senza** aver chiuso la finestra.*
  Don't leave without closing the window.
  ***Prima** di addormentarmi bevo sempre una tazza di camomilla.*
  Before sleeping I always drink a cup of chamomile tea.

With ***dopo*** (after) only the **past infinitive** is used.
***Dopo** aver cenato siamo andati al cinema.* After having dinner we went to the cinema.

Exercises

1 Choose the right alternative.

/6

*Prima di **andare a letto**/essere andato a letto, guardo mezz'oretta la televisione.*

1 Dopo *aver frequentato/frequentare* il corso, eravamo molto bravi a lavorare con il computer.
2 Faccio tanto sport per *dimagrire/essere dimagrito*.
3 Mi ha rimproverato per *comportarmi/essermi comportato* male.
4 Credevo di *aver avuto/avere* un buon risultato, invece mi ha detto che l'esame è andato male.
5 Sperava di *trovare/aver trovato* un buon ristorante, invece mangiò malissimo.
6 Ho preparato le valigie prima di *partire/essere partito*.

2 Match the sentences.

/7

1 Aver visitato quel borgo	☐ a) di chiamare l'idraulico.
2 Scusa, ho dimenticato	☐ b) è stata una bella esperienza.
3 Ho visto i miei vicini	☐ c) prima di comprare il biglietto.
4 Guarda che film c'è	☐ d) di aver fatto un buon lavoro.
5 Sono sicuro	☐ e) dopo aver fatto colazione.
6 Siamo usciti	☐ f) litigare.
7 Temevamo	☐ g) di essere arrivati troppo tardi.

3 Change the sentences replacing the infinitive with the subjunctive.

/6

Crediamo che Pietro <u>avere trovato</u> un cane. ⟶ *Crediamo che Pietro **abbia trovato** un cane.*

1 Speravi che tuo marito *tornare* presto? ....
2 Immaginavate che il film *finire* così? ....
3 Prima che *fare* buio devi bagnare le piante. ....
4 Temeva che il giorno prima il marito la *avere vista* con quell'uomo.
....
5 Speriamo che tu *avere risposto* a tutte le domande che ti hanno rivolto.
....
6 È giusto che voi *rispettare* il regolamento. ....

4 Choose the right alternative.

/5

1 Credevo che Lucia *conosceva/conoscere/conoscesse* lo spagnolo.
2 Pensano che *sia meglio/di essere meglio/essere meglio* andare a casa.
3 Desideravano che gli ospiti *erano/essere/fossero* a loro agio.
4 Temi che Giulio non *volesse/volere/voglia* studiare?
5 Era probabile che la polizia *arrestare/arrestasse/arrestava* il colpevole.

5 Correct the mistake.

/6

Credono <u>che sono i migliori</u>. ⟶ ***di essere i migliori***

Paolo pensava <u>che sua moglie avere preso il pane</u>. ⟶ ***che sua moglie avesse preso il pane.***

1 Speriamo <u>che vinciamo la partita</u>. ....
2 Carla temeva che suo marito la <u>tradire</u>. ....
3 Prima <u>che esca</u> vuole registrare un film. ....
4 Dopo <u>che ha visto Laura</u>, non è più riuscito a scordarla. ....
5 I suoi genitori desideravano <u>che Paolo frequentare l'università</u>. ....
6 Spero <u>che sono arrivato in tempo per la cena</u>. ....

54 So che è arrivato, dice che verrà... Lui ha detto che sarebbe arrivato...
Main clause and object clause

Tense of the main clause: present

- If the action happens **at the same time**.

Main clause (*indicativo presente*)	Dependent clause (*indicativo presente*)
Sappiamo We know	*che Paolo* ***ama*** *la musica.* that Paolo loves music.
Sono certa I'm sure	*che Giulio* ***parte*** *oggi.* that Giulio is leaving today.

- If the action in the dependent clause **happens before** (the one expressed in the main clause).

Main clause (*indicativo presente*)	Dependent clause (*indicativo passato prossimo*)
Mario dice Mario says	*che Carlo* ***ha avuto*** *un incidente.* that Carlo had an accident.

- If the action in the dependent clause **refers to the future** (happens after the one expressed in the main clause).

Main clause (*indicativo presente*)	Dependent clause (*indicativo futuro*)
Sento I feel	*che* ***saremo*** *felici insieme.* we'll be happy together.
È chiaro It's clear	*che Aldo* ***verrà*** *con noi.* Aldo will come with us.

Tense of the main clause: *passto prossimo*

- If the action in the dependent clause happens **at the same time**.

Main clause (*indicativo passato prossimo*)	Dependent clause (*indicativo passato prossimo*)
Lucia ha detto Lucia said	*che Laura* ***ha avuto*** *l'influenza.* that Laura had the flu.

- If the action in the dependent clause **happens before** (the one expressed in the main clause).

Main clause (*indicativo passato*)	Dependent clause (*indicativo trapassato*)
Mario diceva Mario said	*che Lara* ***aveva avuto*** *l'influenza.* that Laura had had the flu.

- If the action in the dependent clause **happens before** (the one expressed in the main clause)

Main clause (*indicativo passato*)	Dependent clause (*condizionale passato*)
Sentivo I felt	*che* ***saremmo stati*** *felici insieme.* that we would be happy together.

In Italian, differently from English, in the subordinate sentence the past (and not the present) conditional is used.

Exercises

1 Complete with the correct form of the verb in brackets. /8

So che Susanna (uscire) → ***è uscita*** *un'ora fa.*

1 Dicono che la loro squadra (*vincere*) .... ieri.
2 Scrive alla moglie che domani (*arrivare*) .... tardi per un impegno improvviso.
3 È chiaro che i loro tentativi (*avere successo*) .... Tutti infatti li hanno applauditi.
4 I nostri vicini affermano che qualcuno (*tentare*) .... di entrare in casa loro ieri.
5 La mail dice che la nostra amica non (*venire*) .... più a trovarci il mese prossimo.
6 Ci raccontano che la prossima settimana (*andare*) .... in visita ai loro amici a Roma.
7 Giuriamo che non (*essere*) .... noi a rompere gli occhiali.
8 Dice che suo fratello (*tornare*) .... a casa tardi ieri notte.

2 Choose the right alternative. /6

1 La prossima settimana potrò finalmente sapere se *avrò preso/prenderò* il massimo dei voti nell'esame che ho fatto.
2 Mi dicono che al colloquio non *ho fatto/faccio* bella figura.
3 Ci riferiscono che ieri mattina *è accaduto/accade* un terribile incidente sulla strada per Pavia.
4 Mi fanno capire che non *sono/sarò stato* adatto al lavoro che mi propongono.
5 Intendi dire che *devo/ho dovuto* uscire subito?
6 Non pensate che il vostro viaggio *sarà/sarà stato* pericoloso?

3 Complete with the correct form of the verb in brackets. /10

Stefano mi ha detto che (studiare) → ***avrebbe studiato*** *quel giorno perché fra un mese deve dare l'esame.*

1 Ci hanno riferito che il presidente della società (*venire*) .... in visita qualche giorno prima.
2 Mi hanno assicurato che il tempo (*essere*) .... bello durante le vacanze, invece ha piovuto sempre.
3 Sapeva che (*essere*) .... inutile, ma lo fece lo stesso.
4 Mi accorsi che la mia amica (*bere*) .... troppo. Non riusciva più neppure a parlare.
5 Ho letto che l'anno scorso (*aumentare*) .... i prezzi.
6 Tutti sapevano che Marco (*partire*) .... il giorno prima.
7 Ero arrabbiata. Mi disse che non (*dovere*) .... arrabbiarmi così.
8 Mi ha scritto che non (*potere*) .... venire a trovarmi. Era stato troppo occupato.
9 Io ho capito che tu non (*volere*) .... partire da solo.
10 Mi hanno detto che il giorno prima Paola mi (*cercare*) .... ma non mi (*trovare*) ....

4 Choose the right alternative. /6

1 Il giornalista ha scritto che il ministro *aveva parlato/avrebbe parlato* il giorno prima.
2 Mio fratello sostiene *che non sarà stato lui/di non essere stato lui* a rompere il vaso.
3 La storia insegna che *dobbiamo/abbiamo dovuto* evitare le guerre.
4 Sentiva che non *potrebbero/sarebbero potuti* essere felici.
5 Si accorse che *dimenticava/aveva dimenticato* il portafoglio e tornò a casa.
6 Capii che *era stato/sarebbe stato* meglio chiamare un dottore e lo feci subito.

55 Se avrò sete berrò, se avessi soldi farei un viaggio, se avessi avuto coraggio ci sarei andato...
Hypothetical period

Periodo ipotetico
della realtà

Periodo ipotetico
della possibilità

Periodo ipotetico
della irrealtà

It is formed by two clauses:
- a dependent clause introduced by ***se*** (if);
- a main clause which indicates **the consequence** of an hypothesis.

There are three **types of hypothesis/consequence situations** in Italian grammar:
- **real** (*periodo ipotetico della realtà*);
- **unlikely** (*periodo ipotetico della possibilità*);
- **no longer possible** (*periodo ipotetico della irrealtà*).

First type: real (*periodo ipotetico della realtà*)

It is used to express **a possible hypothesis**.

Dependent clause (*indicativo presente/futuro*)	**Main clause (*indicativo presente/futuro*)**
*Se **avrò** sete* If I'm thirsty	***berrò** dell'acqua.* I'll drink some water.

Differently from English, it is possible to use two future tenses in the same "period".
*Se **pioverà prenderò** l'ombrello.* If it rains I'll take the umbrella.

Second type: unlikely (*periodo ipotetico della possibilità*)

It is used to refer to something that **might happen** or to talk about very **improbable** (**but possible**) conditions.

Dependent clause (*congiuntivo imperfetto*)	**Main clause (*condizionale presente/imperativo*)**
***Se** avessi più soldi* If I had more money	*mi **comprerei** dei vestiti più costosi.* I'd buy more expensive clothes.

Third type: no longer possible (*periodo ipotetico della irrealtà*)

It is used to express **a possible hypothesis** when the condition refers to the **past**.

Dependent clause (*congiuntivo trapassato*)	**Main clause (*condizionale passato*)**
***Se avessi avuto** più tempo* If I had had more time	***avrei studiato** meglio.* I would have studied better.

Exercises

1 Complete with the verbs in the correct form of the *congiuntivo*. /10

Spero che domani non (piovere) ⟶ ***piova***.

1 Speriamo che voi (*potere*) .... darci una mano. Abbiamo veramente bisogno di aiuto.
2 I miei genitori sono contenti che noi (*avere*) .... un buon lavoro.
3 Ancora Carlo non arriva. Ho paura che gli (*succedere*) .... qualcosa.
4 Si augurano che la festa (*riuscire*) .... bene.
5 È probabile che la polizia (*arrestare*) .... i colpevoli.
6 Sperano che i loro genitori (*divertirsi*) .... durante la crociera del mese scorso.
7 Speriamo che tu (*ricordarsi*) .... di scrivere al tuo professore quando eri in Scozia.
8 Credo che Luigi (*comportarsi*) .... da persona educata in quella occasione.
9 Tanti credono che la crisi non (*cominciare*) .... l'anno scorso ma quest'anno.
10 È tempo che voi (*fare*) .... i bagagli. Presto partiremo.

2 Answer these questions with the *congiuntivo* or *indicativo*. /5

1 Cosa speri che accada nel futuro nella tua città?
Spero che ....
2 Credi che qualcosa cambierà presto nella tua vita?
Credo che ....
3 Credi che la tua squadra preferita vinca l'anno prossimo?
Credo che ....
4 Credi che nei prossimi anni diventerai ricco?
Credo che ....
5 Credi che imparerai l'italiano con questa grammatica?
Credo che ....

3 Complete with the verbs in the *congiuntivo imperfetto* or *trapassato*. /7

Aveva paura che qualcuno lo (seguire) ⟶ ***seguisse***.

1 Credevo che tutto (*essere*) .... più facile una volta terminata l'emergenza.
2 Aveva pensato che Luca non (*avere*) .... un buon lavoro, invece guadagna bene.
3 Credevo che Giulia (*trovare*) .... un appartamento in affitto, invece lo sta ancora cercando.
4 Speravo che Sandro il giorno dopo mi (*telefonare*) .... per avvertire. Ma non lo ha fatto.
5 Credevo che Monica (*uscire*) ...., invece era nell'altra stanza.
6 Pensavamo che Daniele (*laurearsi*) .... il mese prima.
7 Chi poteva immaginare che a Carlo non (*piacere*) .... gli animali?

56 Io sono amato, tu eri amata, lei sarà amata...
Passive form (indicative)

	Active form	Passive form
Presente	*Luca* ***ama*** *Anna.* Luca loves Anna.	*Anna* ***è amata*** *da Luca.* Anna is loved by Luca.
Passato prossimo	*Luca* ***ha amato*** *Anna.* Luca has loved Anna.	*Anna* ***è stata amata*** *da Luca.* Anna has been loved by Luca.
Imperfetto	*Luca* ***amava*** *Anna.* Luca loved Anna.	*Anna* ***era amata*** *da Luca.* Anna was loved by Luca.
Trapassato prossimo	*Luca* ***aveva amato*** *Anna.* Luca had loved Anna.	*Anna* ***era stata amata*** *da Luca.* Anna had been loved by Luca.
Futuro semplice	*Luca* ***amerà*** *Anna.* Luca will love Anna.	*Anna* ***sarà amata*** *da Luca.* Anna will be loved by Luca.
Futuro anteriore	*Luca* ***avrà amato*** *Anna.* Luca will have loved Anna.	*Anna* ***sarà stata amata*** *da Luca.* Anna will have been loved by Luca.
Passato remoto	*Luca* ***amò*** *Anna.* Luca loved Anna.	*Anna* ***fu amata*** *da Luca.* Anna was loved by Luca.
Trapassato remoto	*Luca* ***ebbe amato*** *Anna.* Luca had loved Anna.	*Anna* ***fu stata amata*** *da Luca.* Anna had been loved by Luca.

Usage
In the passive the subject is not who performs the action but the one who **"receives" the action**.

Active	***Luca*** Luca	***ama*** loves	***Anna*** Anna
	soggetto	**verbo attivo transitivo**	**oggetto**

Passive	***Anna*** Anna	***è amata*** is loved	***da Luca*** by Luca
	soggetto	**verbo passivo transitivo**	**agente**

The passive form is formed with the verb ***essere* (to be)** + **past participle** which always **agrees** with the subject in gender and number.

La Divina Commedia ***è stata scritta*** *da Dante Alighieri.*
The Divina Commedia was written by Dante Alighieri.
Queste opere ***sono state composte*** *da Giuseppe Verdi.*
These operas were composed by Giuseppe Verdi.

Exercises

1 Rewrite the sentences in the passive voice. /8

Esattamente un anno fa il terremoto ***ha distrutto*** *questo paese.* → *Esattamente un anno fa questo paese* ***è stato distrutto*** *dal terremoto.*

1 Vendono questa casa a poco prezzo. ....
2 Laveremo il bambino nella vasca da bagno. ....
3 Le donne delle pulizie pulirono la stanza molto bene. ....
4 Arrestarono l'uomo e lo portarono in prigione. ....
5 Farai tutto questo. ....
6 La mamma rimproverava il bambino. ....
7 L'albergo ospitava centinaia di persone. ....
8 Il signor Ferrari non accettò la mia proposta. ....

2 Rewrite the sentences in the passive voice. /6

1 I poliziotti hanno catturato il ladro. ....
2 I Bianchi non ci hanno invitato al matrimonio. ....
3 Le impiegate non avevano aperto la finestra. ....
4 Avevi preparato la pasta per tutti. ....
5 Quelle persone hanno offeso i loro parenti. ....
6 Finalmente quella ditta ha assunto Paola. ....

3 Rewrite the sentences in the active voice. /8

Queste chiese sono visitate da tutti. → ***Tutti visitano queste chiese.***

1 Il computer sul mio tavolo è utilizzato da molti colleghi.
....
2 Dieci frasi sono state tradotte da Nada dall'italiano nella sua lingua.
....
3 Il pacco sarà spedito all'estero dalla segretaria.
....
4 La pop star fu seguita da alcuni fan fino all'albergo.
....
5 Questa lettera non era stata firmata dal direttore.
....
6 Il villaggio fu distrutto da una bomba. ....
7 Il libro era stato scritto da uno scrittore famoso.
....
8 Le poesie sono state recitate dal professore nell'aula conferenze.
....

4 Correct the mistake where necessary. /5

1 Siamo stati mandato qui per verificare degli errori. ....
2 La prossima settimana Francesca sarà assistita da un nuovo insegnante.
....
3 Questa lingua è studiato dappertutto. ....
4 Mi sono stata regalata un libro da Giulio. ....
5 In passato sarà promosso capufficio. ....

57 Viene considerato... Si vendono... Si può aprire...

Passive with the verb *venire* (auxiliary) and with modal verbs; the *si passivante*

Venire

In most cases, the passive form **can be formed by the verb *venire*** (instead of *essere*) + **past participle**, which **agrees with the subject**.

venire amato/a/i/e

*Frank Lloyd Wright **è/viene considerato** uno degli architetti più famosi del mondo.*
Frank Lloyd Wright is considered one of the most famous architects in the world.
*Quell'attrice **era amata** da tutti. Quell'attrice **veniva apprezzata** da tutti.*
That actress was loved by everybody.

Modal verbs (*verbi servili*) with the passive form

With modal verbs it is not possible to form passive sentences.
The passive of a sentence which contains a modal verb is formed in two ways:

- with ***si*** + ***verbo servile*** + **the active form of the infinitive**
  *A colazione **si può** bere una tazza di tè e mangiare dei biscotti.*
  At breakfast you can drink a cup of tea and eat some biscuits.
  *Dove **si può** pranzare qui vicino?*
  Where can we have lunch near here?
- or with ***verbo servile*** + **the passive form of the infinitive**
  *Gli animali **devono essere rispettati**.*
  Animals must be respected.

For the passive form formed with verbs of other modes (subjunctive, conditional etc.) see Appendix.

The *si* with a passive sense (*si passivante*)

The *si passivante* is built with:

- *si* + the verb 3rd person singular (with a singular subject);
- *si* + the verb 3rd person plural (with a plural subject).
  *In Italia **si mangia** molta pasta.*
  In Italy a lot of pasta is eaten. (In Italy people eat a lot of pasta)
  *In quel negozio **si riparano** biciclette.*
  In that shop bicycles are repaired.

Exercises

1 Rewrite the sentences in the passive voice using the verb *venire*. /5

Temono che il cane sia rapito. ⟶ *Temono che il cane **venga rapito**.*

1 Dice che saremo presto mandati via. ....

2 Ho letto che quell'uomo fu imprigionato in una cella. ....

3 Quel tipo di lavoro non era proposto a tutti. ....

4 Il gioiello sarà valutato una grande somma. ....

5 I nonni erano festeggiati da tutti i nipoti. ....

2 Rewrite the sentences in the passive voice using the verb *venire*. /8

Gennaro scrive la lettera a Concetta. ⟶ *La lettera a Concetta **viene scritta** da Gennaro.*

1 Il ragazzo vinse un milione di dollari. ....

2 L'esercito dei Romani sconfiggerà l'esercito nemico. ....

3 La nonna preparava una torta. ....

4 L'editore pubblicherà il libro a marzo. ....

5 La invitano spesso al cinema. ....

6 Il temporale allagò interamente il negozio. ....

7 Il ragazzo mette in ordine la camera. ....

8 Abbasseranno i prezzi. ....

3 Rewrite the sentences in the passive voice using modal verbs. /8

Dovete firmare subito il contratto. ⟶ *Il contratto **deve essere firmato** subito.*

1 Possono avvisare la polizia da un momento all'altro.

....

2 Presto dobbiamo prendere una decisione. ....

3 Carlo deve comprare degli oggetti per la nuova casa.

....

4 Da domani possiamo eleggere i nuovi rappresentanti per il quartiere.

....

5 Puoi sbrigare adesso il tuo lavoro? ....

6 Non potete perdere questa occasione. ....

7 La segretaria non potrà scrivere la lettera prima di domani.

....

8 Non possiamo accettare queste condizioni. Sono impossibili!

....

4 Rewrite the sentences using the *si passivante*. /6

Non possiamo bere bibite dolci. ⟶ *Non **si possono bere** bibite dolci.*

1 Non possiamo visitare siti per adulti in Internet. ....

2 Non possiamo mangiare cioccolato, dolci e caramelle. ....

3 Non possiamo bere caffè. ....

4 Non dobbiamo inviare messaggi agli amici. ....

5 Non possiamo indossare abiti di marca. ....

6 Dobbiamo indossare l'uniforme. .... Che noia!

58 Ma, dunque, cioè...
Coordinating conjunctions

Coordinating conjunctions **combine elements of the same clause** or independent clauses. This is a list of the main coordinating conjunctions.

sia ... sia both ... and	*Martin parla* ***sia*** *il tedesco* ***sia*** *l'italiano.* Martin speaks both German and Italian.
anche also/too	*A Luca piacciono le mele.* ***Anche*** *a me piacciono molto.* Luca likes apples. I like them too.
ma/però/tuttavia but/however	*Non ho finito il lavoro,* ***ma*** *lo farò domani.* I haven't finished my work but I'll do it tomorrow.
inoltre besides	*C'è freddo e sono stanco,* ***inoltre*** *sta per piovere.* It's cold and I'm tired, besides it's going to rain.
né ... né neither ... nor (either/or)	*Non mangio* ***né*** *carne* ***né*** *pesce. Sono vegetariano.* I don't eat either meat or fish. I'm vegetarian.
o/oppure, o ... o either/or	***O*** *vieni* ***oppure*** *andiamo da soli.* Either you come or we'll go alone.
altrimenti otherwise	*Fa' i compiti,* ***altrimenti*** *stasera non vedrai la televisione.* Do your homework, otherwise you won't watch TV tonight.
invece instead	*Mio marito ama il pesce, io* ***invece*** *mangio solo verdura.* My husband loves fish, instead I only eat vegetables.
cioè namely/that's	*Ho una sola preoccupazione,* ***cioè*** *che stiamo spendendo troppo.* I only have one concern, namely that we are spending too much.
infatti in fact/indeed/actually	*E* ***infatti*** *adesso si sa il perché.* And indeed now we know why.
perciò therefore	*Nevica da ieri sera* ***perciò*** *non posso venire a casa tua.* It has been snowing since yesterday evening therefore I cannot come to your house.
quindi/dunque therefore/then	*Ha vissuto sei anni a Roma,* ***quindi*** *capisce l'italiano.* He has lived in Rome for six years, therefore he understands Italian.
non solo ... ma anche not only ... (but) also	***Non solo*** *non ha studiato,* ***ma*** *ha* ***anche*** *rotto una finestra.* ***Not only*** hasn't he studied, he has also broken a window.
e/ed and	*Paolo* ***ed*** *Emma studiano* ***e*** *lavorano.* Paul and Emma study and work.

Exercises

1 Complete the passages with the coordinating conjunctions.

/16

invece • ma • non solo • ma anche • sia • sia

La conoscevo da anni, 1) .... non eravamo mai state amiche, 2) .... perché era antipatica, 3) .... perché tutti la consideravano una secchiona. 4) .... io non la salutavo, 5) .... tutti quelli che abitavano vicino a lei la ignoravano. 6) ...., anni dopo, quando ho cominciato a lavorare, ho capito che era una persona molto in gamba.

però • quindi • o • o • neanche • nemmeno • inoltre

– 7) .... vieni con me 8) .... rimani a casa. Decidi!
– Non rimango a casa! 9) .... per tutto l'oro del mondo!
– 10) .... vieni con me?
– D'accordo, vengo con te, 11) .... non voglio stare fuori tanto. 12) .... se vengo con te, devi comprarmi una cosa.
– Non ci penso 13) ....! Tu vieni e basta!

perciò • invece • infatti

Federico aveva gli occhi azzurri e i capelli biondi, 14) .... tutti lo chiamavano il tedeschino, 15) .... lui era italiano; 16) .... era nato a Cosenza da padre calabrese e madre siciliana.

2 Match the two columns.

/6

1 Siamo interessati sia alla matematica
2 A scuola ha dei pessimi voti
3 Non solo leggono libri
4 Non gioca né a basket
5 Io non partecipo alla conferenza
6 Mangio poco

☐ a) ma anche giornali e riviste.
☐ b) inoltre si comporta male.
☐ c) né a calcio.
☐ d) e neppure Anna ci va.
☐ e) perché non ho mai fame.
☐ f) sia alla chimica.

3 Correct the mistakes using the conjunctions in the list.

/5

infatti • né ... né • altrimenti • perciò • invece

1 Non trovo né il quaderno ma anche il libro.

....

2 È veramente bravo nel suo lavoro. Tuttavia lo pagano molto bene.

....

3 Carlo dorme poco, ma anche Marta dorme molto.

....

4 Bevi subito il tè, tuttavia diventa freddo.

....

5 Era spesso malato, altrimenti andava sempre dal dottore.

....

59 Che, del quale, a cui...
Relative pronouns

Relative pronouns are used **to connect** two clauses.
In Italian they are: ***che, cui, il quale/la quale/i quali/le quali***.

Che is invariabile. It is used for feminine, masculine, singular and plural. It is never preceded by prepositions.

Mia zia ha fatto la torta ***che*** *adoro.*
My aunt has baked the cake I love.
Sono con il ragazzo ***che*** *ho incontrato alla festa.*
I'm with the boy I met at the party.
Ho incontrato Sergio ***che*** *andava al lavoro.*
I met Sergio who was going to work.

Cui is also invariable and it is introduced by prepositions (simple).

Vado dal dentista ***di cui*** *mi hai parlato.*
I'm going to the dentist's you talked about.
Firenze è la città ***in cui*** *è nato Dante Alighieri.*
Florence is the town where Dante Alighieri was born.

Il quale/la quale/i quali/le quali vary in gender and in number.
Il quale → masculine singular
La quale → feminine singular
I quali → masculine plural
Le quali → feminine plural

Also the determinative article and the preposition preceding them vary.

Sonia e Angela, ***alle quali*** *avevo prestato alcuni libri, non me li hanno ancora restituiti.*
Sonia and Angela, to whom I had lent some books, haven't given them back to me yet.
Il ragazzo ***del quale*** *ti ho scritto è spagnolo.*
The boy I wrote you about is Spanish.

They are used **to create emphasis or to be more specific**.

Differently from English the relative pronouns must always be expressed.

La ragazza ***che*** *ho visto alla festa.*
The girl I saw at the party.

Exercises

1 Build sentences using the relative pronoun *che*. /4

Ieri ho comprato un quadro. Il quadro è molto antico. → *Ieri ho comprato un quadro* ***che*** *è molto antico.*

1 Hai fatto una domanda. La domanda è intelligente.

....

2 Sabato sera abbiamo visto un film. Il film era molto divertente.

....

3 Ho conosciuto un ragazzo. Il ragazzo si chiama Aldo.

....

4 Il vigile ha fermato un'automobile. L'automobile era passata con il rosso.

....

2 Complete with the relative pronouns (pay attention to the prepositions!). /6

Ho dato un passaggio a un ragazzo. Il ragazzo era spagnolo. → *Il ragazzo* ***al quale/a cui*** *ho dato un passaggio era spagnolo.*

1 Ho fatto un regalo a mio cugino. Mio cugino ha compiuto gli anni ieri.
Mio cugino, ...

2 I ragazzi sono tedeschi. Noi giochiamo con i ragazzi.
I ragazzi ....

3 I nostri amici arrivano domani. Abbiamo ricevuto un pacco da loro.
I nostri amici ....

4 Il giornalista ha parlato di un libro. Il libro è molto interessante.
Il libro ....

5 Sincerità e onesta sono valori. Non si discute su questi valori.
Sincerità e onestà ....

6 Ho messo le monete in un cassetto. Il cassetto è quello della scrivania.
Il cassetto ....

3 Complete with the relative pronouns. /14

1 In montagna ho raccolto dei funghi, alcuni .... erano velenosi.
2 Filippo, ... ho dato la notizia, era molto contento.
3 L'amico .... gioco a tennis è venezuelano.
4 Il problema .... stiamo discutendo è di difficile soluzione.
5 Il ristorante .... ti ho parlato è in via Roma.
6 L'appartamento .... abita Pamela è piccolo ma grazioso.
7 Gli amici .... sono andato ieri sono molto simpatici.
8 Il farmacista .... ho chiesto l'aspirina mi ha servito rapidamente.
9 Il treno .... arriva mia zia è in ritardo.
10 Il giorno .... mi diverto di più è il giovedì.
11 Qual è la squadra .... fai il tifo?
12 Il camino .... esce quel fumo è quello della casa della nonna.
13 La bicicletta .... vengo a scuola è quella di mia sorella.
14 Il periodo storico .... mi sarebbe piaciuto vivere è quello dell'età classica.

60 Poiché, quando, sebbene...
Subordinating conjunctions (1)

Subordinating conjunctions **connect a main clause with a dependent clause**. Here you find a list of the most important subordinating conjunctions with examples.

Causal
Poiché, perché, visto che, dal momento che, siccome (since, as, because) + indicative mode. (*siccome* must always precede the main clause). They indicate the **cause or the reason of an action**.

Gli ho telefonato ***perché*** volevo parlare con lui.
I phoned him because I wanted to talk to him.
Siccome *sta nevicando, dovrai guidare più piano.*
Since it's snowing, you'll have to drive more slowly.

Final
Affinché, perché (so that) introduce the final cause.

Parlo lentamente ***perché*** *tu possa capire tutto.*
I'm speaking slowly so that you can understand everything.

Temporal
The temporal conjunction explains **when the actions happen**.

- ***Mentre*** (while), ***quando*** (when), ***dopo che*** (after), ***appena*** (as soon as), ***fino a che*** (until), ***da*** (since) + indicative mode.
- ***Prima*** (before) + subjunctive mode.
  Mentre *studia mio fratello ascolta la musica.*
  While studying my brother listens to music.
  Chiamami ***quando*** *sei pronto.*
  Call me when you're ready.
  Torna a casa ***prima che venga*** buio.
  Come back home before it gets dark.

These conjunctions **can also be followed by the infinitive** (corresponding to the English gerund) when the **subject of the main clause is the same as the subject of the dependent clause**.
Mi sono fatto la doccia ***prima di*** *uscire.* I had a shower before going out.

Concessive
They express **a circumstance which is different from the one that is expected** in the main clause.

- ***Benché, sebbene, malgrado, nonostante*** (although, even if, even though) + subjunctive mode.
  Sebbene *sia snella, Anna mangia sempre poco.*
  Although she's thin, Anna always eats little.
- ***Anche se*** + indicative.
  Anche se *è snella, Anna mangia sempre poco.*
  Even if she's thin, Anna always eats little.

Exercises

1 Complete the sentences with the following subordinating conjunctions. /8

mentre • purché • finché • quando • sebbene • prima che • affinché • poiché

1 La nonna va in clinica .... il dottore la possa visitare.
2 .... fa molto freddo nel nostro appartamento, accendiamo il riscaldamento.
3 .... giochino molto bene, i ragazzi non sono stati presi in squadre prestigiose.
4 Non posso allontanarmi da casa .... i miei figli non crescono.
5 Questo lavoro è tuo, ... t'impegni a lavorare tanto.
6 .... sono pronto ti chiamo.
7 Guardo la televisione, ... Carlo scrive al computer.
8 Facciamo delle gite in montagna, ... venga il freddo.

2 Complete the sentences with the following subordinating conjunctions. /8

perché • quando • poiché (2) • sebbene (2) • mentre (2)

- 1) .... torno a casa sono le otto di sera. Entro e vado immediatamente in camera, 2) .... spero che i miei siano ancora occupati a cucinare. Ma 3) .... faccio rumore con i tacchi, mi sentono. Mia mamma arriva di corsa e mi chiede 4) .... sono arrivata così tardi. Io le rispondo che, 5) .... fuori faccia già buio (è novembre!) non è tardi. Sono solo le otto...
- Il cane giocava in giardino, Mario studiava in camera. Ma 6) .... gli volesse ancora bene, Mario non si occupava più dell'animale, 7) .... i suoi genitori la consideravano una perdita di tempo, 8) .... loro non avevano mai amato quell'animale.

3 Complete the sentences with the subordinating and coordinating conjunctions. /11

inoltre • affinché • perciò • poiché • tuttavia • quando (2)

1) .... Lucia perse il lavoro, cominciò a lavorare per una famiglia.
2) .... la famiglia era piuttosto ricca, la casa era bella e grande,
3) .... si trovava in una zona periferica della città. Lucia aveva paura di non arrivare in orario, così partiva un'ora e mezza prima da casa sua, 4) .... la signora non avesse scuse per rimproverarla, così 5) .... arrivava, era già stanca. 6) ...., sull'autobus c'erano spesso dei ragazzacci che le facevano i dispetti. 7) .... qualche mese dopo si mise alla ricerca di un altro lavoro.

inoltre • dopo che • infatti • sebbene

8) .... in casa mia sono entrati i ladri una volta, ho sempre avuto paura a dormire a casa da solo, 9) .... mio padre abbia installato un sistema d'allarme. 10) .... la mia casa si trova in un posto isolato, 11) .... a volte né telefono né cellulare funzionano.

61 Dice che è bello... Diceva che era bello...
Direct and reported speech

Direct speech is used to **report someone's words using quotation marks.**
Reported speech is used **to report someone's words.**
In **reported speech** the **tenses, adjectives** and **pronouns may change.**

Changes of pronouns and adjectives

Pronouns of the **1st** and **2nd** person (singular and plural) ⟶ **3rd** person (singular and plural)

Lui dice: "Sono stanco". ⟶ *Lui* ***dice che è*** *stanco.*
He says: "I'm tired." ⟶ He says that he's tired.

Loro dicono: "La nostra casa è bella". ⟶ *Loro* ***dicono che la loro casa è*** *bella.*
They say: "Our house is beautiful." ⟶ They say that their house is beautiful.

Mode and tense of the verbs

If in the **main clause** the verb is in the **present tense,** the tense of the sentence **in the reported speech doesn't change**.

Marco dice: "Ho sonno perché non ho dormito". ⟶ *Marco dice che* ***ha*** *sonno perché non* ***ha*** *dormito.*
Marco says: "I'm tired because I haven't slept." ⟶ Marco says that he's tired because he hasn't slept.

If in the **main clause** the verb is in the **past tense**:

Presente ⟶ *imperfetto*
Luigi ha detto: "Aldo lavora troppo". ⟶ *Luigi ha detto* ***che Aldo lavorava troppo.***
Luigi said: "Aldo works too much." ⟶ Luigi said **that Aldo worked too much**.

Passato prossimo ⟶ *trapassato prossimo*

Marco diceva: "Domenica sono andato allo stadio". ⟶ *Marco* ***diceva*** *che domenica* ***era andato*** *allo stadio.*
Marco said: "On Sunday I went to the stadium." ⟶ Marco said that on Sunday he had gone to the stadium.

Futuro ⟶ *condizionale passato*

La bambina urlò: "Non metterò mai in ordine la casa!". ⟶ *La bambina* ***urlò che non avrebbe mai messo in ordine*** *la casa.*
The child shouted: "I'll never tidy up the house." ⟶ The child shouted that she would never tidy up the house.

Exercises

1 Transform these sentences into reported speech. /5

Mio nonno dice sempre: "La vita è dura". → *Mio nonno dice sempre* ***che la vita è dura.***

1 Ha sempre detto: "Non sono bello, ma intelligente".

....

2 Mi ha detto: "Parli a voce troppo alta".

....

3 Questo hanno spiegato a tutti: "La campagna pubblicitaria è stata molto lunga e difficile".

....

4 Aveva rivelato ai suoi colleghi: "Presto partirò per la Sardegna".

....

5 Giurava: "Ti amerò per sempre".

....

2 Transform these sentences from direct to reported speech. /11

Paola ha detto: "Non ho imparato l'italiano e perciò non lo so parlare". → *Paola ha detto* ***che non aveva imparato l'italiano e perciò non lo sapeva parlare.***

• Luciano mi ha detto: "1) L'anno scorso ho avuto dei problemi finanziari. Quest'anno però 2) ho trovato un lavoro migliore e ho risolto tutti i problemi. Spero che l'anno prossimo 3) avrò ancora fortuna e che 4) guadagnerò ancora di più".

Luciano mi ha detto che ....

....

....

....

....

....

• La mamma ha detto al figlio: "5) Sono preoccupata perché 6) non stai studiando. 7) Spero che ti metterai presto a studiare di più".

La mamma ha detto che ....

....

....

....

....

• Lo chef ha detto: "8) Ho preparato un piatto che non avevo mai fatto prima. 9) Ho imparato questa ricetta quando ero in Italia. 10) Quando ero in Italia cucinavo sempre cose nuove. Forse in futuro 11) lavorerò lì per qualche mese".

Lo chef ha detto che ....

....

....

....

....

....

62 Abito qui, dice che abita lì... Ieri sono stata, dice che il giorno prima è stata...
Reported speech: peculiarities

Adjective *questo* and adverbs *qui/qua*

- ***Questo*** (this) ⟶ ***quello*** (that)
- ***Qui/qua*** (here) ⟶ ***lì, là*** (there)
  *Dice: "Vivo qui in **questa** casa".* ⟶ *Dice che vive **lì**, in **quella** casa.*
  He says: "I live here in this house." ⟶ He says that he lives there in that house.

Adverbs

- ***Ieri*** (yesterday) ⟶ ***il giorno prima*** (the day before), ***il giorno precedente*** (the previous day)
- ***Oggi*** (today) ⟶ ***quel giorno*** (that day)
- ***Domani*** (tomorrow) ⟶ ***il giorno seguente*** (the following day), ***il giorno successivo*** (the following day)
  *In TV hanno detto: "**Oggi** c'è il sole, **domani** piove".* ⟶ *In TV hanno detto che **quel giorno c'era il sole**, che **il giorno seguente sarebbe piovuto**.*
  On TV they said: "Today it's sunny, tomorrow it will rain." ⟶ On TV they said that day it was sunny, the following day it would rain.

Imperative

The imperative ⟶ ***di*** **+ infinitive**

Il professore dice: "Leggete questo brano". ⟶ *Il professore dice **di leggere** quel brano.*
The teachers says: "Read this passage." ⟶ The teachers says they should read that passage.

Differently from English, if the subject in the main clause is the same as in the dependent clause the **present infinitive** or **past infinitive** preceded by ***di***.

Pensa: "Forse ho mangiato troppo". ⟶ ***Pensa di aver mangiato** troppo.*
He thinks: "Maybe I've eaten too much." ⟶ He thinks that has eaten too much.
Sperava: "Magari incontro Rosanna". ⟶ ***Sperava di incontrare** Rosanna.*
He was hoping: "Perhaps I'll met Rosanna." ⟶ He was hoping to meet Rosanna.
*Il professore dice: "**Mettete** via i libri".* ⟶ *Il professore **dice di mettere** via i libri.*
The teacher tells the students: "Put the books away!" ⟶ The teacher tells the students to put the books away.

Exercises

1 Transform these short sentences from direct to reported speech. /12

Martina dice: "Domani prendo l'autobus". → *Martina dice che* ***domani prenderà*** *l'autobus.*
Martina ha detto che ***il giorno dopo avrebbe preso*** *l'autobus.*

1 Il signor Rossi dice: "Oggi sono proprio stanco".
Il signor Rossi dice che ....
Il signor Rossi ha detto che ....

2 Roberta dice: "I miei amici sono fidati".
Roberta dice che ....
Roberta diceva che ....

3 Il mio collega dice: "Ieri ho sbrigato tutto".
Il mio collega dice che ....
Il mio collega ha detto che ....

4 I miei vicini si lamentano: "In questo palazzo si fa troppo rumore".
I miei vicini si lamentano che ....
I miei vicini si sono lamentati che ....

5 Mi chiedono: "Chi sono quei ragazzi che ti aspettano?".
Mi chiedono ....
Mi hanno chiesto ....

6 Ci domandano: "Dove volete andare domani?".
Ci domandano ....
Ci hanno domandato ....

2 Transform the following passage from direct to reported speech. /7

Eravamo in classe quando entrò un ragazzo. La mia compagna mi chiese: "Sai chi è?".
→ *Mi chiese* ***se sapevo chi fosse****.*

"1) Non l'ho mai visto", risposi io. "2) È veramente carino", disse lei. "3) Sono assolutamente d'accordo", risposi io. Quando finì la lezione, ci trovammo con lui fuori da scuola. La mia compagna, che era molto sfacciata, si avvicinò e gli chiese: "4) Sei nuovo qui?". Lui sorrise e replicò: "5) Sì, sono arrivato soltanto oggi". Poi si presentò dicendo: "6) Sono Tommaso e vengo da Torino". La mia compagna di classe si presentò, poi presentò me. "7) Questa è Luisa", disse. Lui sorrise anche a me, ma di un sorriso molto molto particolare.

....
....
....
....
....
....
....
....
....
....
....

Units 50-62 Summary exercises

1 Complete with the coordinating conjunctions. /6

non solo ... ma anche • infatti • quindi • anche • o • cioè

***Sia** Filippo **sia** Gigi hanno preso l'influenza.*

1 Ti ho già detto di no, ... non insistere.
2 .... Giulio è simpatico, ... gentile.
3 .... a me piace passeggiare nel parco in autunno.
4 Sei sordo .... fingi di non capire?
5 Non sei ordinato, ... perdi sempre tutto!
6 Carlo è un poliglotta, ... conosce molte lingue.

2 Complete with the subordinating conjunctions. /6

se • nonostante • siccome • mentre • prima che • perché

*Ottenne i fondi **cosicché** l'opera poté essere terminata.*

1 Spiegami .... i tuoi amici escono così spesso.
2 Siamo tornati a casa .... facesse buio.
3 .... sono distratto, perdo un sacco di tempo a cercare le mie cose.
4 Qualcuno ha rubato loro le scarpe .... riposavano.
5 .... non chiudi la finestra, entrerà l'acqua quando comincerà a piovere.
6 Luca sembra sereno .... abbia molti problemi.

3 Rewrite the sentences in the passive form. /5

Lo zio ha regalato a Silvia un orologio per il suo compleanno.
→ *Un orologio **è stato regalato dallo zio a Silvia** per il suo compleanno.*

1 I bambini non amano le verdure.

....

2 I vincitori otterranno una medaglia.

....

3 La nonna ha appena cucinato una torta.

....

4 Avevate scritto voi l'indirizzo sulla busta?

....

5 I Greci vinsero la guerra di Troia grazie all'inganno del cavallo di legno.

....

4 Change the sentences to the past. /5

Se mi dessi ascolto, non sbaglieresti. → *Se mi **avessi dato** ascolto, non **avresti sbagliato**.*

1 Se fosse ricco, smetterebbe di lavorare.

....

2 Se non lo amassero, non lo sopporterebbero.

....

3 Farei il giro del mondo, se non avessi paura di volare.

....

4 Non fareste tutti quegli errori, se vi concentraste di più.

....

5 Se avessimo diciotto anni, andremmo via da casa.

....

5 Complete with the infinitive (present or past).

/5

Hai portato i documenti? Sì, credo di ***averli portati****.*

1 A che ora ti vuoi alzare domani? Voglio .... presto per partire con il fresco.
2 Quando scriverai a me e ai nonni? Penso di .... appena sarò arrivato a Parigi.
3 Hai lasciato il numero di telefono a Nora? No, temo di non ....
4 Accompagnate voi Paolo? Sì, pensiamo di .... noi.
5 Quando mi presenti la tua ragazza? Pensavo di .... a breve.

6 Complete with the relative pronoun.

/5

Non vedo i ragazzi ***di cui*** *mi hai parlato.*

1 Il medico .... sono andato è molto bravo.
2 Il film .... ho visto ha avuto l'Oscar.
3 Abbiamo comprato un caffè .... etichetta riporta una provenienza straniera.
4 Quelli .... parli male sono i miei amici.
5 È ottimo il ristorante .... mangiamo ogni giorno.

7 Translate into Italian.

/8

1 Julie says that she has never been to the States.

....

2 If you loved me you would write me more often.

....

3 If it rains I'll take the umbrella.

....

4 If I were you I'd buy a big house at the seaside.

....

5 Since you're here I want to ask you a question.

....

6 This house was built last year.

....

7 This is the boy who speaks three languages.

....

8 Even if the weather is bad we'll go to the seaside.

....

CELI 1 • Livello A2

1 Ricostruire le frasi divise in due parti. Scegliere il completamento corretto.

1 Prendi il tram
2 Se vieni da me domenica
3 Quando vedo il professore
4 Filippo non esce mai di sera
5 Quando mangio troppo
6 Ogni giorno lavora e poi
7 Devo lavare le magliette

a) perché sono sporche.
b) va a correre.
c) se vuoi arrivare prima.
d) il giorno dopo mi sento male.
e) senza chiedere il permesso ai suoi genitori.
f) gli devo parlare dei voti.
g) anche se piove.
h) mangia troppo.
i) prendiamo un caffè insieme.
l) per sentire la musica.
m) per andare dal dentista.

2 Ricostruire le frasi divise in due parti. Scegliere il completamento corretto.

1 Se mi presti il tuo maglione
2 Questi arnesi servono
3 Prima mangio
4 Mi piace molto
5 Che cosa hai intenzione
6 Marta ha una macchina
7 Non ho visto Mario a scuola

a) e poi vado a trovare Giorgio.
b) che è molto piccola e vecchia.
c) andare in barca.
d) non c'è il sole.
e) se fosse bello.
f) dove vuoi.
g) di fare questo weekend?
h) perché era malato.
i) a sciare.
l) io ti presto la mia borsa.
m) per lavorare la terra.

3 Abbinare a ogni domanda la risposta corretta.

1 Dove vai?
2 A che ora partiremo?
3 Che cosa posso regalare a Mario?
4 Preferisci pesce o carne?
5 Hai comprato le scarpe?
6 A che cosa stai pensando?

a) Nessuno dei due. Sono vegetariana.
b) Moltissimo.
c) Credo alle quattro. Devo controllare.
d) Un bel maglione.
e) No, per niente.
f) Sì, in un negozio vicino alla stazione.
g) A casa.
h) Non ancora.
i) È mio fratello.
l) Alla mia ragazza.

4 Completare con la parola mancante.

Esempio di risposta: 0 ⟶ Ho

IL LAVORO

- Sono Pablo. 0) .... 22 anni e vengo 1) .... Madrid, in Spagna. Lavoro 2) .... un bar, ma il mio sogno 3) .... di lavorare in televisione.
- Io sono Michele e mi piacerebbe diventare 4) .... famoso giocatore di calcio. Adesso gioco a calcio 5) .... una squadra 6) .... mia città. 7) .... credete che riuscirò?
- Il mio nome è Veronica. 8) .... studiato matematica all'università e adesso insegno. Ma questo lavoro non 9) .... piace molto. E adesso 10) .... cercando qualcosa d'altro.

5 Scrivere una lettera. Usare il passato. *(Da un minimo di 80 a un massimo di 90 parole.)*

Paola è andata in vacanza. In questa lettera racconta a un'amica che cosa ha fatto (Sì) e che cosa non ha fatto (No).

SÌ

✔ andare al mare ogni giorno
✔ prendere il sole
✔ leggere riviste in spiaggia
✔ nuotare molto
✔ conoscere gente nuova
✔ uscire ogni sera con gli amici
✔ divertirsi molto

NO

✔ studiare
✔ fare ginnastica
✔ telefonare a qualcuno
✔ mangiare (mai) a mezzogiorno
✔ annoiarsi (mai)

Cara Marina

Sono stata in vacanza. Sono ...

....

....

....

....

....

....

....

....

....

....

....

....

CELI 2 • Livello B1

1 Completare le frasi da 1 a 5 con la parola opportuna tra le quattro proposte. Una sola è la scelta possibile.

1 Carlo, stasera vediamo la televisione .... usciamo con gli amici?

a) oppure b) anche c) sia d) perché

2 .... vediamo i nostri colleghi, possiamo andare a mangiare con loro.

a) finché b) quando c) perché d) allora

3 .... stai? Vorrei saperlo.

a) perché b) se c) quando d) come

4 .... non mangi qualcosa starai male.

a) come b) quando c) se d) allora

5 .... di voi parla italiano?

a) che cosa b) chi c) quale d) quando

2 Completare il testo. Scegliere la parola opportuna fra le quattro proposte. Una sola è la scelta possibile.

Esempio di risposta: 0 ⟶ c)

Vi voglio (0) .... della vacanza 1) .... che ho trascorso nella mia vita.
Dovevo partire di mattina alle otto, ma l'aereo 2) .... un ritardo di sei ore e 3) ....
di pomeriggio alle due.
4) .... sei ero arrivato a Casiria, una 5) .... località di mare.
Sono andato direttamente 6) .... albergo che avevo prenotato. Ma la mia camera non era come era illustrato in Internet. Era piccola e sporca, il letto era troppo corto e non c'era il balcone. Ho protestato, ma non ho ottenuto 7) .... La mattina dopo 8) .... andato al mare, però anche qui 9) .... aspettava un'altra brutta sorpresa: non si poteva nuotare 10) .... il mare era pieno di meduse!
La spiaggia era estremamente affollata e il cibo al ristorante dell'albergo era 11) ....
Una settimana dopo sono tornato a casa, non sono stato mai 12) .... contento nella mia vita che una vacanza fosse finita!

0	a) parla	b) parlando	c) parlare	d) parlerò
1	a) male	b) il più peggiore	c) pessimo	d) peggiore
2	a) era	b) aveva	c) fu	d) ebbe avuto
3	a) partiva	b) partivo	c) ero partito	d) sono partito
4	a) con le	b) a	c) alle	d) dalle
5	a) bel	b) bella	c) bell'	d) bello
6	a) all'	b) al	c) allo	d) ad
7	a) nessuno	b) no	c) niente	d) non niente
8	a) ho	b) sono	c) ebbi	d) avevo
9	a) me	b) a me	c) mi	d) a me mi
10	a) che	b) dove	c) anche se	d) perché
11	a) peggiore	b) pessimo	c) il peggiore	d) il più peggiore
12	a) molto	b) così	c) tanta	d) a

3 Completare il testo. Scegliere la parola opportuna fra le quattro proposte. Una sola è la scelta possibile.

Esempio di risposta: 0 ⟶ a)

Ieri ho trascorso 0) .... bella giornata con i 1) .... amici. Abbiamo fatto una gita 2) .... montagna. Siamo partiti da casa 3) .... otto e siamo tornati 4) .... sera tardi. In montagna abbiamo camminato a lungo, per più 5) .... cinque ore. Ci siamo fermati 6) .... mangiare in una baita. Il cibo era buono e genuino.
Poi ci siamo rimessi in cammino, 7) .... alcuni del nostro gruppo erano stanchi e allora abbiamo deciso di prendere una funivia 8) .... scendere a valle. Ci siamo fermati in un bar. Abbiamo bevuto qualcosa e dei ragazzi del posto 9) .... hanno chiesto se volevamo giocare a carte con loro. Io e un mio amico abbiamo giocato, le ragazze 10) .... sono andate in paese a fare shopping. Siamo ripartiti alle nove di sera 11) .... aver mangiato una pizza in un locale. La prossima settimana vorremmo fare una gita 12) .... mare!

0 a) una	b) la	c) un	d) qualche
1 a) suoi	b) miei	c) mio	d) nostri
2 a) alla	b) nella	c) in	d) su
3 a) alla	b) nelle	c) a	d) alle
4 a) nella	b) di	c) per	d) in
5 a) delle	b) a	c) di	d) che
6 a) a	b) di	c) nel	d) al
7 a) e	b) ma	c) quindi	d) quando
8 a) a	b) per	c) di	d) su
9 a) vi	b) gli	c) ti	d) ci
10 a) però	b) che	c) invece	d) ma
11 a) dopo	b) prima	c) quando	d) per
12 a) sul	b) al	c) a	d) nel

APPENDIX

Phonology and ortography

The Italian alphabet is composed by **21 letters** : **5 vowels** and **16 consonants** + five letters from **other languages**.
They are written in grey in the chart below.

small letters	a	b	c	d	e	f	g	h	i	j	k	l	m	n	o	p	q	r	s	t	u	v	w	x	y	z
CAPITAL LETTERS	A	B	C	D	E	F	G	H	I	J	K	L	M	N	O	P	Q	R	S	T	U	V	W	X	Y	Z

The letter *h*

The ***h*** at the beginning of the word is not pronounced. After the ***c*** and ***g*** it has a **harsh sound**: *chitarra* (guitar), *poche* (few), *righe* (lines), *luoghi* (places).

The group *sce-scie*

The words that contain the group ***sce*** are written without ***i***: *scena* (scene), *conoscenza* (knowledge).
The words deriving from *scienza* are written with ***i***: *scienza* (science), *scienziato* (scientist), *coscienza* (conscience).

The double consonant

There aren't precise rules about the use of the double consonant. The vowel that precedes a double consonant has a longer sound: *cartello* (sign), *pollo* (chicken).
The consonants ***g*** and ***z*** never double before ***-ione***: *stazione* (station), *nazione* (nation), *regione* (region).
The consonant ***b*** never doubles before ***-ile***: *automobile* (automobile), *disabile* (disabled person).

The apostrophe

The apostrophe is used with:

- ***uno*, *nessuno* ⟶ *un'*, *nessun'*** + feminine noun beginning with a vowel, even if it is accompanied by an adjective beginning with a vowel: *un'attrice* (an actress), *nessun'amica* (no friend), *un'incredibile esperienza* (an incredible experience);
- ***lo*, *la* ⟶ *l'*** + feminine or masculine noun or adjective beginning with a vowel: *l'amica* (the friend), *l'attore* (the actor);
- ***dello*, *allo*, *sullo*, *in* ⟶ *dell'*, *all'*, *sull'*, *nell'*** + feminine or masculine noun only singular, if accompanied by an adjective beginning with a vowel or ***h***: *dell'amore* (of love), *all'hotel* (at the hotel), *nell'elegante locale* (in the elegant hotel);
- ***questo*, *quello*, *bello*, *grande* ⟶ *quest'*, *quell'*, *bell'*, *grand'*** + feminine or masculine noun beginning with a vowel: *quest'anno* (this year), *quell'impiegata* (that clerk), *bell'idea* (great idea), *grand'uomo* (big man);
- ***ci*, *come*** + verb *to be* in the expressions beginning with ***e* ⟶ *c'***: *c'è* (there is), *c'erano* (there were), *com'è* (as/how it is).

These forms of the imperative are written with the apostrophe (2nd person singular): ***dire***: *di'!* (**to say**: say!), ***fare***: *fa'!* (**to do**: do!), ***andare***: *va'!* (**to go**: go!), ***dare***: *da'!* (**to give**: give!).

The accent

The accent falls on the **last syllable** with words like: *città* (city), *caffè* (coffee), *perché* (because/why).
The following **monosyllabic** words are written **with the accent**: *sì* (yes), *là*, *lì* (there), *è* (third person of the verb *to be*), *sé* (self).
Also the following **monosyllabic** words are written **with the accent**: *già* (already), *può* (can), *più* (more), *ciò* (this), *giù* (down).
The **first and the third person singular of some verbs** in the *passato remoto* are written **with the accent**: *io amerò* (I'll love), *lui prenderà* (he'll take), *lei andò* (she went) etc.

Punctuation

Full stop [.]

Monica ama molto gli animali. ***D****a piccola aveva un gatto che si chiamava Michele.*
Monica loves animals very much. As a child she had a cat who was called Michele.
It indicates a short pause, to divide two short sentences. It is used in lists and to isolate a concept.

Comma [,]

Ho incontrato Paolo, che è il mio migliore amico, poi Anna, Luca, Gianni e Mario.
I met Paolo, who's my best friend, then Anna, Luca, Gianni and Mario.
It indicates a short pause, to divide two short clauses in a sentence. It is used in lists and to isolate a concept.

Semicolon ;

*Il venerdì è il giorno della settimana che preferisco**;** il lunedì, invece, lo detesto.*
Friday is the day of the week that I prefer; instead, I hate Monday.
It indicates a pause, it divides two (not very short) sentences.

Colon :

*Ho comprato**:** mele, pere e banane.* I bought: apples, pears and bananas.
*Anna disse**:** "Eccomi!"* Anna said: "Here I am."
A colon is used to introduce an explanation, a list or direct speech.

Question mark ?

*Dove vai**?** Vado al cinema.* Where are you going? I'm going to the cinema.
It is used to introduce a question. After the question mark a capital letter is necessary.

Exclamation mark !

*Che bella giornata**!*** What a beautiful day! *Fa' silenzio**!*** Be silent! *Ah, che male**!*** Ouch, that hurts!
It is used to express wonder, enthusiasm or pain and also to express an order when the verb is in the imperative.

Ellipsis ...

*Avrei voluto dirglielo, ma**...*** I wish I could tell you, but...
The ellipsis consists of three dots to indicate words that you leave out to shorten a quotation, or because you don't want to or can't say them.

Inverted commas " "

*Le ho chiesto: **"**Quanti anni hai?**"**.* I asked her: "How old are you?"
*Giulio è un **"**mago**"** del computer.* Giulio is a "computer wiz".
Inverted commas, or quotation marks, are used to mark the beginning and end of direct speech or to indicate a particular meaning of a word, especially when used in a different context.

Interjections

Interjections express in a very immediate and lively way feelings or a state of mind. They are used in particular in the spoken language.

Joy	**Oh! Ah!**	***Oh**, che bella città!* What a beautiful city! ***Ah**, che sorpresa!* How surprising!
Anger	**Ah!**	***Ah!** Che noia!* Oh, what a bore!
Pain	**Ahi! Ahimè!**	***Ahi!** Mi hai fatto male!* Ouch, you hurt me!
Boredom	**Uffa!**	***Uffa!** È da un'ora che aspetto...* How boring! I've been waiting for an hour.
Wonder	**Toh!**	***Toh!** Sei qui!* Wow! You're here!
Doubt	**Ehm...**	***Ehm...** non ricordo bene la risposta...* Hum... I don't remember the answer...
Exhortation	**Su! Suvvia!**	***Su**, sbrigati, dobbiamo partire!* Come on, we have to leave! ***Suvvia**, non ti arrabbiare!* Come on, don't get angry!

The article

Determinative article

	Singular	Plural
Masculine	il, lo, l'	i, gli,
Feminine	la, l'	le

Indeterminative article

	Singular	Plural
Masculine	un, uno	dei, degli
Feminine	una, un'	delle

Partitive article

It is used to indicate a part of a group or a set of objects. The plural of the partitive articles corresponds to the plural of the indeterminate articles.

	Singular	Plural
Masculine	del, dello, dell'	dei, degli
Feminine	della, dell'	delle

Remember!

The article is not used:

- with names like Mario, James, Anna;
- with possessive adjectives.
  Vivo con mio fratello, mia sorella e i miei genitori.
  I live with my brother, my sister and my parents.
- ***Un*** + masculine noun doesn't take the apostrophe. *Un amico.* A friend.
- ***Un*** + feminine noun always requires the apostrophe. *Un'amica.* A female friend.

Rules for the use of the article

				Singular	Plural
il	plural **i**	before **masculine nouns** beginning with a consonant		***il*** *cane* ***il*** *bambino*	***i*** *cani* ***i*** *bambini*
lo	plural **gli**	before **masculine nouns** beginning with:	y-, z-, x-, j-	***lo*** *yogurt* ***lo*** *zoccolo*	***gli*** *yogurt* ***gli*** *zoccoli*
			s- + consonant	***lo*** *studente* ***lo*** *sbaglio* ***lo*** *sport*	***gli*** *studenti* ***gli*** *sbagli* ***gli*** *sport*
			ps-, gn-, pn-	***lo*** *psicologo* ***lo*** *gnomo*	***gli*** *psicologi* ***gli*** *gnomi*
la	plural **le**	before **feminine nouns** beginning with a consonant		***la*** *gatta*	***le*** *gatte*
l'	plural **gli, le**	before **masculine** and **feminine nouns** beginning with a vowel or *h-*		***l'****amico* ***l'****amica*	***gli*** *amici* ***le*** *amiche*

un	plural **dei, degli**	before **masculine nouns** beginning with a consonant or a vowel		***un*** *cane* ***un*** *amico*	***dei*** *cani* ***degli*** *amici*
uno	plural **degli**	before **masculine nouns** beginning with:	y-, z-, x-, j-	***uno*** *yogurt* ***uno*** *zoccolo*	***degli*** *yogurt* ***degli*** *zoccoli*
			s- + consonant	***uno*** *studente* ***uno*** *sbaglio* ***uno*** *sport*	***degli*** *studenti* ***degli*** *sbagli* ***degli*** *sport*
			ps-, gn-, pn-	***uno*** *psicologo* ***uno*** *gnomo*	***degli*** *psicologi* ***degli*** *gnomi*
una	plural **delle**	before **feminine nouns** beginning with a consonant		***una*** *gatta*	***delle*** *gatte*
un'	plural **delle**	before **feminine nouns** beginning with a vowel		***un'****amica*	***delle*** *amiche*

The article ***del, dello, dell'*** etc follows the rules of the determinative article.
Ho comprato ***del*** *pane.* I bought some bread.
Siamo ***degli*** *studenti.* We are (some) students.
Vorrei ***della*** *pasta.* I'd like some pasta.

The noun

Masculine	
Singular	**Plural**
bambin-**o** can-**e**	bambin-**i** can-**i**

Feminine	
Singular	**Plural**
bambin-**a** chiav-**e**	bambin-**e** chiav-**i**

Nouns with an irregular plural

Singular	Plural	Example
Feminine in -***ca***, -***ga***	-***che***, -***ghe***	*colle**ghe***
Masculine in -***ca***, -***go***	-***chi***, -***ghi***, -***ci***, -***gi***	*alber**ghi**, medi**ci***
Masculine in -***io***	-***ii***/-***i***	*add**ii**, stud**i***
Feminine in -***cia***, -***gia***	-***cie***/-***gie***, -***ce***/-***ge***	*cilie**gie**, aran**ce**, nevral**gie***
Masculine in -***logo***	-***logi*** (things), -***loghi*** (people)	*psico**logi**, cata**loghi***

Peculiarities

Nouns that have two plurals with different meanings

Singular	Plural	
il braccio	*le braccia* (arms; *of the human body*)	*i bracci* (arms; *mechanical*)
l'osso	*ossa* (bones; *of the human body*)	*ossi* (bones; *of animals*)
il membro	*membra* (limbs; *of the human body*)	*membri* (members; *of a family, a club etc.*)
labbro	*le labbra* (lips; *of the mouth*)	*i labbri* (edges; *of a wound*)

Masculine nouns in the singular, feminine in the plural

Masculine singular: -o	*il dit-**o***	*il pai-**o***	*il migliaio-**o***	*l'uov-**o***	*il centinai-**o***	*l'url-**o***
Femminile plurale: -a	*le dit-**a***	*le pai-**a***	*le migliai-**a***	*le uov-**a***	*le centinai-**a***	*le url-**a***

Nouns that have only the plural form

Masculine	Feminine
i pantaloni, gli occhiali, i viveri	*le mutande, le ferie, le forbici, le stoviglie*

Nouns that have only the singular form

Masculine	Feminine
il latte, il pane, il riso, il sangue, il coraggio	*la sete, la fame, la prole*

Nouns with the same singular and plural

	Masculine	Feminine
Nouns of foreign origin ending with a consonant	*il bar, i bar*	*la star, le star*
Nouns of only one syllable	*il re, i re*	*la gru, le gru*
Nouns ending with -*i*	*il brindisi, i brindisi*	*l'ipotesi, le ipotesi*
Nouns with the accent on the last syllable	*il caffè, i caffè*	*la città, le città*

Irregular nouns in the feminine

Masculine	*il principe*	*il dottore*	*l'eroe*	*l'attore*	*il dio*	*il re*
Feminine	*la principessa*	*la dottoressa*	*l'eroina*	*l'attrice*	*la dea*	*la regina*

Nouns with two different forms for the masculine and for the feminine

Masculine	*il maiale*	*il montone*	*l'uomo*	*il padre/papà*	*il marito*	*il genero*
Feminine	*la scrofa*	*la pecora*	*la donna*	*la madre/mamma*	*la moglie*	*la nuora*

Compound nouns

Adjective + noun Verb + masculine noun	only the noun takes the plural	*il francobollo, i francobolli il passaporto, i passaporti*
Verb + feminine noun Verb + verb	doesn't change	*il salvagente, i salvagente*
Noun + noun of the same gender	only the second noun takes the plural	*la ferrovia, le ferrovie*
Nouns + noun of a different gender	only the firt noun takes the plural	*il pescespada, i pescispada*
Noun + adjective	both take the plural form	*la cassaforte, le casseforti*
Adjective + adjective	the second adjective takes the plural	*il pianoforte, i pianoforti*

Modification of the noun

Diminutive	***-ino, -ello, -etto***	*scarpina, alberello, lavoretto*
Augmentative	***-one***	*pentolone*
Pejorative	***-accio, -astro, -aglia***	*ragazzaccio, giovinastro, gentaglia*
Modification to express endearment	***-uccio, -uzzo, -ino***	*reuccio, labbruzzo, nasino*

The adjective

<table>
<tr><td rowspan="7">QUALIFYING</td><td>Positive</td><td colspan="2"></td><td>forte</td></tr>
<tr><td rowspan="3">Comparative</td><td colspan="2">"di uguaglianza"</td><td>tanto forte quanto</td></tr>
<tr><td colspan="2">"di maggioranza"</td><td>più forte di</td></tr>
<tr><td colspan="2">"di minoranza"</td><td>meno forte di</td></tr>
<tr><td rowspan="2">Superlative</td><td colspan="2">"assoluto"</td><td>fortissimo, molto forte</td></tr>
<tr><td colspan="2">"relativo"</td><td>il/la/i/le più forte/i dei/
degli/delle/della/del</td></tr>
<tr><td colspan="4"></td></tr>
<tr><td rowspan="4">POSSESSIVE</td><td colspan="2">Masculine</td><td colspan="2">Feminine</td></tr>
<tr><td>Singular</td><td>Plural</td><td>Singular</td><td>Plural</td></tr>
<tr><td>mio, tuo, suo
nostro, vostro,
proprio/loro</td><td>miei, tuoi, suoi
nostri, vostri,
propri/loro</td><td>mia, tua, sua
nostra, vostra,
propria/loro</td><td>mie, tue, sue,
nostre, vostre,
proprie/loro</td></tr>
<tr><td colspan="4">unchangeable: altrui</td></tr>
<tr><td rowspan="3">DEMONSTRATIVE</td><td colspan="2">Masculine</td><td colspan="2">Feminine</td></tr>
<tr><td>Singular</td><td>Plural</td><td>Singular</td><td>Plural</td></tr>
<tr><td>questo, quello, stesso,
medesimo, tale, quale,
codesto</td><td>questi, quelli,
stessi, medesimi,
tali, quali, codesti</td><td>questa, quella,
stessa, medesima,
tale, quale, codesta</td><td>queste, quelle,
stesse, medesime,
tali, quali, codeste</td></tr>
<tr><td rowspan="3">NUMERAL</td><td>Cardinal</td><td colspan="3">uno/una, due, dieci, venti, mille ecc.</td></tr>
<tr><td>Ordinal</td><td colspan="3">primo/a/i/e, secondo/a/i/e, terzo/a/i/e ecc.</td></tr>
<tr><td>Moltiplicative</td><td colspan="3">doppio/a/i/e, triplo/a/i/e, duplice/i ecc.</td></tr>
<tr><td rowspan="4">INDEFINITE</td><td colspan="2">Masculine</td><td colspan="2">Feminine</td></tr>
<tr><td>Singular</td><td>Plural</td><td>Singular</td><td>Plural</td></tr>
<tr><td>molto, poco,
parecchio, tutto,
alcuno, alcun, ciascuno,
ciascun, nessuno,
nessun</td><td>molti, pochi,
parecchi, tutti,
alcuni
-
-</td><td>molta, poca,
parecchia, tutta,
alcuna, alcun',
ciascuna, ciascun',
nessuna, nessun'</td><td>molte, poche,
parecchie, tutte,
alcune
-
-</td></tr>
<tr><td colspan="4">Ogni and qualche: indeclinable, they take the singular noun and verb.
Alcuno, ciascuno and nessuno: they are used the same way as the article un, uno etc.</td></tr>
<tr><td>INTERROGATIVE</td><td colspan="4">Che? Quale/quali? Quanto/i/a/e?</td></tr>
<tr><td>EXCLAMATORY</td><td colspan="4">Che! Quale/i! Quanto/i/a/e!</td></tr>
</table>

Agreement of adjectives

	Masculine singular	Masculine plural	Feminine singular	Feminine plural
First group	piccolo-**o**	piccolo-**i**	piccolo-**a**	piccolo-**e**
Second group	felic-**e**	felic-**i**	felic-**e**	felic-**i**
Adjective in -*a*	ottimist-**a**	ottimist-**i**	ottimist-**a**	ottimist-**e**

Irregular plurals

Singular	Plural	Rule	Example	Masculine plural	Feminine plural
-co	-chi	if the tonic accent falls on the penultimate syllable	*stàn-**co***	*stan-**chi***	*stan-**che***
	-ci	if the tonic accent doesn't fall on the penultimate syllable	*simpàti-**co***	*simpati-**ci***	*simpati-**che***
-go	-ghi		*lun-**go***	*lun-**ghi***	*lun-**ghe***
-io	-ii	if the tonic accent falls on the *i*	*nat-**ìo***	*nat-**ìi***	*nat-**ìe***
	-i	if the tonic accent doesn't fall on the *i*	*grig-**io***	*grig-**i***	*grig-**ie***

Irregular comparative and superlative forms

Positive	Comparative	Superlative
buono	*migliore*	*ottimo/a/i/e*
cattivo	*peggiore*	*pessimo/a/i/e*
grande	*maggiore*	*massimo/a/i/e*

Positive	Comparative	Superlative
piccolo	*minore*	*minimo/a/i/e*
poco	*meno*	*pochissimo/a/i/e*
molto	*più*	*moltissimo/a/i/e*

Modification of the adjective

Diminutive	***-ino, -ello, -etto***	*bellino, grandicello, poveretto*
Augmentative	***-one, -acchione***	*grassone, furbacchione*
Pejorative	***-accio, -astro, -ognolo***	*cattivaccio, golosastro, amarognolo*
Modification to express endearment	***-uccio, -otto, -olino***	*calduccio, bassotto, verdolino*

Numeral adjectives

Cardinal		Ordinal	
uno	1	*primo*	I
due	2	*secondo*	II
tre	3	*terzo*	III
quattro	4	*quarto*	IV
cinque	5	*quinto*	V
sei	6	*sesto*	VI
sette	7	*settimo*	VII
otto	8	*ottavo*	VIII
nove	9	*nono*	IX
dieci	10	*decimo*	X
undici	11	*undicesimo*	XI
dodici	12	*dodicesimo*	XII
tredici	13	*tredicesimo*	XIII
quattordici	14	*quattordicesimo*	XIV
quindici	15	*quindicesimo*	XV
sedici	16	*sedicesimo*	XVI
diciassette	17	*diciassettesimo*	XVII
diciotto	18	*diciottesimo*	XVIII
diciannove	19	*diciannovesimo*	XIX
venti	20	*ventesimo*	XX
ventuno	21	*ventunesimo*	XXI
ventidue etc.	22	*ventiduesimo etc.*	XXII

Cardinal		Ordinal	
trenta	30	*trentesimo*	XXX
trentuno	31	*trentunesimo*	XXXI
trentadue etc.	32	*trentaduesimo etc.*	XXXII
quaranta	40	*quarantesimo*	XL
cinquanta	50	*cinquantesimo*	L
sessanta	60	*sessantesimo*	LX
settanta	70	*settantesimo*	LXX
ottanta	80	*ottantesimo*	LXXX
novanta	90	*novantesimo*	XC
cento	100	*centesimo*	C
centouno	101	*centunesimo*	CI
duecento	200	*duecentesimo*	CC
cinquecento	500	*cinquecentesimo*	D
mille	1000	*millesimo*	M
diecimila	10.000	*decimillesimo*	$\overline{X}$
centomila	100.000	*centomillesimo*	$\overline{C}$
un milione	1.000.000	*milionesimo*	$\overline{M}$

The pronoun

	Masculine		Feminine	
	Singular	Plural	Singular	Plural
POSSESSIVE PRONOUNS	*Il mio, il tuo, il suo, il nostro, il vostro, il proprio, il loro*	*i miei, i tuoi, i suoi, i nostri, i vostri, i propri, i loro*	*la mia, la tua, la sua, la nostra, la vostra, la propria, la loro*	*le mie, le tue, le sue, le nostre, le vostre, le proprie, le loro*
	Masculine		**Femminile**	
	Singular	**Plural**	**Singular**	**Plural**
DEMONSTRATIVE PRONOUNS	*questo, quello* *lo stesso, il medesimo,* *il tale, costui, colui,* *ciò* (for objects)	*questi, quelli* *gli stessi, i medesimi,* *i tali, costoro, coloro* -	*questa, quella* *la stessa, la medesima,* *la tale, costei, colei* -	*queste, quelle* *le stesse, le medesime,* *le tali, costoro, coloro* -

	Only singular	Only plural
INDEFINITE PRONOUNS	*ciascuno/a, ciascun/ciascun', ognuno/a, uno/a, qualcuno/a, chiunque, nessuno/a, nessun/nessun', niente, nulla, qualcosa*	*molti/e, pochi/e, parecchi/e, tutti/e, alcuni/e*
INTERROGATIVE PRONOUNS	*Che? Chi? Quale/quali? Quanto/a/i/e?*	
EXCLAMATORY PRONOUNS	*Che! Chi! Quale/i! Quanto/a/i/e!*	

	Masculine		Feminine	
	Singular	**Plural**	**Singular**	**Plural**
RELATIVE	*il quale*	*i quali*	*la quale*	*le quali*
	quale/quali preceeded by prepositional articles (*al quale, dei quali, sulle quali* etc.)			
	che, cui preceeded by prepositions (*a cui, di cui, con cui* etc.)			
	Subject	**Direct**	**Indirect**	**Indirect combined**
PERSONAL	*io*	*mi/me*	*mi*	*me lo, me la, me l', me li, me le, me ne*
	tu	*ti/te*	*ti*	*te lo, te la, te l', te li, te le, te ne*
	lui/egli/esso *lei/ella/essa* *lui/lei (riflessivo)*	*lo/l'/lui* *la/l'/lei* *si/sé*	*gli, ne* *le, ne* *si*	*glielo, gliela, gliel', glieli, gliele, gliene*
	noi	*ci/noi*	*ci*	*ce lo, ce la, ce l', ce li, ce le, ce ne*
	voi	*vi/voi*	*vi*	*ve lo, ve la, ve l', ve li, ve le, ve ne*
	loro (maschile) - essi *loro (femminile) - esse*	*li/loro* *le/loro*	*loro/gli, ne* *loro/gli, ne*	*glielo, gliela, gliel', glieli, gliele, gliene*

Prepositions and prepositional articles

PREPOSITIONS	PREPOSITIONAL ARTICLES						
	Determinative articles						
di	*del*	*dell'*	*dello*	*della*	*dei*	*degli*	*delle*
a	*al*	*all'*	*allo*	*alla*	*ai*	*agli*	*alle*
da	*dal*	*dall'*	*dallo*	*dalla*	*dai*	*dagli*	*dalle*
in	*nel*	*nell'*	*nello*	*nella*	*nei*	*negli*	*nelle*
con	*con il, col*	*con l', coll'*	*con lo*	*con la*	*con i, coi*	*con gli*	*con le*
su	*sul*	*sull'*	*sullo*	*sulla*	*sui*	*sugli*	*sulle*
per	*per il*	*per l'*	*per lo*	*per la*	*per i*	*per gli*	*per le*
tra/fra	*tra il/fra il*	*tra l'/fra l'*	*tra lo/fra lo*	*tra la/fra la*	*tra i/fra i*	*tra gli/fra gli*	*tra le/fra le*

Improper prepositions: *dietro, dopo, dentro (a), insieme a/con, davanti a, vicino a, fuori da, lontano da, prima di.*

Use of prepositions

- **Possession**: *la valigia* ***di*** *Marco* (Marco's suitcase), *l'ufficio* ***del*** *direttore* (the manager's office).
- **Means of transport**: ***in*** *macchina* (by car), ***in*** *pullman* (by coach), ***in*** *treno* (by train) ecc., *but*: ***a*** *piedi* (on foot).
- **Means of communication**: *ti avviso* ***per*** *telefono* (I'll phone you), *è arrivata* ***per*** *posta* (it arrived/came by mail).
- **Origin**: *esco* ***da*** *casa* (I'm leaving home), *viene* ***da*** *Parigi* (he comes from Paris), ma: *sono* ***di*** *Roma* (I'm from Rome).
- **Time**: *aspetto* ***da*** *un'ora* (I've been waiting for one hour), *vive qui* ***da*** *due anni* (he's been living here for two years); *arrivo* ***fra/tra*** *dieci minuti* (I'll come in ten minutes), *parte* ***fra/tra*** *due ore* (he'll leave in two hours).
- ***Andare/vivere...*** **+ city**: ***a*** *Milano* (in Milan), ***a*** *New York* (in New York), + **countries and regions**: ***in*** *Italia* (in Italy), ***in*** *Germania* (in Germany), ***in*** *Toscana* (in Tuscany), ***negli*** *Stati Uniti* (in the United States); ... + **persons**: ***da*** *Carlo* (at Carlo's), ***dal*** *dottore* (at the doctor's), ***dal*** *macellaio* (at the butcher's), ***al*** *cinema* (at the cinema), ***a*** *teatro* (at the theatre); but ***partire*** + ***per***: *partiamo* ***per*** *Venezia* (I'm leaving for Venice).
- ***Andare*** **+ places ending in -*teca* or -*eria***: ***in*** *pizzeria* (to the pizzeria), ***in*** *biblioteca* (to the library).
- **Materials**: *maglia* ***di*** *lana* (woolen pullover), *fazzoletto* ***di*** *cotone* (cotton handkerchief), *tavolo* ***di*** *legno* (table of wood/wooden table).
- **Ore del giorno**: ***alle*** *3* (at three), ***a*** *mezzogiorno* (at midday), ***a*** *mezzanotte* (at midnight).
- **Cause**: *trema* ***per*** *il freddo,* ***per*** *la fame,* ***per*** *la paura* (he trembles with cold, hunger, fear), but *muoio* ***di*** *freddo,* ***di*** *fame,* ***di*** *paura* (I'm freezing,I'm starving, I'm scared to death).

The adverb

Types of adverbs

- **Manner**: *bene* (well), *male* (badly), *piano* (slowly), *forte* (loud), *chiaramente* (clearly) etc.
- **Place or location**: *qui/qua* (here), *lì/là* (there), *su* (up/above), *giù* (down), *laggiù/lassù* (over there), *vicino* (nearby), *lontano* (far), *fuori* (outside), *dentro* (inside), *sopra* (up/on/on top/above), *sotto* (under/below), *dappertutto* (everywhere), *ovunque* (everywhere) etc.
- **Statement**: *sì* (yes), *sicuramente* (certainly), *davvero* (indeed), *certo* (surely) etc.
- **Negation**: *no* (no), *non* (not), *affatto* (at all/not at all) ecc.
- **Doubt**: *forse* (maybe), *probabilmente* (probably), *magari* (perhaps/maybe) ecc.
- **Time**: *ora/adesso* (now), *sempre* (always), *mai* (never), *quasi mai* (almost never), *spesso* (often), *talvolta/a volte* (sometimes), *raramente* (seldom), *prima* (first), *poi* (then), *presto* (soon/early), *tardi* (late) etc.
- **Quantity**: *troppo* (too much), *molto/tanto* (a lot), *parecchio* (a lot of), *abbastanza* (plenty), *piuttosto* (quite), *un po'* (a little/not much), *poco* (little/not much), *per niente* (not at all) etc.
- **Interrogative**: *come?* (how?), *dove?* (where?), *quando?* (when?), *quanto?* (how much?), *perché?* (why?), etc.

Formation of adverbs

Adjective		Adverb
First group	*lento-**o***	*lent-**a-mente***
Second group	*dolc-**e***	*dolc-**e-mente***
Adjective ending in -*le*	*cordia**l-e***	*cordial-**mente***
Adjective ending in -*re*	*regolar-**e***	*regolar-**mente***

The degrees of adverbs

Positive		*velocemente*
Comparative	"di uguaglianza"	*tanto velocemente quanto*
	"di maggioranza"	*più velocemente di*
	"di minoranza"	*meno velocemente di*
Superlative	"assoluto"	*velocissimamente, molto velocemente*
	"relativo"	*il più velocemente possibile*

Adverbs with irregular comparatives and superlatives

	Positive	Comparative	Superlative
Adjective	*buono*	*migliore*	*ottimo/a/i/e*
Adverb	*bene*	*meglio*	*ottimamente (benissimo)*
Adjective	*cattivo*	*peggiore*	*pessimo/a/i/e*

	Positive	Comparative	Superlative
Adverb	*male*	*peggio*	*pessimamente (malissimo)*
Adjective	*grande*	*maggiore*	*massimo/a/i/e*
Adverb	*grandemente*	*maggiormente*	*massimamente (moltissimo)*
Adjective	*poco, piccolo*	*minore*	*minimo/a/i/e, pochissimo*
Adverb	*poco*	*meno*	*minimamente (pochissimo)*
Adjective	*molto*	*più*	*moltissimo/a/i/e*
Adverb	*molto*	*più*	*moltissimo*

Alteration of adverbs

It follows the same rules as the adjective.

Diminutive (smaller, prettier)	*più piccolo, grazioso*	**-*ino*, -*etto***	*pochino, pochetto*
Augmentative (bigger, larger)	*più grande*	**-*one***	*benone*
Pejorative (uglier, more unpleasant)	*più brutto, spiacevole*	**-*accio***	*malaccio*
Modification to express endearment (dearer, pleasant, pretty)	*più caro, piacevole, grazioso*	**-*uccio***	*maluccio*

The conjunction

Coordinating conjunctions

Conjunction	Use	Example
e(d), anche, pure, inoltre (affermative), *né, neppure, neanche, nemmeno* (negative)	They link two elements	*Paolo è simpatico, **inoltre** è un tipo atletico. Mio figlio non mangia gli spinaci **neppure** se lo obbligo.*
o, oppure, altrimenti	They express an alternative	*Preferisci il pesce **o/oppure** la carne? Spostati, **altrimenti** non vedo nulla!*
ma, però, anzi, invece, eppure, tuttavia, piuttosto	They express a contrast	*Prenderei il dolce **ma/però** ho paura di ingrassare. Fa ancora freddo, **eppure/tuttavia** è già aprile.*
cioè, ossia, infatti	They explain what was told	*Il cane è un quadrupede, **cioè/ossia** ha quattro zampe. Le previsioni erano buone, **infatti** c'è il sole.*
dunque, perciò, pertanto, quindi	They express a consequence	*Non trova le chiavi, **quindi/dunque/pertanto/perciò** non può aprire la porta.*
o ... o, sia ... sia, tanto ... quanto, e ... e, né ... né, non solo ... ma anche	The put two elements in relation	*Detesto **sia** il rosso **sia** il nero. **Non solo** sono in ritardo, **ma** ho **anche** dimenticato i biglietti!*

Subordinating conjunctions

Conjunction	Use	Example
che	They explain what was told in the main clause	*Sai **che** Paola si è sposata? Ho paura **che** mio marito non arrivi in tempo.*
perché, poiché, siccome + indicativo	They indicate a cause	*Sono stanca **perché/poiché** ho dormito poco. **Siccome** non amo volare, viaggio sempre in treno.*
affinché, perché + congiuntivo	They indicate an aim/a goal	*Ti presto la mia bicicletta **affinché/poiché/perché** possa partecipare anche tu alla gita.*
così ... che/da, tanto ... che/da	They indicate a consequence	*Era **così** debole **che** non riusciva a parlare. Aveva pianto **tanto da** non avere più lacrime.*
quando, mentre, finché, prima che, dopo che, appena	They express time	*Mi rassereno, **quando** sento il canto dei grilli. **Mentre** lavava i piatti, il marito le leggeva il giornale.*
se, qualora, nel caso che	They express an hypothesis	***Se** supero l'esame, pago da bere per tutti! Chiedetemi pure spiegazioni **qualora** fosse necessario.*

Conjunction	Use	Example
sebbene, benché, nonostante, malgrado, per quanto + congiuntivo, *anche se* + indicativo	They indicate an opposing condition which doesn't prevent the action	***Sebbene/nonostante/malgrado/benché*** *preferisca i gatti, amo molto anche i cani.* ***Anche se*** *non lo vuole ammettere, Anna è delusa.*
come (se), quasi,	They express a comparison	*Hai fatto* ***come*** *ti ho chiesto?* *Perché parli piano* ***quasi*** *fosse mezzanotte?*
tranne, fuorché, eccetto che, a meno che, senza che	They express an exclusion or an exception	***A meno che*** *lo abbia dimenticato, verrà anche Gianni.* *Preparò ogni cosa* ***senza che*** *il marito se ne accorgesse.*

The verb

Modes and tenses

Modes: *indicativo, congiuntivo, condizionale imperativo, infinito, gerundio, participio.*
Tenses: *presente, imperfetto, passato remoto, futuro semplice, passato prossimo, trapassato prossimo, trapassato remoto, futuro anteriore.*

Auxiliary verbs

The auxiliary is the verb that is used to build compound tenses. *Essere* and *avere* are auxiliary verbs.
Essere **(to be)**. Examples: *sono detti, è preso, erano usciti, fu scritto, siano amati, sarà fatto, fosse visto, essere nati, sarebbe andato.*
Avere **(to have)**. Examples: *ho detto, abbiamo fatto, aveva scritto, ebbe letto, abbia parlato, avesse preso, avere mangiato, avrebbe dato.*

Conjugations

There are three verb conjugations.
- ***-are*** 1st *am-**are***
- ***-ere*** 2nd *vend-**ere***
- ***-ire*** 3rd *sent-**ire***

Reflexive verbs
- ***-arsi*** 1st *am-**arsi***
- ***-ersi*** 2nd *sed-**ersi***
- ***-irsi*** 3rd *vest-**irsi***

ESSERE			
Indicativo		**Congiuntivo**	
Presente	**Passato prossimo**	**Presente**	**Passato**
io sono	io sono stato	che io sia	che io sia stato
tu sei	tu sei stato	che tu sia	che tu sia stato
lui/lei/Lei è	lui/lei/Lei è stato	che lui/lei/Lei sia	che lui/lei/Lei sia stato
noi siamo	noi siamo stati	che noi siamo	che noi siamo stati
voi siete	voi siete stati	che voi siate	che voi siate stati
loro sono	loro sono stati	che loro siano	che loro siano stati
Imperfetto	**Trapassato prossimo**	**Imperfetto**	**Trapassato**
io ero	io ero stato	che io fossi	che io fossi stato
tu eri	tu eri stato	che tu fossi	che tu fossi stato
lui/lei/Lei era	lui/lei/Lei era stato	che lui/lei/Lei fosse	che lui/lei/Lei fosse stato
noi eravamo	noi eravamo stati	che noi fossimo	che noi fossimo stati
voi eravate	voi eravate stati	che voi foste	che voi foste stati
loro erano	loro erano stati	che loro fossero	che loro fossero stati
Passato remoto	**Trapassato remoto**	**Condizionale**	
io fui	io fui stato	**Presente**	**Passato**
tu fosti	tu fosti stato	io sarei	io sarei stato
lui/lei/Lei fu	lui/lei/Lei fu stato	tu saresti	tu saresti stato
noi fummo	noi fummo stati	lui/lei/Lei sarebbe	lui/lei/Lei sarebbe stato
voi foste	voi foste stati	noi saremmo	noi saremmo stati
loro furono	loro furono stati	voi sareste	voi sareste stati
		loro sarebbero	loro sarebbero stati

Futuro semplice	Futuro anteriore	Imperativo	
		Presente	
io sarò	io sarò stato	–	
tu sarai	tu sarai stato	sii (tu)	
lui/lei/Lei sarà	lui/lei/Lei sarà stato	sia (lui/lei/Lei)	
noi saremo	noi saremo stati	siamo (noi)	
voi sarete	voi sarete stati	siate (voi)	
loro saranno	loro saranno stati	siano loro)	

Infinito		Gerundio		Participio	
Presente	Passato	Presente	Passato	Presente	Passato
essere	essere stato	essendo	essendo stato	(ente)	stato

AVERE			
Indicativo		Congiuntivo	
Presente	Passato prossimo	Presente	Passato
io ho	io ho avuto	che io abbia	che io abbia avuto
tu hai	tu hai avuto	che tu abbia	che tu abbia avuto
lui/lei/Lei ha	lui/lei/Lei ha avuto	che lui/lei/Lei abbia	che lui/lei/Lei abbia avuto
noi abbiamo	noi abbiamo avuto	che noi abbiamo	che noi abbiamo avuto
voi avete	voi avete avuto	che voi abbiate	che voi abbiate avuto
loro hanno	loro hanno avuto	che loro abbiano	che loro abbiano avuto
Imperfetto	Trapassato prossimo	Imperfetto	Trapassato
io avevo	io avevo avuto	che io avessi	che io avessi avuto
tu avevi	tu avevi avuto	che tu avessi	che tu avessi avuto
lui/lei/Lei aveva	lui/lei/Lei aveva avuto	che lui/lei/Lei avesse	che lui/lei/Lei avesse avuto
noi avevamo	noi avevamo avuto	che noi avessimo	che noi avessimo avuto
voi avevate	voi avevate avuto	che voi aveste	che voi aveste avuto
loro avevano	loro avevano avuto	che loro avessero	che loro avessero avuto
Passato remoto	Trapassato remoto	Condizionale	
		Presente	Passato
io ebbi	io ebbi avuto	io avrei	io avrei avuto
tu avesti	tu avesti avuto	tu avresti	tu avresti avuto
lui/lei/Lei ebbe	lui/lei/Lei ebbe avuto	lui/lei/Lei avrebbe	lui/lei/Lei avrebbe avuto
noi avemmo	noi avemmo avuto	noi avremmo	noi avremmo avuto
voi aveste	voi aveste avuto	voi avreste	voi avreste avuto
loro ebbero	loro ebbero avuto	loro avrebbero	loro avrebbero avuto
Futuro semplice	Futuro anteriore	Imperativo	
		Presente	
io avrò	io avrò avuto	–	
tu avrai	tu avrai avuto	abbi (tu)	
lui/lei/Lei avrà	lui/lei/Lei avrà avuto	abbia (lui/lei/Lei)	
noi avremo	noi avremo avuto	abbiamo (noi)	
voi avrete	voi avrete avuto	abbiate (voi)	
loro avranno	loro avranno avuto	abbiano (loro)	

Infinito		Gerundio		Participio	
Presente	Passato	Presente	Passato	Presente	Passato
avere	avere avuto	avendo	avendo avuto	avente	avuto

AMARE - 1ª CONIUGAZIONE			
ATTIVO			
Indicativo		**Congiuntivo**	
Presente	**Passato prossimo**	**Presente**	**Passato**
io amo	io ho amato	che io ami	che io abbia amato
tu ami	tu hai amato	che tu ami	che tu abbia amato
lui/lei/Lei ama	lui/lei/Lei ha amato	che lui/lei/Lei ami	che lui/lei/Lei abbia amato
noi amiamo	noi abbiamo amato	che noi amiamo	che noi abbiamo amato
voi amate	voi avete amato	che voi amiate	che voi abbiate amato
loro amano	loro hanno amato	che loro amino	che loro abbiano amato
Imperfetto	**Trapassato prossimo**	**Imperfetto**	**Trapassato**
io amavo	io avevo amato	che io amassi	che io avessi amato
tu amavi	tu avevi amato	che tu amassi	che tu avessi amato
lui/lei/Lei amava	lui/lei/Lei aveva amato	che lui/lei/Lei amasse	che lui/lei/Lei avesse amato
noi amavamo	noi avevamo amato	che noi amassimo	che noi avessimo amato
voi amavate	voi avevate amato	che voi amaste	che voi aveste amato
loro amavano	loro avevano amato	che loro amassero	che loro avessero amato
Passato remoto	**Trapassato remoto**	**Condizionale**	
io amai	io ebbi amato	**Presente**	**Passato**
tu amasti	tu avesti amato	io amerei	io avrei amato
lui/lei/Lei amò	lui/lei/Lei ebbe amato	tu ameresti	tu avresti amato
noi amammo	noi avemmo amato	lui/lei/Lei amerebbe	lui/lei/Lei avrebbe amato
voi amaste	voi aveste amato	noi ameremmo	noi avremmo amato
loro amarono	loro ebbero amato	voi amereste	voi avreste amato
		loro amerebbero	loro avrebbero amato
Futuro semplice	**Futuro anteriore**	**Imperativo**	
io amerò	io avrò amato	**Presente**	
tu amerai	tu avrai amato	–	
lui/lei/Lei amerà	lui/lei/Lei avrà amato	ama (tu)	
noi ameremo	noi avremo amato	ami (lui/lei/Lei)	
voi amerete	voi avrete amato	amiamo (noi)	
loro ameranno	loro avranno amato	amate (voi)	
		amino (loro)	

Infinito		**Gerundio**		**Participio**	
Presente	**Passato**	**Presente**	**Passato**	**Presente**	**Passato**
amare	avere amato	amando	avendo amato	amante	amato

VENDERE - 2ª CONIUGAZIONE			
ATTIVO			
Indicativo		**Congiuntivo**	
Presente	**Passato prossimo**	**Presente**	**Passato**
io vendo	io ho venduto	che io venda	che io abbia venduto
tu vendi	tu hai venduto	che tu venda	che tu abbia venduto
lui/lei/Lei vende	lui/lei/Lei ha venduto	che lui/lei/Lei venda	che lui/lei/Lei abbia venduto
noi vendiamo	noi abbiamo venduto	che noi vendiamo	che noi abbiamo venduto
voi vendete	voi avete venduto	che voi vendiate	che voi abbiate venduto
loro vendono	loro hanno venduto	che loro vendano	che loro abbiano venduto
Imperfetto	**Trapassato prossimo**	**Imperfetto**	**Trapassato**
io vendevo	io avevo venduto	che io vendessi	che io avessi venduto
tu vendevi	tu avevi venduto	che tu vendessi	che tu avessi venduto
lui/lei/Lei vendeva	lui/lei/Lei aveva venduto	che lui/lei/Lei vendesse	che lui/lei/Lei avesse venduto
noi vendevamo	noi avevamo venduto	che noi vendessimo	che noi avessimo venduto
voi vendevate	voi avevate venduto	che voi vendeste	che voi aveste venduto
loro vendevano	loro avevano venduto	che loro vendessero	che loro avessero venduto

VENDERE - 2ª CONIUGAZIONE			
ATTIVO			
Indicativo		**Congiuntivo**	
		Condizionale	
Passato remoto	**Trapassato remoto**	**Presente**	**Passato**
io vendetti, vendei tu vendesti lui/lei/Lei vendette, vendé noi vendemmo voi vendeste loro vendettero, venderono	io ebbi venduto tu avesti venduto lui/lei/Lei ebbe venduto noi avemmo venduto voi aveste venduto loro ebbero venduto	io venderei tu venderesti lui/lei/Lei venderebbe noi venderemmo voi vendereste loro venderebbero	io avrei venduto tu avresti venduto lui/lei/Lei avrebbe venduto noi avremmo venduto voi avreste venduto loro avrebbero venduto
Futuro semplice	**Futuro anteriore**	**Imperativo**	
		Presente	
io venderò tu venderai lui/lei/Lei venderà noi venderemo voi venderete loro venderanno	io avrò venduto tu avrai venduto lui/lei/Lei avrà venduto noi avremo venduto voi avrete venduto loro avranno venduto	– vendi (tu) venda (lui/lei/Lei) vendiamo (noi) vendete (voi) vendano (loro)	

Infinito		**Gerundio**		**Participio**	
Presente	**Passato**	**Presente**	**Passato**	**Presente**	**Passato**
vendere	avere venduto	vendendo	avendo venduto	(vendente)	venduto

SENTIRE - 3ª CONIUGAZIONE			
ATTIVO			
Indicativo		**Congiuntivo**	
Presente	**Passato prossimo**	**Presente**	**Passato**
io sento tu senti lui/lei/Lei sente noi sentiamo voi sentite loro sentono	io ho sentito tu hai sentito lui/lei/Lei ha sentito noi abbiamo sentito voi avete sentito loro hanno sentito	che io senta che tu senta che lui/lei/Lei senta che noi sentiamo che voi sentiate che loro sentano	che io abbia sentito che tu abbia sentito che lui/lei/Lei abbia sentito che noi abbiamo sentito che voi abbiate sentito che loro abbiano sentito
Imperfetto	**Trapassato prossimo**	**Imperfetto**	**Trapassato**
io sentivo tu sentivi lui/lei/Lei sentiva noi sentivamo voi sentivate loro sentivano	io avevo sentito tu avevi sentito lui/lei/Lei aveva sentito noi avevamo sentito voi avevate sentito loro avevano sentito	che io sentissi che tu sentissi che lui/lei/Lei sentisse che noi sentissimo che voi sentiste che loro sentissero	che io avessi sentito che tu avessi sentito che lui/lei/Lei avesse sentito che noi avessimo sentito che voi aveste sentito che loro avessero sentito
Passato remoto	**Trapassato remoto**	**Condizionale**	
		Presente	**Passato**
io sentii tu sentisti lui/lei/Lei sentì noi sentimmo voi sentiste loro sentirono	io ebbi sentito tu avesti sentito lui/lei/Lei ebbe sentito noi avemmo sentito voi aveste sentito loro ebbero sentito	io sentirei tu sentiresti lui/lei/Lei sentirebbe noi sentiremmo voi sentireste loro sentirebbero	io avrei sentito tu avresti sentito lui/lei/Lei avrebbe sentito noi avremmo sentito voi avreste sentito loro avrebbero sentito

SENTIRE - 3ª CONIUGAZIONE			
ATTIVO			
Futuro semplice	**Futuro anteriore**	**Imperativo**	
		Presente	
io sentirò tu sentirai lui/lei/Lei sentirà noi sentiremo voi sentirete loro sentiranno	io avrò sentito tu avrai sentito lui/lei/Lei avrà sentito noi avremo sentito voi avrete sentito loro avranno sentito	– senti (tu) senta (lui/lei/Lei) sentiamo (noi) sentite (voi) sentano (loro)	

Infinito		Gerundio		Participio	
Presente	**Passato**	**Presente**	**Passato**	**Presente**	**Passato**
sentire	avere sentito	sentendo	avendo sentito	(sentente)	sentito

PASSIVO							
Indicativo							
	1ª coniug.	2ª coniug.	3ª coniug.		1ª coniug.	2ª coniug.	3ª coniug.
Presente				**Passato prossimo**			
io sono	amato/a	venduto/a	sentito/a	io sono stato	amato/a	venduto/a	sentito/a
tu sei	amato/a	venduto/a	sentito/a	tu sei stato	amato/a	venduto/a	sentito/a
lui/lei/Lei è	amato/a	venduto/a	sentito/a	lui/lei/Lei è stato	amato/a	venduto/a	sentito/a
noi siamo	amati/e	venduti/e	sentiti/e	noi siamo stati	amati/e	venduti/e	sentiti/e
voi siete	amati/e	venduti/e	sentiti/e	voi siete stati	amati/e	venduti/e	sentiti/e
loro sono	amati/e	venduti/e	sentiti/e	loro sono stati	amati/e	venduti/e	sentiti/e
Imperfetto				**Trapassato prossimo**			
io ero	amato/a	venduto/a	sentito/a	io ero stato/a	amato/a	venduto/a	sentito/a
tu eri	amato/a	venduto/a	sentito/a	tu eri stato/a	amato/a	venduto/a	sentito/a
lui/lei/Lei era	amato/a	venduto/a	sentito/a	lui/lei/Lei era stato/a	amato/a	venduto/a	sentito/a
noi eravamo	amati/e	venduti/e	sentiti/e	noi eravamo stati/e	amati/e	venduti/e	sentiti/e
voi eravate	amati/e	venduti/e	sentiti/e	voi eravate stati/e	amati/e	venduti/e	sentiti/e
loro erano	amati/e	venduti/e	sentiti/e	loro erano stati/e	amati/e	venduti/e	sentiti/e
Passato remoto				**Trapassato remoto**			
io fui	amato/a	venduto/a	sentito/a	io ero stato/a	amato/a	venduto/a	sentito/a
tu fosti	amato/a	venduto/a	sentito/a	tu eri stato/a	amato/a	venduto/a	sentito/a
lui/lei/Lei fu	amato/a	venduto/a	sentito/a	lui/lei/Lei era stato/a	amato/a	venduto/a	sentito/a
noi fummo	amati/e	venduti/e	sentiti/e	noi eravamo stati/e	amati/e	venduti/e	sentiti/e
voi foste	amati/e	venduti/e	sentiti/e	voi eravate stati/e	amati/e	venduti/e	sentiti/e
loro furono	amati/e	venduti/e	sentiti/e	loro erano stati/e	amati/e	venduti/e	sentiti/e
Futuro semplice				**Futuro anteriore**			
io sarò	amato/a	venduto/a	sentito/a	io sarò stato/a	amato/a	venduto/a	sentito/a
tu sarai	amato/a	venduto/a	sentito/a	tu sarai stato/a	amato/a	venduto/a	sentito/a
lui/lei/Lei sarà	amato/a	venduto/a	sentito/a	lui/lei/Lei sarà stato/a	amato/a	venduto/a	sentito/a
noi saremo	amati/e	venduti/e	sentiti/e	noi saremo stati/e	amati/e	venduti/e	sentiti/e
voi sarete	amati/e	venduti/e	sentiti/e	voi sarete stati/e	amati/e	venduti/e	sentiti/e
loro saranno	amati/e	venduti/e	sentiti/e	loro saranno stati/e	amati/e	venduti/e	sentiti/e

PASSIVO

Indicativo

Congiuntivo

	1ª coniug.	2ª coniug.	3ª coniug.		1ª coniug.	2ª coniug.	3ª coniug.
Presente				**Passato**			
io sia	amato/a	venduto/a	sentito/a	io sia stato	amato/a	venduto/a	sentito/a
tu sia	amato/a	venduto/a	sentito/a	tu sia stato	amato/a	venduto/a	sentito/a
lui/lei/Lei sia	amato/a	venduto/a	sentito/a	lui/lei/Lei sia	amato/a	venduto/a	sentito/a
noi siamo	amati/e	venduti/e	sentiti/e	noi siamo stati	amati/e	venduti/e	sentiti/e
voi siamo	amati/e	venduti/e	sentiti/e	voi siate stati	amati/e	venduti/e	sentiti/e
loro siano	amati/e	venduti/e	sentiti/e	loro siano stati	amati/e	venduti/e	sentiti/e
Imperfetto				**Trapassato**			
io fossi	amato/a	venduto/a	sentito/a	io fossi stato/a	amato/a	venduto/a	sentito/a
tu fossi	amato/a	venduto/a	sentito/a	tu fossi stato/a	amato/a	venduto/a	sentito/a
lui/lei/Lei fosse	amato/a	venduto/a	sentito/a	lui/lei/Lei fosse stato/a	amato/a	venduto/a	sentito/a
noi fossimo	amati/e	venduti/e	sentiti/e	noi fossimo stati/e	amati/e	venduti/e	sentiti/e
voi foste	amati/e	venduti/e	sentiti/e	voi foste stati/e	amati/e	venduti/e	sentiti/e
loro erano	amati/e	venduti/e	sentiti/e	loro erano stati/e	amati/e	venduti/e	sentiti/e

Condizionale

	1ª coniug.	2ª coniug.	3ª coniug.		1ª coniug.	2ª coniug.	3ª coniug.
Presente				**Passato**			
io sarei	amato/a	venduto/a	sentito/a	io sarei stato/a	amato/a	venduto/a	sentito/a
tu saresti	amato/a	venduto/a	sentito/a	tu saresti stato/a	amato/a	venduto/a	sentito/a
lui/lei/Lei sarebbe	amato/a	venduto/a	sentito/a	lui/lei/Lei sarebbe stato/a	amato/a	venduto/a	sentito/a
noi saremmo	amati/e	venduti/e	sentiti/e	noi saremmo stati/e	amati/e	venduti/e	sentiti/e
voi sareste	amati/e	venduti/e	sentiti/e	voi sareste stati/e	amati/e	venduti/e	sentiti/e
loro sarebbero	amati/e	venduti/e	sentiti/e	loro sarebbero stati/e	amati/e	venduti/e	sentiti/e

Imperativo

	1ª coniug.	2ª coniug.	3ª coniug.
Presente			
–	amato/a	venduto/a	sentito/a
sii (tu)	amato/a	venduto/a	sentito/a
sia (lui/lei/Lei)	amato/a	venduto/a	sentito/a
siamo (noi)	amati/e	venduti/e	sentiti/e
siate (voi)	amati/e	venduti/e	sentiti/e
siano (loro)	amati/e	venduti/e	sentiti/e

Infinito

	1ª coniug.	2ª coniug.	3ª coniug.		1ª coniug.	2ª coniug.	3ª coniug.
Presente				**Passato**			
essere	amato/a amati/e	venduto/a venduti/e	sentito/a sentiti/e	essere stato/a/i/e	amato/a amati/e	venduto/a venduti/e	sentito/a sentiti/e

Congiuntivo

	1ª coniug.	2ª coniug.	3ª coniug.		1ª coniug.	2ª coniug.	3ª coniug.
Presente				**Passato**			
essendo	amato/a amati/e	venduto/a venduti/e	sentito/a sentiti/e	essendo stato/a/i/e	amato/a amati/e	venduto/a venduti/e	sentito/a sentiti/e

Participio

Passato			
stato/a stati/e	amato/a/ amati/e	venduto/a venduti/e	sentito/a sentiti/e

Main verbs with an irregular present indicative

Infinito	io	tu	lui/lei	noi	voi	loro
andare	vado	vai	va	andiamo	andate	vanno
apparire	appaio	appari	appare	appariamo	apparite	appaiono
bere	bevo	bevi	beve	beviamo	bevete	bevono
dare	do	dai	dà	diamo	date	danno
dire	dico	dici	dice	diciamo	dite	dicono
dovere	devo	devi	deve	dobbiamo	dovete	devono
fare	faccio	fai	fa	facciamo	fate	fanno
morire	muoio	muori	muore	moriamo	morite	muoiono
obbedire	obbedisco	obbedisci	obbedisce	obbediamo	obbedite	obbediscono
ottenere	ottengo	ottieni	ottiene	otteniamo	ottenete	ottengono
piacere	piaccio	piaci	piace	piacciamo	piacete	piacciono
porre	pongo	poni	pone	poniamo	ponete	pongono
produrre	produco	produci	produce	produciamo	producete	producono
riempire	riempio	riempi	riempie	riempiamo	riempite	riempiono
rimanere	rimango	rimani	rimane	rimaniamo	rimanete	rimangono
salire	salgo	sali	sale	saliamo	salite	salgono
sapere	so	sai	sa	sappiamo	sapete	sanno
scegliere	scelgo	scegli	sceglie	scegliamo	scegliete	scelgono
sciogliere	sciolgo	sciogli	scioglie	sciogliamo	sciogliete	sciolgono
sedere	siedo	siedi	siede	sediamo	sedete	siedono
sostituire	sostituisco	sostituisci	sostituisce	sostituiamo	sostituite	sostituiscono
spegnere	spengo	spegni	spegne	spegniamo	spegnete	spengono
stare	sto	stai	sta	stiamo	state	stanno
tacere	taccio	taci	tace	tacciamo	tacete	tacciono
tenere	tengo	tieni	tiene	teniamo	tenete	tengono
togliere	tolgo	togli	toglie	togliamo	togliete	tolgono
tossire	tossisco	tossisci	tossisce	tossiamo	tossite	tossiscono
Verbs ending in -***urre*** drop the -***rre*** and add -***c*** before conjugating.						
tradurre	traduco	traduci	traduce	traduciamo	traducete	traducono
trarre	traggo	trai	trae	traiamo	traete	traggono
uscire	esco	esci	esce	usciamo	uscite	escono
venire	vengo	vieni	viene	veniamo	venite	vengono
Verbs ending in ***–care*** or ***–gare*** add an -***h*** in the second person singular and in the 1st person plural.						
cercare	cerco	cerchi	cerca	cerchiamo	cercate	cercano
giocare	gioco	giochi	gioca	giochiamo	giocate	giocano
pagare	pago	paghi	paga	paghiamo	pagate	pagano
obbligare	obbligo	obblighi	obbliga	obblighiamo	obbligate	obbligano

Past participle of the main irregular verbs with the auxiliary *avere*

Infinito	Participio passato
accendere	acceso
assumere	assunto
bere	bevuto
chiedere	chiesto
chiudere	chiuso
conoscere	conosciuto
correggere	corretto
correre	corso

Infinito	Participio passato
fare	fatto
leggere	letto
mettere	messo
muovere	mosso
nascondere	nascosto
offendere	offeso
offrire	offerto
perdere	perso

Infinito	Participio passato
risolvere	risolto
rispondere	risposto
rompere	rotto
scegliere	scelto
scrivere	scritto
soffrire	sofferto
spegnere	spento
tradurre	tradotto

Infinito	Participio passato
cuocere	cotto
decidere	deciso
dire	detto
dividere	diviso

Infinito	Participio passato
piangere	pianto
prendere	preso
produrre	prodotto
ridere	riso

Infinito	Participio passato
uccidere	ucciso
vedere	visto
vincere	vinto
vivere	vissuto

Past participle of the main irregular verbs with the auxiliary *essere*

Infinito	Participio passato
apparire	apparso
essere	stato
morire	morto
giungere	giunto
nascere	nato
piacere	piaciuto
rimanere	rimasto
scendere	sceso
succedere	successo
venire	venuto

Past participle of the main regular verbs with the auxiliary *essere*

Infinito	Participio passato
andare	andato
arrivare	arrivato
cadere	caduto
entrare	entrato
partire	partito
uscire	uscito

Main verbs with an irregular *passato remoto*

Infinito	io	tu	lui/lei	noi	voi	loro
accendere	accesi	accendesti	accese	accendemmo	accendeste	accesero
bere	bevvi	bevesti	bevve	bevemmo	beveste	bevvero
cadere	caddi	cadesti	cadde	cademmo	cadeste	caddero
chiedere	chiesi	chiedesti	chiese	chiedemmo	chiedeste	chiesero
chiudere	chiusi	chiudesti	chiuse	chiudemmo	chiudeste	chiusero
conoscere	conobbi	conoscesti	conobbe	conoscemmo	conosceste	conobbero
correre	corsi	corresti	corse	corremmo	correste	corsero
crescere	crebbi	crescesti	crebbe	crescemmo	cresceste	crebbero
dare	diedi	desti	diede	demmo	deste	diedero
decidere	decisi	decidesti	decise	decidemmo	decideste	decisero
dire	dissi	dicesti	disse	dicemmo	diceste	dissero
fare	feci	facesti	fece	facemmo	faceste	fecero
leggere	lessi	leggesti	lesse	leggemmo	leggeste	lessero
mettere	misi	mettesti	mise	mettemmo	metteste	misero
nascere	nacqui	nascesti	nacque	nascemmo	nasceste	nacquero
nascondere	nascosi	nascondesti	nascose	nascondemmo	nascondeste	nascosero
perdere	persi	perdesti	perse	perdemmo	perdeste	persero
piacere	piacqui	piacesti	piacque	piacemmo	piaceste	piacquero

Infinito	io	tu	lui/lei	noi	voi	loro
piangere	piansi	piangesti	pianse	piangemmo	piangeste	piansero
prendere	presi	prendesti	prese	prendemmo	prendeste	presero
ridere	risi	ridesti	rise	ridemmo	rideste	risero
rimanere	rimasi	rimanesti	rimase	rimanemmo	rimaneste	rimasero
rispondere	risposi	rispondesti	rispose	rispondemmo	rispondeste	risposero
rompere	ruppi	rompesti	ruppe	rompemmo	rompeste	ruppero
sapere	seppi	sapesti	seppe	sapemmo	sapeste	seppero
scegliere	scelsi	scegliesti	scelse	scegliemmo	sceglieste	scelsero
scrivere	scrissi	scrivesti	scrisse	scrivemmo	scriveste	scrissero
spendere	spesi	spendesti	spese	spendemmo	spendeste	spesero
stare	stetti	stesti	stette	stemmo	steste	stettero
tacere	tacqui	tacesti	tacque	tacemmo	taceste	tacquero
tradurre	tradussi	traducesti	tradusse	traducemmo	traduceste	tradussero
vedere	vidi	vedesti	vide	vedemmo	vedeste	videro
venire	venni	venisti	venne	venimmo	veniste	vennero
vincere	vinsi	vincesti	vinse	vincemmo	vinceste	vinsero
vivere	vissi	vivesti	visse	vivemmo	viveste	vissero
volere	volli	volesti	volle	volemmo	voleste	vollero

Main verbs with an irregular *imperfetto*

Infinito	io	tu	lui/lei	Infinito	io	tu	lui/lei
bere	bevevo	bevevi	beveva ecc.	**fare**	facevo	facevi	faceva ecc.
dire	dicevo	dicevi	diceva ecc.	**tradurre**	traducevo	traducevi	raduceva ecc

Main verbs with an irregular future indicative and present conditional

Infinito	Indicativo futuro			Condizionale presente		
andare	io andrò	tu andrai	lui/lei andrà ecc.	io andrei	tu andresti	lui/lei andrebbe ecc.
avere	io avrò	tu avrai	lui/lei avrà ecc.	io avrei	tu avresti	lui/lei avrebbe ecc.
bere	io berrò	tu berrai	lui/lei berrà ecc.	io berrei	tu berresti	lui/lei berrebbe ecc.
cadere	io cadrò	tu cadrai	lui/lei cadrà ecc.	io cadrei	tu cadresti	lui/lei cadrebbe ecc.
dare	io darò	tu darai	lui/lei darà ecc.	io darei	tu daresti	lui/lei darebbe ecc.
dovere	io dovrò	tu dovrai	lui/lei dovrà ecc.	io dovrei	tu dovresti	lui/lei dovrebbe ecc.
essere	io sarò	tu sarai	lui/lei sarà ecc.	io sarei	tu saresti	lui/lei sarebbe ecc.
fare	io farò	tu farai	lui/lei farà ecc.	io farei	tu faresti	lui/lei farebbe ecc.
potere	io potrò	tu potrai	lui/lei potrà ecc.	io potrei	tu potresti	lui/lei potrebbe ecc.
rimanere	io rimarrò	tu rimarrai	lui/lei rimarrà ecc.	io rimarrei	tu rimarresti	lui/lei rimarrebbe ecc.
sapere	io saprò	tu saprai	lui/lei saprà ecc.	io saprei	tu sapresti	lui/lei saprebbe ecc.
stare	io starò	tu starai	lui/lei starà ecc.	io starei	tu staresti	lui/lei starebbe ecc.
tenere	io terrò	tu terrai	lui/lei terrà ecc.	io terrei	tu terresti	lui/lei terrebbe ecc.
tradurre	io tradurrò	tu tradurrai	lui/lei tradurrà ecc.	io tradurrei	tu tradurresti	lui/lei tradurrebbe ecc.
vedere	io vedrò	tu vedrai	lui/lei vedrà ecc.	io vedrei	tu vedresti	lui/lei vedrebbe ecc.
venire	io verrò	tu verrai	lui/lei verrà ecc.	io verrei	tu verresti	lui/lei verrebbe ecc.
vivere	io vivrò	tu vivrai	lui/lei vivrà ecc.	io vivrei	tu vivresti	lui/lei vivrebbe ecc.
volere	io vorrò	tu vorrai	lui/lei vorrà ecc.	io vorrei	tu vorresti	lui/lei vorrebbe ecc.
I verbi in -*care*, -*gare* prendono la -***h***- in tutte le persone.						
cercare	io cercherò	tu cercherai	lui/lei cercherà ecc.	io cercherei	tu cercheresti	lui/lei cercherebbe ecc.
pagare	io pagherò	tu pagherai	lui/lei pagherà ecc.	io pagherei	tu pagheresti	lui/lei pagherebbe ecc.

Infinito	Indicativo futuro			Condizionale presente		
I **verbi in** ***-ciare***, ***-giare*** perdono la ***-i-*** in tutte le persone.						
cominciare	io comincerò	tu comincerai	lui/lei comincerà ecc.	io comincerei	tu cominceresti	lui/lei comincerebbe ecc.
mangiare	io mangerò	tu mangerai	lui/lei mangerà ecc.	io mangerei	tu mangeresti	lui/lei mangerebbe ecc.

Main verbs with an irregular present subjunctive

Infinito	Congiuntivo presente	Infinito	Congiuntivo presente
andare	io, tu, lui/lei vada ecc.	**sapere**	io, tu, lui/lei sappia ecc.
avere	io, tu, lui/lei abbia ecc.	**scegliere**	io, tu, lui/lei scelga ecc.
bere	io, tu, lui/lei beva ecc.	**spegnere**	io, tu, lui/lei spenga ecc.
dare	io, tu, lui/lei dia ecc.	**stare**	io, tu, lui/lei stia ecc.
dire	io, tu, lui/lei dica ecc.	**tacere**	io, tu, lui/lei taccia ecc.
dovere	io, tu, lui/lei debba ecc.	**tenere**	io, tu, lui/lei tenga ecc.
essere	io, tu, lui/lei sia ecc.	**togliere**	io, tu, lui/lei tolga ecc.
fare	io, tu, lui/lei faccia ecc.	I **verbi in** ***-urre*** aggiungono la ***-c-*** nel tema.	
morire	io, tu, lui/lei muoia ecc.	**tradurre**	io, tu, lui/lei traduca ecc.
potere	io, tu, lui/lei possa ecc.	**uscire**	io, tu, lui/lei esca ecc.
rimanere	io, tu, lui/lei rimanga ecc.	**venire**	io, tu, lui/lei venga ecc.
salire	io, tu, lui/lei salga ecc.	**volere**	io, tu, lui/lei voglia ecc.

Main verbs with an irregular imperfect subjunctive

Infinito	Congiuntivo imperfetto	Infinito	Congiuntivo imperfetto
bere	io, tu bevessi, lui/lei bevesse ecc.	**fare**	io, tu facessi, lui/lei facesse ecc.
dare	io, tu dessi, lui/lei desse ecc.	**stare**	io, tu stessi, lui/lei stesse ecc.
dire	io, tu dicessi, lui/lei dicesse ecc.	I **verbi in** ***-urre*** aggiungono la ***-c-*** nel tema.	
essere	io, tu fossi, lui/lei fosse ecc.	**tradurre**	io, tu traducessi, lui/lei traducesse ecc.

Main irregular direct imperatives

Infinito	tu	voi
avere	abbi	abbiate
essere	sii	siate
andare	va'	
dare	da'	
dire	di'	
fare	fa'	
sapere	sa'	sappiate
stare	sta'	

KEY TO EXERCISES

Unit 1

1 **1** noi **2** lei, noi **3** lui **4** voi, loro **5** lo **6** lei

2 **1** sono **2** sono, è **3** sono **4** sono, sono **5** siamo **6** siete, siamo **7** è

3 **1**c **2**a **3**d **4**e **5**b **6**f

4 **1** ci sono **2** c'è **3** c'è **4** ci sono **5** ci sono **6** c'è

Unit 2

1 **1** ho **2** ha **3** ha, ha **5** ha

2 **1** avete **2** avete **3** avete **4** abbiamo

4 **1** ha **2** ho, è **3** hai, hai, è **4** hai, sono

5 **1** sono **2** sono **3** sono **4** è **5** sono **6** ho **7** è **8** hai **9** ho **10** ho **11** è **12** hai

Unit 3

1 **1, 2, 4, 5, 6**

2 **1** è **2** ha **3** è **4** ha **5** è **6** ha **7** è

3 **1** ha **2** è **3** ha **4** non ha **5** è

4 **1** ha **2** sei **3** è **4** hai **5** hai

Unit 4

1 **1** abitano **2** disegnate **3** cucina **4** imparate **5** torna **6** parlano

2 **1** Studiate italiano? **2** Lavori? **3** Cantate spesso? **4** Mangia al ristorante?

3 **2**e **3**c **4**b **5**a

4 **1** cuciniamo **2** arrivo **3** amo **4** lavorate **4** mangia **6** non ricordo

Unit 5

1 **1** cercate, cerchiamo **2** paghi, pago **3** gioca **4** dimentichiamo

2 **1** stai **2** sta **3** sta **4** stiamo **5** state **6** stanno

3 **1** do **2** danno **3** date **4** diamo

4 **1** va **2** andiamo **3** vanno **4** andate **5** andiamo

5 **1** fa la doccia **2** fai il caffè **3** fa sport **4** fanno shopping **5** fa i compiti

Unit 6

1 **1** leggono, leggo **2** scrive **3** prendono **4** vende **5** chiude

2 **1** bevono, V **2** chiudono, V **3** puliscono, V **4** conoscono, F **5** parlano, F

3 **1** Vivi a Roma? **2** Conoscete Paolo? **3** Mangiano carne? **4** Anna corre ogni giorno? **5** Spendi molto?

4 **1** dici **2** dà **3** stanno **4** salite **5** rimani

Unit 7

1 **1**b **2** b **3**c **4**c **5**a

2 **1** vengo **2** vengono **3** venite, veniamo **4** vengono **5** viene

3 **1** Dove andate? **2** Quando arrivate? **3** Quando vieni da me? **4** Quanto partite? **5** Dove vai?

Unit 8

1 lo studente, il biglietto, il fiume, la mamma, il genitore, la città, l'ombrello, la famiglia, il padre, la madre, l'amica, la moglie, il marito, lo zio, la classe, il pesce, il mare, il bicchiere, la forchetta, l'estate, la tovaglia, la stagione, il gatto, il cane, il sole, la sete, la gamba, l'amore, il sale, il fiume, il monte, il piatto, il cuore, lo sbaglio, l'errore

2 **1** il **2** le **3** la **4** la **5** le **6** le **7** i **8** la **9** la **10** i **11** il

3 **1** il **2** gli **3** il **4** l' **5** lo **6** il **7** gli **8** gli

4 **1** il, i **2** gli **3** la **4** il **5** gli, i **6** il, il, lo

Unit 9

1 **1** un' **2** una **3** una **4** una **5** una **6** una **7** un' **8** una **9** una **10** una **11** un **12** un **13** un **14** un **15** uno **16** uno **17** un **18** un **19** un **20** uno

2 **1** una **2** un' **3** un **4** una **5** una **6** un' **7** una **8** una **9** una **10** un **11** un **12** un **13** un **14** un' **15** un **16** una **17** un **18** un **19** un **20** una

3 **1** una, una **2** la **3** una **4** un, l' **5** uno **6** la, il **7** il, un, una

4 **1**a **2**b **3**a **4**b **5**a **6**a **7**a **8**b **9**a **10**a **11**a **12**b **13**a **14**b **15**b

Unit 10

1 **1** matite **2** segretarie **3** zaini **4** ponti **5** lavori **6** porte **7** pesci **8** studenti **9** leggi **10** appartamenti

2 **1** -e **2** -i **3** -e **4** -o, -e **5** -e **6** -e, -e **7** -i **8** -e **9** -i, -o, -e

3 **2**g **3**h **4**p **5**i **6**l **7**c **8**m **9**o **10**a **11**f **12**e **13**d **14**n

4 **1** letti **2** sedie **3** pettini **4** bicchieri **5** semafori **6** farfalle

Summary exercises 1-10

1 **1** siete, siamo **2** sei, sono, ho **3** ci sono, c'è **4** hai, ho **5** sta, sto, stai **6** hanno, è **7** ha

2 **1** trovo **2** abita **3** risponde **4** cominciano **5** accende **6** parte **7** ascoltano **8** sentite **9** prendono, prendiamo

3 **1** vai, vado **2** capiamo, preferiamo **3** vieni, andate, veniamo **4** bevete, noi beviamo **5** conoscono **6** hanno **7** spende **8** chiediamo

4 **1** guardiamo **2** bevono **3** vieni **4** andate **5** è **6** è **7** sta, ha **8** chiudono, fa

5 **1** la cena **2** a letto **3** la televisione **4** alla stazione **5** la finestra

6 **1** -i **2** -e **3** -i, -e **4** -e **5** -e, -e, -o **6** -i **7** -e **8** -e, -a **9** -e

7 **1** un, una **2** un, una **3** lo, i, il **4** la, un' **5** le, un' **6** le, un **7** lo, il, i **8** gli, un'

8 **1** C'è il sole oggi **2** Ci sono due libri qui **3** C'è un regalo per me? **4** Ti piace l'Italia? **5** Mi piace il formaggio **6** Paul capisce l'italiano e il francese **7** Parliamo spagnolo **8** Ho una penna. Hai un quaderno?

Unit 11

1 **1** uomini **2** dei **3** climi **4** braccia **5** dita **6** poeti **7** autobus **8** serie **9** brindisi **10** città **11** foto **12** re

2 **1** serie **2** poeti **3** telegrammi **4** hotel **5** mani **6** papà **7** auto **8** ipotesi

3 **1** farmacie **2** cataloghi **3** amici **4** maghi **5** maghe **6** astrologi **7** cuoche **8** cuochi

4 **1** alberghi **2** medici **3** colleghe **4** nemici **5** addii **6** ciliegie **7** arance **8** psicologi

Unit 12

1 **1** perché **2** perché **3** come **4** come **5** come

2 **1** perché **2** come mai **3** sta, ha **4** sto

3 **1** Dove andate? **2** Quando/A che ora arrivate? **3** Quando vieni da me? **4** Quando partite? **5** Dove vai?

4 **1** abbastanza **2** per niente **3** abbastanza **4** molto **5** troppo **6** molto **7** un po'

Unit 13

1 **1** facilmente **2** improvvisamente **3** diligentemente **4** lentamente **5** velocemente **6** profondamente **7** cordialmente **8** stupidamente

2 **1** talvolta **2** spesso **3** mai **4** sempre

3 **1** dappertutto **2** giù **3** sopra **4** là dentro **5** lontano **6** qua

4 **1** sì, certo **2** certamente **3** davvero **4** probabilmente **5** magari **6** certamente

Unit 14

1 **1** -e **2** -a **3** -i **4** -a **5** -o **6** -e, -a **8** -o, -o

2 **1** -o, -o, -a, -a, -a **2** -a, -a, -o, -o, -o **3** -a, -i, -i **4** -e, -i

3 **1** -a, -i **2** -o, -o **3** -o, -o **4** -e **5** -i, -i

4 **1** scuri **2** fredda **3** pieni **4** curiose **5** noioso **6** famosi

Unit 15

1 **1** -e **2** -e, -o **3** -a, -a, -e **4** -e, -a **5** -e, -e **6** -e, -i **7** -e **8** -e **9** -e, -o **10** -e

2 **1** nubile **2** inutile **3** infelice **4** maschile **5** meridionale **6** forte **7** difficile

3 **1**e **2**d **3**i **4**b **5**c **6**a **7**f **8**g **9**h

4 **1**b **2**a **3**d **4**c **5**e

Unit 16

1 **1** egoista **2** pari **3** rosa **4** blu **5** entusiasta **6** ottimista

2 **2** stanchi **3** simpatici **4** seri **6** lunghi **7** antinebbia

3 **1** bello **2** buona **3** bell' **4** buon **5** bell'

4 **1** grand' **2** grandi **3** gran **4** grande **5** grandi

5 **1** Gli armadi sono antichi, i tavoli sono recenti **2** I bambini non mangiano verdure crude **3** I problemi di matematica sono facili, gli esercizi di geometria sono difficili **4** Non ci sono formaggi freschi? **4** Le anziane signore sono dolci e simpatiche **6** Perché bevete le birre analcoliche?

Unit 17

1 **1** vogliamo **2** vuoi **3** volete **4** voglio **5** vuole **6** vogliono, vuole

2 **1** posso **2** potete, possiamo **3** possono, possono **4** posso **5** può, posso

3 **1** dovete, dobbiamo **2** devi **3** deve, devono **4** devi, dovete

4 **1** posso **2** puoi **3** puoi **4** dovete **5** deve **6** devo **7** devo **8** possiamo **9** potete **10** posso **11** vuoi **12** vogliamo

Unit 18

1 **1** giocando **2** leggendo **3** dicendo **4** finendo **5** aspettando **6** mettendo **7** facendo **8** partendo

2 **1** Noi stiamo mandando una mail **2** I miei colleghi stanno leggendo il giornale **3** Che cosa stai pensando? **4** Giovanni sta dicendo una bugia **5** Voi state arrivando? **6** Dove sta lavorando adesso, signora Torti?

3 **1** state facendo? Stiamo scrivendo **2** stai studiando **3** sta andando **4** sta guardando **5** stanno facendo, stanno telefonando **6** state partendo, stiamo prendendo **7** sta bevendo

Unit 19

1 **1** si fa **2** mi taglio **3** si arrabbia **4** vi trovate **5** ci sentiamo **6** si divertono

2 **1** si chiama **2** ci addormentiamo **3** si trova **4** ci rilassiamo **5** mi preoccupo

3 **1** ti alzi **2** si veste **3** ci pettiniamo **4** si rilassano **5** vi sedete

4 **1** mi **2** mi **3** mi **4** si **5** si **6** si **7** ti **8** ti **9** ti

Summary exercises 11-19

1 **1** dici, dico **2** usciamo, rimango **3** noi saliamo **4** vengo, fa **5** rimango, finisco **6** voi sapete, dà

2 **1** paghi **2** fate **3** cerchiamo **4** faccio **5** escono, c'è **6** spengo **7** facciamo

3 **1** posso, devo **2** potete, dovete **3** vuoi **4** possiamo, dobbiamo **5** volete **6** può, vuole, devono **7** vogliono, possono, devono

4 **1** carne **2** estate **2** squadre **4** occhiali **5** affitto **6** negozi **7** esami **8** appuntamento

5 **1** luminosa **2** amaro **3** grassa **4** caro, ricchi **5** fredda, pesanti **6** socievole **7** divertenti **8** sporco **9** meridionale

6 **1** piccoli **2** verdi, grandi **3** interessante, noiosa **4** vecchia, comoda **5** bollenti, macchiati **6** aperte **7** intelligenti **8** ricca

7 **1** I bambini non amano i cibi piccanti **2** Noi non facciamo mai una colazione abbondante **3** Voi fate una bella passeggiata? **4** Voi preferite le donne bionde o brune? **5** Noi dobbiamo comprare vestiti pesanti e scarpe nuove

8 **1** Marco è un uomo intelligente **2** Ho amici interessanti **3** Parlo lentamente **4** I maghi per la festa dei bambini sono qui **5** Luca e Martina mangiano poco, Sebastiano mangia molto **6** Cosa posso fare per te? **7** Susanna vuole andare a una festa **8** Devo ancora comprare i regali per Natale

Unit 20

1 **1** a, di **2** d' **3** a, di **4** di, di **5** di **6** di **7** a **8** di **9** a **10** d', d' **11** di

2 **1** di **2** di **3** d' **4** d' **5** a **6** a

3 **1**d **2**a **3**e **4**c **5**b

4 **1** da **2** in **3** in, in **4** da **5** in **6** da **7** da **8** da, da

Unit 21

1 **1**a **2**a **3**b **4**a **5**a **6**c

2 **1** tra **2** per **3** tra **4** in **5** tra **6** per

3 **1** di **2** da **3** da, a, in **4** in **5** da **6** da **7** da **8** da **9** di

4 **1** per **2** per **3** tra **4** per, per

5 **1**b **2**d **3**a **4**c

Unit 22

1 **1**c **2**a **3**b **4**a **5**b

2 **1** con **2** con **3** per **4** tra **5** con **6** tra **7** con **8** su

3 **1** dietro **2** davanti **3** lontano **4** fuori **5** sotto **6** dentro

Unit 23

1 **1** ti, mi **2** ti, mi **3** vi **4** vi **5** vi **6** mi **7** mi **8** ci, ci **9** vi **10** ti

2 **1**c **2**a **3**b **4**e **5**d **6**f

3 **1**a **2**b **3**a **4**a **5**a **6**b **7**a **8**b

4 **1** non la conosco **2** lo preferiamo **3** La prepariamo **4** la guardo **5** li uso **6** le compro **7** lo mangio **8** lo sappiamo **9** non la facciamo **10** la diciamo

Unit 24

1 **1**ci **2** ti **3** vi **4** ci **5** vi **6** ti **7** mi

2 **1** ve la diamo **2** vi aspettiamo **3** mi scrivono spesso **4** non ti accompagno **5** ci chiama

3 **1** le amo **2** li ama **3** le passo **4** le conosco **5** lo parla

Unit 25

1 **1** ne **2** la **3** ne **4** ne **5** lo **6** ne **7** ne **8** li

2 **1** la **2** li **3** l' **4** la **5** la **6** li

3 **1** lo **2** lo **3** la **4** la, la/ci **6** la

4 **1** Le camicie? Le lascio dentro ai cassetti **2** Non salutiamo quelle ragazze perché non le conosciamo **3** I colleghi delle mie sorelle sono simpatici **4** Sopra i tavoli ci sono le tovaglie con i piatti, i bicchieri, le forchette e i cucchiai **5** Non mangiamo formaggi freschi perché li detestiamo

Unit 26

1 **1** Gliele spiega? **2** Glielo consigliate? **3** Glielo mostri? **4** Gliela fai vedere? **5** Glielo regalate? **6** Glieli hai dati?

2 **1** glielo **2** gliele **3** glieli **4** gliel' **5** glieli, glieli **6** gliele

3 **1** gliel'ho chiesta **2** ce lo hanno dato **3** non glieli hanno spediti **4** glieli ho fatti **5** ne ha compiuti 23 **6** non te l'ho chiesto **7** ne abbiamo comprati **8** non ve lo abbiamo consegnato

4 **1** lo abbiamo **2** ve lo diamo **4** glielo consegniamo **5** ne ho molte

Unit 27

1 **1** si guida **2** si va **3** non si fa **4** non si lavora **5** ci si alza

2 **1** ci si rilassa **2** si dorme **3** si mangia **4** si tiene **5** si legge **6** si innamora

3 **1** noi giochiamo **2** tu compri **3** si parte **4** paghi due e compri tre **5** ci si veste bene

Unit 28

1 **1** il suo fidanzato **2** la vostra proposta **3** i loro CD **4** il suo zaino **5** il suo numero di telefono **6** la sua sorellina **7** i suoi occhi **8** i suoi cugini **9** il suo quadro **10** i suoi genitori

2 **1** suo **2** suoi **3** suo **4** nostra **5** loro

3 **1** i suoi **2** la tua **3** i suoi **4** i nostri **5** le mie

4 **1** la mia **2** la nostra **3** i vostri **4** il nostro, il vostro **5** il tuo **6** le nostre **7** la sua

Unit 29

1 **1** questa **2** questa **3** questo **4** quest' **5** quest' **6** queste

2 **1** quegli **2** quelle **3** quella **4** quelle **5** quell', quei **6** quel

3 **1** questo, quello **2** quegli **3** quest', quello **4** quest', quella **5** queste, quegli **6** questo

4 **1** Desidero quei maglioni, per favore **2** Quell'animale è malato **3** Quegli alberi hanno più di 100 anni **4** Quest'amico abita a Genova **5** Quell'ora di lezione è divertente **6** Quelle ragazze sono molto carine

Summary exercises 20-29

1 **1** a, in, con **2** da, in **3** in, a, in **4** su **5** con **6** con **7** con, per **8** a, con **9** di, di, in

2 **1** da, di **2** a, in **3** a, di **4** a, in **5** di **6** in **7** in

3 **1** mi piacciono **2** le telefoniamo **3** non lo leggo **4** li cerco **5** lo abbiamo **6** non lo sappiamo **7** ci parlo **8** gli racconto

4 **1** si diventa **2** si capisce **3** ci si veste **4** si legge **5** si cena **6** si parla **7** si fuma **8** ci si alza

6 **1** della **2** dei **3** della **4** dei **5** del

7 **1** Questo è il mio libro. Che cos'è quello? **2** I miei amici sono qui **3** Vuoi del latte? Sì, un po' **4** Mi dici la verità? Te la dico **5** Vado a casa di mio zio **6** Lily sta a casa mia **7** La scuola è vicina alla stazione **8** Gli alberi sono dietro all'università

Unit 30

1 **1** sette **2** nove **3** diciassette **4** diciannove **5** quattro

6 quindici **7** dieci **8** diciotto **9** quattordici **10** due **11** cinque **12** sedici **13** dodici **14** zero **15** tredici **16** undici

2 **1** settecentoquarantacinque **2** cinquecentosettantotto **3** centosedici **4** milletrecentonovantasei **5** cinquemilaseicentosessantotto

3 **1** tre tre otto cinque quattro tre sette sei cinque zero **2** zero tre quattro sette otto sei cinque quattro tre **3** quattro quattro zero sei sei sette otto nove quattro tre

Unit 31

1 **1** sesto **2** decimo **3** quattordicesimo **4** novantanovesimo **5** millesimo **6** sessantesimo **7** cinquantacinquesimo **8** primo **9** duecentotrentesimo **10** quinto

2 **1** dieci **2** centotredici **3** tre **4** cinquantuno **5** uno **6** ottantadue

3 **1** sesto **2** terzo **3** quinto **4** primo **5** quattordicesimo **6** ottavo **7** seconda **8** sedicesimo

4 **1** nona **3** i primi, i terzi **4** quarta **5** terzo **6** mille **7** settimo **8** il centesimo

Unit 32

1 **1** pulito **2** potuto **3** telefonato **4** disegnato **5** cantato **6** voluto **7** saputo **8** pagato **9** creduto **10** dovuto **11** contato **12** parlato

2 **1** avete comprato **2** abbiamo finito **3** hanno ballato **4** avete sentito **5** avete dato **6** abbiamo avuto

3 **1**d **2**c **3**e **4**b **5**a

4 **1** ho avuto **2** ho trovato **3** ha invitato **4** ho incontrato **5** noi abbiamo ballato **6** abbiamo mangiato **7** abbiamo portato **8** abbiamo chiacchierato **9** ho capito **10** ho domandato **11** ha dato **12** ho telefonato

Unit 33

1 **1** ho giocato, hanno vinto, ho perso **2** abbiamo scritto, ha risposto **3** avete letto **4** abbiamo visto, abbiamo pianto

2 **1** abbiamo sempre capito **2** hai mandato **3** hanno avuto **4** ha raccontato

4 **1** Voi avete messo le bottiglie in frigorifero? **2** Lui ha bevuto una tazza di tè **3** Lei ha riso perché lui ha raccontato una barzelletta **4** Tu hai chiesto a Claudia se ha portato i piatti di plastica? **5** Quando ho perso gli orecchini d'oro ho pianto come una fontana!

Unit 34

1 **1** I miei pesci rossi sono diventati grandi **2** Il nonno di Paul è tornato in Scozia **3** È arrivata tardi perché non è stata bene **4** Dove sei stata tutto il pomeriggio? **5** Ieri la mia amica è andata al cinema a vedere un film giallo

2 **1** è andata **2** sei uscita **3** è salito **4** è stata, è venuta **5** si è alzato

3 **1** siamo arrivati **2** siamo entrati **3** sono piaciuti **4** sono sembrati **5** sono stata **6** ho potuto **7** ho dimenticato

4 **1** sto **2** sono stata **3** hai avuto **4** ho avuto **5** sei stata **6** è stato **7** ha dato **8** fa **9** vado

Unit 35

1 **1** -o **2** -a, -a **3** -i **4** -a, -a, -a **5** -i, -i, -i

2 **1** abbiamo perso **2** è piaciuto **3** ha avuto, è caduta **4** ha speso, ha chiesto **5** ci siamo alzati, è suonata

3 **1** sono successe **2** ho avuto **3** sono arrivata **4** sono passati **5** abbiamo vissuto **6** è piaciuta **7** ha trovato **8** ci siamo trasferiti **9** ho dovuto **10** ho conosciuto **11** sono trovata **12** ho fatto **13** ho capito **14** ho ancora raccontato **15** ho incontrato **16** l'ho conosciuto **17** ho visto **18** è piaciuto **19** ho ancora finito **20** è successo

Unit 36

1 **1** parlavano **2** vedevi **3** finiva **4** credeva **5** cantavate **6** studiava **7** sentivano **8** andavo **9** lavorava **10** piangevano

2 **1** disegnava, ascoltava, cantava **2** ci divertivamo, preparavano **3** vivevi, mangiavi **4** lavorava, si occupava, abitava **5** costruivano, andavano **6** usciva, piaceva

3 **1** era **2** aveva **3** vedeva **4** veniva **5** leccava **6** abbaiava **7** erano **8** amavamo **9** coccolavo **10** viziavamo **11** diceva **12** era **13** volevo **14** piaceva

Unit 37

1 **1** dicevi **2** facevamo **3** traducevate **4** eravamo **5** dovevamo **6** potevo **7** eri **8** beveva **9** facevate **10** dicevano

2 **1** faceva **2** abitavo **3** bevevo **4** voleva **5** diceva **6** faceva **7** mangiava **8** era

3 **1** andava **2** ho visto, è piaciuto **3** leggeva, ha messo, abbiamo riso **4** c'era, avevano, morivano **5** leggeva **6** abitavano, avevano

4 **1** dormivo **2** mangiavo **4** ha studiato

Unit 38

1 **1** mangia!, mangiate! **2** dormi!, dormite! **3** scrivi!, scrivete! **4** parla!, parlate! **5** corri!, correte! **6** gioca!, giocate! **7** ascolta!, ascoltate! **8** finisci!, finite! **9** traduci!, traducete! **10** usa!, usate!

2 **1** prendi **2** aspetta **3** non studiate **4** pulite **5** lava **6** non guardate

3 **1** Parlate a bassa voce, per favore! **2** Spegni la televisione, per favore! **3** Apparecchia la tavola, per favore! **4** Non aprite la finestra, per favore!

4 **1** non sedetevi **2** svegliati **2** lavatevi **4** tornare **5** spostatevi **6** uscire

Unit 39

1 **1** abbi **2** abbiate **3** sii **4** non avere **5** non siate **6** non abbiate

2 **1** va' **2** di' **3** da' **4** fa' **5** sii **6** sta' **7** abbi **8** sappi

3 **1** va' **2** state **3** abbi **4** non abbiate **5** sii **6** scrivile

4 **1** dovete dargliela **2** non devi telefonarle **4** devi comperarlo **5** non dovete riferirla **5** devi scriverle

5 **1** di' **2** diccele **3** fallo **4** va' **4** dillo **5** fare

Summary exercises 31-39

1 **1** terzo **2** secondo **3** mille **4** tredici, diciassette **5** quinto **6** cento **7** quaranta **8** diciotto

2 **1** brindiamo, abbiamo brindato **2** pulisci, hai pultio **3** posso, ho potuto **4** litighiamo, abbiamo mai litigato **5** capisci, hai capito

3 **1** entrano, sono entrati **2** si addormentano, si sono addormentati **3** esci, sei uscito **4** si alzano, si sono sempre alzati **5** spedisco, ho sempre spedito

4 **1** dove sei stata **2** ha bevuto **3** accendete **4** non abbiamo ancora letto, avete scritto **5** ha sciolto, siamo rimasti, siamo venuti **6** avete speso, avete chiesto

5 **1** eravamo, aiutava, stava **2** ha detto, ha rotto, giocavano **3** ho perso, parcheggiavo **4** ha tolto, faceva **5** ha fatto, era

6 **1** Lunedì è il primo giorno della settimana **2** Ieri siamo andati a una festa **3** Dove sei andata la scorsa settimana, Roxana? **4** Sabato notte Adriano non ha dormito a casa **5** Fred è uscito con Paul **6** Vieni qui e ascoltami! **7** Va' a casa! È tardi **8** Stavo lavando i piatti quando è suonato il telefono

Unit 40

1 **1** dell' **2** della **3** del **4** della **5** dell' **6** dello **7** dello **8** dell' **9** del **10** del **11** dello **12** dell'

2 **1** degli **2** delle **3** dei **4** delle **5** degli **6** degli **7** degli **8** dei

3 **1** delle **2** degli **3** dell' **4** della **5** del **6** delle **7** dei **8** del **9** delle **10** del **11** della **12** delle **13** degli **14** del **15** del **16** degli **17** del **18** dei **19** dei **20** dei

4 **1** del **2** del **3** della **4** dei **5** dell'

5 **1** al, alle **2** al, al **3** alla **4** alla **5** alle, all' **6** alla, alle

Unit 41

1 **1** dalla **2** dallo **3** dalla **4** dalla **5** dall' **6** dal, dal

2 **1** dal fruttivendolo **2** dal dentista **3** alla stazione **4** al cinema **5** al supermercato **6** dal panettiere

3 **1** nel **2** nell' **3** nei **4** nel **5** nelle **6** nei

4 **1** sugli **2** sull' **3** sulla **4** sul **5** sugli **6** sulla

5 **1** alle (sulle) **2** coi **3** tra **4** con **5** sulla **6** nei **7** sullo **8** nella **9** di **10** nell'

Unit 42

1 **1** partiranno **2** scriverò **3** apriranno **4** arriverà **5** passeremo **6** finirò **7** smetterà **8** laveremo **9** comprerò **10** uscirà

2 **1** diventerà **2** comprerà **3** si sposerà **4** abiterà **5** viaggerà

3 **1** No, non partirò/Sì, partirò **2** No, non passerò/Sì, passerò **3** No, non visiterò/Sì, visiterò **4** No, non mi divertirò/Sì, mi divertirò **5** No, non leggerò/Sì, leggerò **6** No, non mangerò/Sì, mangerò

Unit 43

1 **1** sarai **2** avrò **3** sarà **4** mangerò **5** farà, pioverà **6** usciremo **7** vedrò

2 **1** lavoreranno **2** parleranno **3** vivranno **4** sarà **5** avranno

3 **1** siamo andati **2** pago, pagherai **3** partiremo **4** dimenticherò **5** saprete **6** siamo stati

4 **1** inviterò **2** rimarrò **3** prenderò **4** giocherò **5** uscirò **6** dormirò

Unit 44

1 **1** Il mare è più vicino della montagna. Il mare è vicino come la montagna. Il mare è meno vicino della montagna **2** Mio fratello è più alto di Claudio. Mio fratello è alto come Claudio. Mio fratello è meno alto di Claudio **3** Questa camera è più bella della nostra. Questa camera è bella come la nostra. Questa camera è meno bella della nostra **4** Noi siamo più ricchi di voi. Noi siamo ricchi come voi. Noi siamo meno ricchi di voi **5** Il vino è più costoso della birra. Il vino è costoso come la birra. Il vino è meno costoso della birra **6** L'inglese è più difficile del francese. L'inglese è difficile come il francese. L'inglese è meno difficile del francese

2 **1** Il fiume Po **2** Cioccolato **3** Bahamas **4** Una poltrona **5** Milano **6** Le Piramidi

3 **1** più, del **2** meno, della **3** famoso come **4** meno, che **5** caldo come

4 **1** di **2** che **3** che **4** di **5** di

Unit 45

1 **1** Paolo è il più alto della famiglia **2** Il nostro appartamento è il più pulito di tutti **3** Questa città è la più ricca d'Italia **4** I musei di Firenze sono i più interessanti della Toscana **5** L'aeroplano è il mezzo più veloce di tutti **6** Questo quartiere è il più elegante della città **7** Il tuo caffè è il migliore di tutti **8** Questo locale èil più brutto del quartiere **9** Il tempo di questa settimana è il peggiore di tutta l'estate **10** Sergio è il più piccolo dei (tra i) miei fratelli

2 **1** molto raffinati/raffinatissimi **2** molto veloce/velocissimo **3** molto luminosa/luminosissima **4** molto divertente/divertentissimo **5** molto magro/magrissimo

3 **1** molto velocemente **2** moltissimo **3** molto lentamente **4** molto presto/prestissimo **5** molto male/malissimo

4 **1** Il fiume Reno è più lungo del Po **2** Il Po è il fiume più lungo d'Italia **3** Qual è il monte più alto d'Italia? **4** Il Monte Rosa è più alto del Cervino? Sì, è più alto del Cervino **5** Abbiamo mangiato i piatti più buoni/migliori del ristorante **6** La mia auto è più veloce della tua. Però l'auto del signor Rossi è la più veloce di tutte **7** Ho visto il quadro più interessante della mostra **8** I dipinti di Raffaello sono secondo me più belli di quelli di Michelangelo **9** Franco è lo studente più pigro della classe. Non credo. Maria è ancora più pigra di Franco **10** I vestiti di marca sono i più cari di tutti

Unit 46

1 **1** tutti **2** qualcosa, niente **3** ciascuno, niente **4** qualsiasi **5** nessuno **6** ogni **7** tutti **8** qualcuno **9** qualcosa **10** qualsiasi

2 **1** qualunque **2** alcune **3** nessun **4** pochi **5** qualcosa **6** qualche **7** qualche **8** ogni

3 **1** pochi **2** tutti **3** nessuno **4** molti **5** qualche **6** dei

Unit 47

1 **1** partimmo **2** tornammo **3** ci divertimmo **4** cominciò **5** finì **6** morirono **7** emigrarono **8** trovarono **9** fu **10** dormii **11** ebbi **12** mi svegliai **13** mi alzai **14** incontrammo **15** capimmo **16** andaste **17** mi portarono **18** fu **19** tornammo **20** trovò **21** fu **22** viaggiasti **23** arrivasti **24** spediste **25** ricevemmo **26** ebbe **27** operò **28** fu **29** è guarì **30** passarono **31** rallentarono **32** furono

2 **1** bevemmo **2** mangiammo **3** ballammo **4** lessero **5** conobbi **6** fu **7** accadde **8** si scontrarono **9** rimase **10** venne **11** riuscì **12** chiamammo

Unit 48

1 **1** era successo **2** avevo guardato **3** avevi scritto **4** avevano visto **5** avevamo offerto **6** avevo capito **7** avevate mangiato **8** aveva consigliato **9** erano usciti **10** avevano ordinato

2 **1** avevo visto **2** aveva trovato **3** ero mai stato **4** avevo sentito **5** avevi regalato

3 **1** sei stato **2** sono stato **3** ho telefonato **4** hanno detto **5** eri uscito **6** sono stato **7** è uscito **8** ha avuto **9** hanno parlato **10** hai prestato **11** è suonato **12** ho risposto

4 **1** avevo lavorato, sono rimasta **2** avevamo appena finito, è entrato **3** ci siamo alzati, ci siamo addormentati **4** hai mai conosciuto **5** eravate appena usciti, è arrivata

Unit 49

1 **1** parlerei **2** pioverebbe **3** regaleremmo **4** prendereste **5** crederebbero **6** camminerebbero **7** finiresti **8** seguireste **9** lavorerei **10** si sveglierebbe

2 **1** spenderei **2** lascerei **3** lavorerei **4** investirei

3 **1** dareste **2** vorrebbero **3** potresti **4** sapremmo **5** saresti **6** saremmo **7** potrei **8** vorrebbe **9** potreste **10** vorrebbero **11** mangeresti **12** berrebbe **13** tradurrei **14** tradurreste **15** faresti **16** farebbero **17** avrei **18** avrebbero **19** berrebbero **20** mangeremmo

4 **1** vorrei **2** potrebbe **4** berremmo **5** piacerebbe

Summary exercises 40-49

1 **1** dagli **2** alle, alla **3** sui **4** dell', del, dei **5** nelle, nell' **6** sulla, in, del **7** negli **8** dalle, alle **9** al, dai **10** dei

2 **1** verranno **2** sarò, viaggerò **3** farete, avremo, andremo **4** scriveranno **5** potrà **6** dovrai **7** partiranno

3 **1** disse **2** vide **3** fu **4** uscì **5** diedero **6** fece **7** lesse **8** andarono **9** dormirono **10** ebbero

4 **1** siete andati **2** aveva già visto, era piaciuto **2** ha comprato, aveva fatto, aveva trovato **3** abbiamo risposto, ha capito **4** ha sgridato, aveva preso **5** è arrivata, era già morto **6** avete mai mangiato **7** sono andata, avevo finito

5 **1** più popolosa **2** più lungo **3** più alto **4** è grande come **6** più piccolo

6 **1** più **2** la più **3** come **4** più **5** i più

7 **1** Comprerò dei vestiti per il tuo compleanno **2** Verrai alla mia festa in discoteca? **3** Ben è più alto di suo fratello **4** Non voglio niente per me **5** C'è qualcuno a casa? **6** Qualcuno è sempre a casa **7** Potresti telefonarmi domani? **8** Vorrei vendere la mia casa il più presto possibile

Unit 50

1 **1** accetti **2** dorma **3** aspettiate **4** parta **5** prendiate **6** scendiate **7** si impegnino

2 **1** si senta **2** parla **2** parte **4** scriviate **5** pensano **6** torni **7** lavorate

3 **1** si informi **2** accettino **3** migliorano **4** si mettano **5** scade **6** lavora **7** prendano

4 **1** diamo, dessimo **2** dia, dessi **3** sappiate, sapeste **4** sappiano, sapessero **5** stiate, steste **6** stia, stessi **7** traducano, traducessero **8** traduca, traducesse **9** beviate, beveste **10** beva, bevesse **11** beviamo, bevessimo **12** dicano, dicessero **12** vadano, andassero **14** io vada, andassi **15** venga, venissi

Unit 51

1 **1** vedessi **2** mangiassero **3** credessimo **4** telefonassi **5** guardasse **6** pensaste **7** abitassi **8** uscissi **9** mettessero **10** vendereste **11** mentissi **12** partissi

2 **1** Temevo che Luca perdesse **2** Speravamo che Sergio avesse **3** Era meglio che tu decidessi **4** Credevate che Lucia potesse

3 **1** arrivasse **2** salissero **3** ascoltassi **4** si comportasse **5** aspettaste **6** sapesse

4 **1** cucinasse **2** recitino **3** partisse **4** capissero **5** arrabbiassi **6** veniste

Unit 52

1 **1** abbia creduto/avessi creduto **2** siamo usciti/fossimo usciti **3** siano tornati/fossero tornati **4** sia stato/fossi stato **5** abbia detto/avesse detto **6** abbiate saputo/aveste saputo **7** abbiate ricevuto/aveste ricevuto **8** sia partito/fosti partito **9** abbiano fatto/avessero fatto **10** abbiano voluto/avessero voluto

2 **1** fosse **2** aveva **3** era **4** dicano

3 **1** tenessero **2** riuscisse **3** telefonasse **4** avesse avuto **5** fossero preparati **6** si fossero sbagliati **7** si fossero sposati **8** avesse preso

4 **1** il marito fosse andato al cinema **2** Luca le avesse nascosto qualcosa **3** le ragazze non avrebbero dovuto indossare i pantaloni **4** Andrea sapesse giocare a scacchi **5** tutti avessero finito il lavoro

Unit 53

1 **1** aver frequentato **2** dimagrire **3** essermi comportato **4** aver avuto **5** aver trovato **6** partire

2 **1**b **2**a **3**f **4**c **5**d **6**e **7**g

3 **1** tornasse **2** finisse **3** faccia **4** l'avesse vista **5** abbia risposto **6** rispettiate

4 **1** conoscesse **2** sia meglio **3** fossero **4** voglia **5** arrestasse

5 **1** di vincere **2** la tradisse **3** di uscire **4** aver visto **5** frequentasse **6** di essere arrivato

Unit 54

1 **1** ha vinto **2** arriverà **3** hanno avuto successo **4** ha tentato **5** verrà **6** andranno **7** siamo stati **8** è tornato

2 **1** avrò preso **2** ho fatto **3** è accaduto **4** sono **5** devo **6** sarà

3 **1** verrà **2** sarebbe stato **3** sarebbe stato **4** aveva bevuto **5** sono aumentati **6** sarebbe partito **7** dovevo **8** poteva **9** volevi **10** aveva cercato, aveva trovato

4 **1** aveva parlato **2** di non essere stato lui **3** dobbiamo **4** sarebbero potuti **5** aveva dimenticato **6** sarebbe stato

Unit 55

1 **1** possiate **2** abbiamo **3** sia successo **4** riesca **5** abbia arrestato **6** si siano divertiti **7** ti sia ricordato **8** si sia comportato **9** sia cominciata **10** facciate

3 **1** fosse **2** avesse **3** avesse trovato **4** telefonasse **5** fosse uscita **6** si fosse laureato **7** piacessero

Unit 56

1 **1** Questa casa è stata venduta a poco prezzo **2** Il bambino sarà lavato nella vasca da bagno **3** La stanza fu pulita molto bene dalle donne delle pulizie **4** L'uomo fu arrestato e fu portato in prigione **5** Tutto questo sarà fatto **6** Il bambino è stato rimproverato dalla mamma **7** Centinaia di persone erano ospitate nell'albergo **8** La mia proposta non fu accettata dal signor Ferrari

2 **1** Il ladro è stato catturato dai poliziotti **2** Non siamo stati invitati al matrimonio dai Bianchi **3** La finestra non era stata aperta dalle impiegate **4** La pasta era stata preparata per tutti **5** I parenti sono stati offesi da quelle persone **6** Paola è stata assunta da quella ditta

3 **1** Molti colleghi utilizzano il computer sul mio tavolo **2** Nada ha tradotto dieci frasi dall'italiano nella sua lingua **3** La segretaria spedirà il pacco all'estero **4** Alcuni fan seguirono la pop star fino all'albergo **5** Il direttore non aveva firmato quella lettera **6** Una bomba distrusse il villaggio **7** Uno scrittore famoso aveva scritto il libro **8** Il professore ha recitato le poesie nell'aula conferenze

4 **1** siamo stati mandati **3** è studiata **4** mi è stato regalato **5** è stato promosso/fu promosso

Unit 57

1 **1** verremo presto mandati **2** venne imprigionato **3** veniva proposto **4** verrà valutato **5** venivano festeggiati

2 **1** Un milione di dollari venne vinto dal ragazzo **2** L'esercito nemico verrà sconfitto dall'esercito dei Romani **3** Una torta veniva preparata dalla nonna **4** Il libro verrà pubblicato a marzo **5** Viene spesso invitata al cinema **6** Il negozio fu allagato interamente dal temporale **7** La camera viene messa in ordine dal ragazzo **8** I prezzi verranno abbassati

3 **1** La polizia può essere avvisata **2** Una decisione deve essere presa presto **3** Degli oggetti per la nuova casa devono essere comprati da Carlo **4** I nuovi rappresentanti per il quartiere possono essere eletti da domani **5** Il tuo lavoro può essere sbrigato adesso? **6** Questa occasione non può essere persa **7** La lettera non potrà essere scritta dalla segretaria prima di domani **8** Queste condizioni non possono essere accettate

4 **1** Non si possono visitare **2** Non si possono mangiare **3** Non si può bere **4** Non si devono inviare **5** Non si possono indossare **6** Non si può indossare

Unit 58

1 **1** ma **2** sia **3** sia **4** non solo **5** ma anche **6** invece **7** o **8** o **9** nemmeno **10** quindi **11** però **12** quindi **13** neanche **14** perciò **15** invece **16** infatti

2 **1**f **2**b **3**a **4**c **5**d **6**e

3 **1** né il quaderno né il libro **2** perciò **3** invece **4** altrimenti **5** infatti

Unit 59

1 **1** Hai fatto una domanda che è intelligente **2** Sabato sera abbiamo visto un film che era molto divertente **3** Ho conosciuto un ragazzo che si chiama Aldo **4** Il vigile ha fermato un'automobile che era passata con il rosso

2 **1** a cui ho fatto un regalo, ha compiuto gli anni ieri **2** con cui giochiamo sono tedeschi **3** da cui abbiamo ricevuto un pacco, arrivano domani **4** di cui ha parlato il giornalista è molto interessante **5** sono valori su cui non si discute **6** in cui ho messo le monete è quello sulla scrivania

3 **1** dei quali **2** a cui/al quale **3** con cui/con il quale **4** di cui/del quale **5** di cui/del quale **6** in cui/nel quale **7** da cui/dai quali **8** a cui/al quale **9** con cui/con il quale **10** in cui/nel quale **11** per cui/per la quale **12** da cui/dal quale **13** con cui/con la quale **14** in cui/nel quale

Unit 60

1 **1** affinché **2** poiché **3** sebbene **4** finché **5** purché **6** quando **7** mentre **8** prima che

2 **1** quando **2** mentre **3** poiché **4** perché **5** sebbene **6** sebbene **7** mentre **8** poiché

3 **1** quando **2** poiché **3** inoltre **4** affinché **5** quando **6** tuttavia **7** perciò **8** dopo che **9** sebbene **10** infatti **11** inoltre

Unit 61

1 **1** che non sono bello ma intelligente **2** che parlo a voce troppo alta **3** che la campagna pubblicitaria era stata lunga e difficile **4** che presto sarebbe partito per la Sardegna **5** che lo avrebbe amato per sempre

2 **1** l'anno scorso aveva avuto **2** ha trovato **3** avrebbe avuto **4** avrebbe guadagnato **5** che era preoccupata **6** non stava studiando **7** che si sarebbe messo a studiare **8** che aveva preparato **9** che aveva imparato **10** cucinava **11** avrebbe lavorato

Unit 62

1 **1** oggi è proprio stanco, quel giorno era proprio stanco **2** i suoi amici sono fidati, i suoi amici erano fidati **3** il giorno prima ha sbrigato tutto, il giorno prima aveva sbrigato tutto **4** in questo palazzo si fa troppo rumore, in questo palazzo si faceva troppo rumore **5** chi sono quei ragazzi che mi aspettano, chi erano quei ragazzi che mi aspettavano **6** dove vogliamo andare domani, dove volevano andare il giorno dopo

2 **1** Io risposi che non lo avevo mai visto **2** Lei disse che era veramente carino **3** Io risposi che ero assolutamente d'accordo **4** E gli chiese se era di nuovo lì **5** Lui sorrise e replicò che sarebbe arrivato quel giorno **6** Si presentò dicendo che era Tommaso e veniva da Torino **7** Disse che quella era Luisa

Summary exercises 50-62

1 **1** quindi **2** non solo, ma anche **3** anche **4** o **5** infatti **6** cioè

2 **1** perché **2** prima che **3** siccome **4** mentre **5** se **6** nonostante

3 **1** Le verdure non sono amate dai bambini **2** Una medaglia sarà ottenuta dai vincitori **3** Una torta è stata appena cucinata dalla nonna **4** L'indirizzo sulla busta era stato scritto da voi? **5** La guerra di Troia fu vinta dai Greci grazie all'inganno del cavallo di legno

4 **1** Se fossi stato ricco, avrei smesso di lavorare **2** Se non lo avessero amato, non lo avrebbero sopportato **3** Avrei fatto il giro del mondo, se non avessi avuto paura di volare **4** Non avreste fatto tutti quegli errori, se vi foste concentrati di più **5** Se avessimo avuto diciotto anni, saremmo andati via da casa

5 **1** alzarmi **2** scrivervi **3** averglielo lasciato **4** accompagnarlo **5** presentartela

6 **1** da cui **2** che **3** la cui **4** di cui **5** nel quale

7 **1** Giulia dice che non è mai stata negli Stati Uniti **2** Se tu mi amassi, mi scriveresti più spesso **3** Se piove, prendo l'ombrello **4** Se fossi in te, comprerei una grande casa sul mare **5** Dal momento che sei qui, ti voglio chiedere una cosa **6** Questa casa è stata costruita l'anno scorso **7** Questo è il ragazzo che parla tre lingue **8** Anche se il tempo è brutto, andremo al mare

Finito di stampare nel mese di settembre 2022
presso LegoDigit S.r.l., Lavis (Trento)